Library of
Davidson College

Towards Full Employment: a policy appraisal

Towards Full Employment:
A Policy Appraisal

Ciaran Driver

ROUTLEDGE & KEGAN PAUL
London and New York

339.5
D782t

First published in 1987 by
Routledge & Kegan Paul Ltd
11 New Fetter Lane, London EC4P 4EE

Published in the USA by
Routledge & Kegan Paul Inc.
in association with Methuen Inc.
29 West 35th Street, New York, NY 10001

Set in Imprint
by Hope Services Ltd.
and printed in Great Britain
by Richard Clay Ltd.,
Bungay, Suffolk

© Ciaran Driver 1987

No part of this book may be reproduced in
any form without permission from the publisher
except for the quotation of brief passages
in criticism

Library of Congress Cataloging in Publication Data
Driver, Ciaran.
Towards Full Employment: a policy appraisal
Bibliography: p.
Includes indexes. 88-8759
1. Employment stabilization.   2. Full employment
policies.   3. Unemployment.   I. Title.   II. Title:
Making the jobs go around.
HD5713.2.D75   1987   339.5   87-9814
ISBN 0-7102-0918-5

Contents

	Foreword	vii
	Preface	xi
1	No future?	1
2	Workshop and the world	31
3	High road or low road?	55
4	New jobs and old	71
5	Ways and means	94
6	Small wonder?	127
7	Special measures	151
8	Making the jobs go round	169
9	Summing up	199
	Notes	205
	Bibliography	215
	Index of names	231
	Index of subjects	234

Foreword

For the past sixty years or more, unemployment has been the dominant problem of the British economy. Following the publication of Keynes' General Theory it was believed that the solution had been discovered. Keynes argued that unemployment was largely the result of deficient real aggregate demand, and could be removed by appropriate fiscal and monetary policy. Of course, solving the unemployment problem was only one part of macroeconomics. There remained the issue of inflation, which, in fact, is made more difficult in conditions of full employment. In addition, there has always been the problem of the supply side of Britain's relatively low productivity and growth rate.

In the 1970s, however, the economic climate changed dramatically for the worse. The rise in the real price of oil, and the response to it, led to a serious intensification of inflation, and a lower growth rate. Coupled with disinflationary demand side policies, the outcome was stagflation. New policy initiatives were called for. Instead of responding to this, the government reverted to that most classic of interventions, the the creation of a permanent army of some three million unemployed. Inflation has been brought under control for the time being and the economy has been enabled to resume its normal growth path, but the real cost has been enormous. And even then the balance of payments on the current account has been allowed to slip into deficit.

Economists have not been slow to recognise that the phenomenon of stagflation requires some new analysis, though this does not mean the abandonment of fundamental principles. It is a triviality to say that the maintenance of full employment always requires that the corresponding output must be bought at home or abroad. It is also the case that this will not happen automatically, but requires a correct combination of fiscal and monetary policy, and a competitive exchange rate. Furthermore, if there is not to be runaway inflation and continuous devaluation, there must be a policy for incomes.

Other considerations must also be brought to bear. These are connected, to a considerable extent, with the structural imbalances resulting from persistent depression. As compared with a minor recession, industry's recovery possibilities are limited in the short term. In technical parlance, the short run aggregate supply curve is not flat. New enterprises need to be created, and existing ones take time to adjust to more buoyant circumstances. The chronically unemployed need to adapt themselves to a working environment once more, and must be retrained. An extra difficulty is that there are major technological changes occuring throughout the world economy, leaving much of British industry obsolete and calling for new industrial initiatives.

All of this means that the recovery programme must be targeted at particular groups of workers, firms, and regions. That is the way to make overall expansion more efficacious and less inflationary. In addition, it is a mistake to concentrate just on the immediate future. There must be plans spanning the medium and longer terms. Those who say that we will never get back to full employment again are far too pessimistic. But they are right to point out that, if we go on as we are, we will be part of the Third World in the twenty-first century. Moreover, even with the best policies, it is realistic to say that a full recovery will take ten years or more, and will hardly be completed before the new century begins.

It is also apparent that recovery must be based on a continuation of the mixed economy, in which both the public and private sectors have a part to play. Government policy intervention is of great importance at both the micro- and macroeconomic levels, but it must be in a form which enables the private sector to respond to the demands that will confront it.

All of this is made clear in Ciaran Driver's admirable book. What is especially valuable about it is the extent to which it is firmly embedded in actual experience and research. This is true of such topics as the labour market, the structure of industry, and the way the problem varies from region to region. Of course, the tone of the book is interventionist in the sense that it is not based on the proposition that all that is required is to leave free markets to get on with things. But it is a good deal less doctrinaire than might be expected; very few economists would disagree with it nowadays. All in all, this is an important book which makes a significant contribution to the continuing debate on employment policy.

Maurice Preston

Preface

It is not easy to write a book on unemployment. On one side the terrain slopes steeply over vacuous good intent, while on the other the hard rock of austere theory overshadows the route. The reader, hopefully, will have an easier ride. The book is informed by theory and develops it where appropriate, but there is no recourse to unnecessary or unproductive abstraction. And while Hobsbawm's assertion may be true that 'hidden in every economist . . . is a politician struggling to be let out', I have tried to minimise argument that cannot be supported within these covers.

Unemployment is of general concern and this book is aimed at a wide readership. The general reader will find the argument accessible in all but a few places that can be skipped as necessary. Technical argument that is of more interest to specialists is separated out from the text.

Part of my motivation – and indeed opportunity – for writing this book stemmed from my experience in assessing the unemployment question as part of the 'New Jobs' exercise at the National Economic Development Office. But although I learned a lot from this period and was stimulated by it, this book is in no sense an exposition or record of official thought. The debt of gratitude owed to my former colleagues must be tempered by saying that many will not agree with much of what is argued.

Special thanks are due to those who have read and commented on the various chapters – Jerry Coakley, Phivos Arestis, Chris Whitbread, Malcolm Sawyer and Al Eicher.

Bob Rowthorn stimulated my thinking in respect of material in Chapter 3. Peter Chalk talked to me about computers. Anne Phillips not only commented thoughtfully on three of the chapters but also erred on the side of generosity in doing her half of childcare. Other friends contributed more indirectly by tolerating my long periods of introspection and preoccupation.

Finally, in a period of budget restrictions on education, I would like to thank Thames Polytechnic for the modicum of research time able to be allocated to allow me to finish the book.

1 No future?

Mass unemployment re-emerged in developed countries in the 1970s. On some estimates, it has already lasted longer than the similar experience of the 1930s. Over a hundred million years of potential labour supply has been unused in the OECD area alone. Thirty million people are officially classified as out of work, one tenth of them in Britain, where long-term unemployment is still static despite special measures to alleviate it. Nearly a million and a half people have not found work after more than a year's search.

In Britain, a climate of acquiescence in mass unemployment is already developing. Some have begun to question the basis of unemployment figures, suggesting that a true count would be lower. Many commentators now argue that we must learn to live with a different notion of work to that of permanent employment for all. Certainly most of the long-term economic forecasts of the UK economy expect no significant fall in unemployment on present policies by the end of the decade. This has even been accepted by government departments as a working assumption (Department of Trade and Industry, 1986). And the general pessimism seems to be shared by the unemployed; one in five of these, questioned in late 1985, expected that they would never work again.[1]

What has caused mass unemployment? This book attributes it to a weakening in economic growth generally, for reasons explained later. It is not the case that the huge increase in job losses and job seekers has been caused by an increased labour force.[2] Nor is it true that there is now a greater proclivity for leisure and that much unemployment is 'voluntary'.[3] It may of course be that there is less of a stigma attached to unemployment when jobs are difficult to find and this may have had some effect on people's willingness to work, especially in the case of young people or those on low pay.[4] Mass unemployment will also have caused depression and lethargy, with a resultant effect on capacity to work. However, these phenomena are consequences not causes. The main reason for high unemployment must be found in the weak growth of output and in the reduced labour requirement to produce that output.

It is possible to distinguish three broadly differing positions in policy-making circles accounting for the emergence and persistence of unemployment and slow growth.

The first view, which is sometimes termed 'classical', sees the problem as arising in the labour market, with real wages too high and profitability correspondingly low. This results in less expansionary investment and a greater reliance on labour-saving techniques.[5] Inflationary pressures also work to keep unemployment high. The route to this can be direct, as when prices rise and demand falls, or indirect, due to contradictionary measures to contain inflation. Attempts to generate fuller employment by stimulating demand will, on this view, be self-defeating. Unemployment will persist until the real wage moderates or until technical change or a reduction in costs improves profitability and induces expansion.

The second view, which will be termed Keynesian, is dominated by a consideration of the role of autonomous demand on output growth. It is recognised that some elements of autonomous demand – say an increase in North–South trade – are not susceptible to policies of individual states. A number of Keynesians will even admit to a belief that the long-run level of demand is completely endogenous. However there is a unified belief that short-run policy measures can at least prevent an economy sticking in an under-employment state below that long-run level of demand. The main constraint on policy is inflation; it is widely accepted that this is in large part attributable to real-wage pressure, which is seen as having intensified considerably during the 1970s. Keynesians prefer to concentrate not on the source but on the transmission of that pressure via money, wages and prices. The real constraint on policy is thus the ability of institutional methods to resolve social conflict over distribution, especially in the presence of external shocks which disturb accustomed claims on output:

> the characteristics of pay setting, together with the institutional arrangements and methods associated with collective bargaining, coupled with shocks to the economic system and policies designed to bring inflation under control tend to generate high and persistent levels of unemployment. (Morris and Sinclair, 1985, p. 11)

The two views just outlined do not necessarily conflict, and Layard and Nickell (1985a) have called the debate fruitless since it is quite possible for real-wage pressure to be a serious problem without actual real wages being too high. This is explainable by the role of government deflationary measures in containing price rises. It is then very difficult to know whether demand or wages should be identified as the culprit. It is important to note, however, that the Layard and Nickell synthesis of classical and Keynesian views singles out the labour market – and its failure to operate without building up real-wage pressure – as the villain of the piece.[6]

The structural view

This is where the third view (advanced in this book) parts company with the traditional approach just outlined. This third view, which will be termed 'structural', differs from the others in that it does not locate the origin of the unemployment in the labour market. The problems of an imperfect labour market are not new and it is difficult to understand why they should now wreak such havoc on employment opportunities. Economists such as Bruno and Sachs (1985) have gone to great lengths to document possible factors behind the increase in real-wage pressure in the 1970s, instancing such factors as incomes policies in the 1960s, the 'May events' (France, 1968) and the 'hot Autumn' (Italy, 1969), but the discussion seems more descriptive than analytical.

It is difficult to see labour-market problems as a *causa*

causans in the sense of being independent of other pressures. For instance, it is known that labour mobility between jobs lessened dramatically at the end of the 1970s; however, this was not caused by a sudden malfunctioning of the labour market but by the fear of unemployment, consequent on slow growth.[7]

The structural view argues that economic development is punctuated by periods of unusual structural change to which market economies find it difficult to adapt because of heightened uncertainty over the direction of change. Such periods are characterised by unbalanced preoccupation with cost-cutting rather than exploiting new opportunities for expansion inherent in new technologies and ways of working. There are thus three propositions which need to be argued in defence of the relevance to current economic conditions of the structural view. Firstly, that structural change is unusually high; secondly, that cost-cutting has become a priority for firms; and thirdly, that uncertainty over the future evolution of economic variables has risen. Each of these points is supported below.

Structural change

The notion that structural change is at an unusually high level may strike some observers as obvious, especially in the case of Britain in the last few years. Nevertheless, it is important to establish this point as it has become a controversial one among economists.[8] Some economists, especially those with an interest in technology, do argue that unemployment has a significant structural element, in the sense of increased mismatch in skills, regional location and types of capital goods, as a result of greater technical change (Soete and Freeman, 1982). But this is not generally accepted by others. For instance, Nickell (1985) has argued that 'the current period has a level of structural change which is quite unremarkable' (p. 108). Nickell's view is based on a very long view of the data, which may not be appropriate given changes in industrial classification, but even on his own figures, structural change has risen perceptibly since the late 1960s. Furthermore there is more than one method of measuring structural change, and

> **Panel 1.1**
>
> **Structural Change**
>
> Indices of structural change in the whole economy since 1948 are considered here. The index is constructed by summing across twenty-three sectors the absolute value of the change in employment proportions that occurs over each time period. Nickell's view is based on differences over one year, as calculated by Newell (1984). However, this will include a lot of noise due to purely cyclical variation and it seems more appropriate to use longer periods for differencing. Figure 1.1 shows how the index of structural change has increased in recent years, especially when longer differencing periods are taken. The dip in the early 1970s confirms the results of Layard, Nickell and Jackman (1984), who observed such a fall in a number of OECD countries using cyclically averaged data. It would appear that the accommodatory policies used in the wake of the first OPEC price rise, and the subsequent moderate expansion in the OECD area, may have dampened structural change, with companies preferring a cautious approach.

reliable indicators suggest a much increased level for the 1980s. Panel 1.1 details the evidence.

It is important to note that the high level of structural change does not connote a successful transition to a new industrial structure. The index of change counts negative and positive movements (i.e. losses and gains in capacity) equally and a sharp loss of capacity in some industries, unbalanced by any major gains, will also show up as unusual structural change. Nevertheless, it does appear that change has accelerated and this has implications for economic policy that will be brought out later in the book, in particular the necessity for increased attention to education and training and the justification that it offers for higher public borrowing.

Cost-cutting

Fixed investment in many countries has become biased towards cost-saving rather than new expansion. Some see this as resulting from wage push, but it is more likely that the most powerful stimulus to this type of investment is increased uncertainty in product markets, as discussed later.

OECD sources pointed to this emphasis on cost-cutting even before the second oil-price hike in the late 1970s. The McCracken report (1977) commented on 'a fall in the share of investment going to extensions of capacity' and went on to cite business survey data in support of this claim. In Germany, for example, the proportion of manufacturing companies giving expansion of capacity as the principal reason for investment fell from over half in 1960 to only 15 per cent in the late 1970s, and, although it then rose, it was still only 30 per cent by early 1986.

In the United States, OECD statistics based on the McGraw-Hill survey of business plans suggest that, in the wake of the second oil shock, the 1980 figure for the proportion of modernisation in total investment was the highest since 1961. A similar story can be read from the figure on the proportion of capital stock accounted for by modernisation investment; this was at an all-time high in 1980, following a climb from a twenty-year stable average up to the mid-1970s.[9]

Evidence for the UK is more indirect, but still striking. Since the last quarter of 1979, the CBI Industrial Trends Survey has recorded whether investment is for capacity expansion or for increased efficiency. This data reveals a sharp rise in the proportion of efficiency investment after 1979, and it would be of interest to observe earlier figures. While these cannot be obtained directly, it has proved possible to infer the general historical pattern, which again confirms a swing away from expansionary investment. This is detailed in Panel 1.2.

For all these countries it appears then that there is evidence of a bias towards cost-saving investment within manufacturing. One major consequence of this has been an increasingly

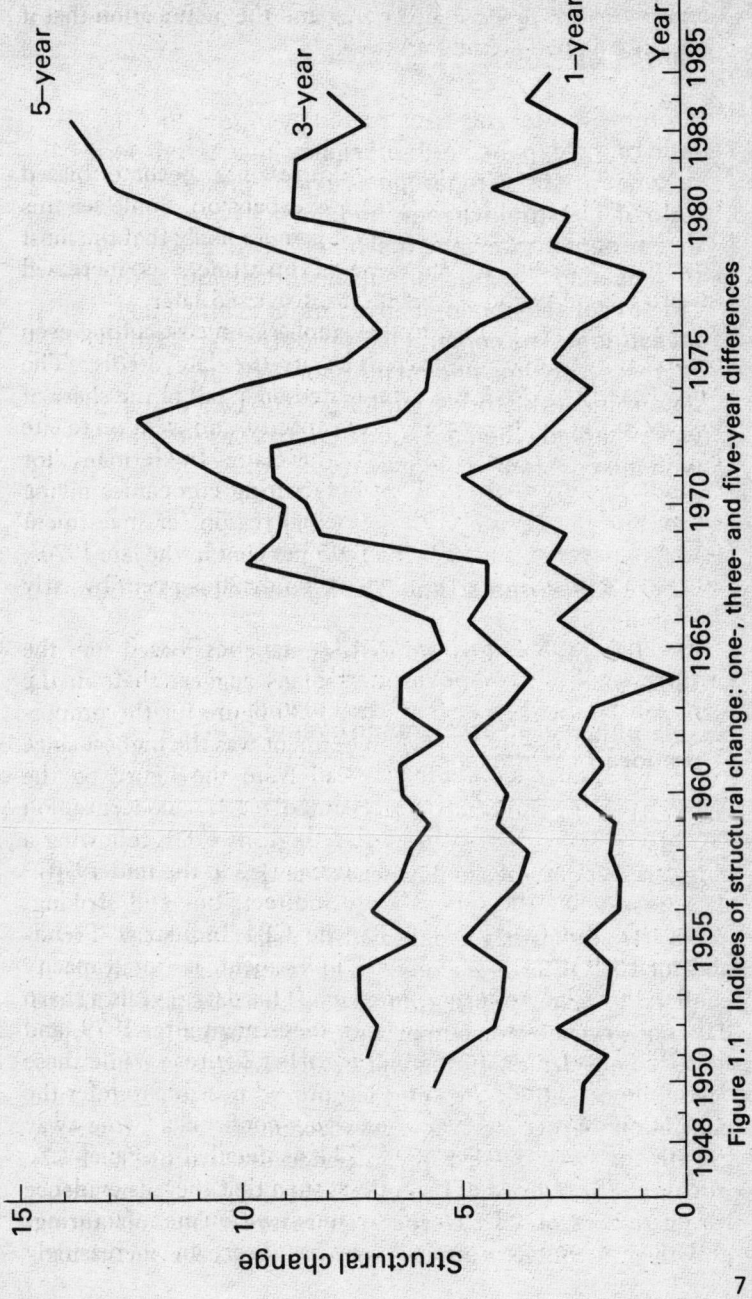

Figure 1.1 Indices of structural change: one-, three- and five-year differences

> **Panel 1.2**
>
> A simple model was constructed by regressing the ratio of the expansion-to-efficiency investment series on what might be regarded as a good proxy – the ratio of investment in new building and works to investment in plant and machinery. The results were then used to construct annual historical figures for the ratio of capacity building investment to efficiency investment. The constructed series (ACE) was then regressed on time and on the square of time to determine its historical evolution. The best equation was obtained when the squared term was entered with the constant, giving:
>
> $$ACE = 0.56 - 0.00085T^2$$
> $$(16.25) \quad (-6.00)$$
>
> Where T represents Time. The figures in brackets are 't' statistics.
> $R^2 = 0.61$; DW = 1.51; annual constructed data 1962–83
>
> This suggests an acceleration over time in the proportion of efficiency investment.

sluggish response of employment to output growth in recent decades.

Several studies have confirmed this shift, both for Britain and for the OECD generally.[10] The testing has usually been confined to manufacturing, in view of the unreliability of the data on service-sector output and employment; some results for UK non-manufacturing will be discussed later.

An important finding of the studies has been that the generation of net new jobs now requires a higher output growth than was needed in earlier decades (Cornwall, 1977; Michl, 1985). Cornwall has calculated that for the manufacturing sectors of OECD countries in the 1950s, an output growth in manufacturing of a mere 1.7 per cent would have resulted in employment growth. By the end of the 1960s he calculated the corresponding figure to be 2.8 per cent. It now appears, however, that the latter was very much an underestimate. Work done by Michl suggests that a figure of approximately 7 per cent would be more appropriate for the 1970s and late 1960s, despite the fall-off in productivity growth.[11] As the actual output growth rate was only half this figure, large job losses in manufacturing were inevitable.

For the economy as a whole, and particularly the service sector, the picture is somewhat more clouded. The EEC Commission has argued that a growth rate of 6 per cent a year was required to keep employment rising up to 1973. By contrast, it is claimed that a figure as low as 2 per cent would have created employment in the period 1977–85, though even this was not achieved (Commission of the European Communities, 1985a). These statistics raise problems of interpretation. The low figure for the later period is a reflection of the fact that many new jobs are likely to be part time. While this may prove a pointer to the need to reduce average working hours (see Chapter 8), it also disguises the severity of the present problem, in that a rise in part-time work will not solve structural employment in the context of present institutional arrangements. For this reason it may be of more interest to analyse the behaviour of full-time equivalent (FTE) employment which adjusts for hours worked.

In the British case the employment output relationship has not been well determined for the service sector in recent years. Employment growth and output growth now appear to have no significant correlation.[12] An exception to this finding appears to be the case of consumer services such as leisure and household services (see Panel 1.3). It is also possible that areas such as public services, where no reliable output measures exist, may still have a well-determined response of employment to output.

Uncertainty

The third proposition of the structural view is that uncertainty has risen as a consequence of structural change. Indeed it is this that explains the lack of commitment to expansionary in-

> **Panel 1.3**
>
> The following equation was estimated for consumer services, excluding retailing, public services and banking.
>
> $$e = 4.41 + 0.24q + 0.34q(-1) + 0.87\,T$$
> $$\quad\;\;(8.77)\quad\;(2.15)\quad\;\;\;(2.80)\quad\;\;\;(5.82)$$
>
> $R^2 = 0.93;\; DW = 2.10$
>
> where e and q are natural logarithms of employment and output respectively; T is time. Figures in brackets are 't' statistics.
>
> The measure of employment used was a full-time equivalent index where part time is counted as half full-time. Regressions were attempted over a run of years for which consistent data was available (1972–82). Estimation was performed for the public sector (where measurable – mainly transport); for those parts of the following services where reliable output measures exist – producer, distribution and financial services; and for consumer services not included in the previous categories. Only in the last case was a clear relationship between employment and output apparent.

vestment noted above. It is of interest that in the UK, net investment by non-North Sea companies fell as a proportion of net capital stock, from 5 per cent in the mid-1960s to 2 per cent in the mid-1970s and was negative in the first half of the 1980s.

A considerable element of 'downside' risk exists for investors. Among the more obvious elements of risk are: the prospects for East–West arms control, with implications for the US budget deficit; the effect of continued high real interest rates on LDC (less developed countries) debt negotiations; commodity prices; exchange-rate volatility; and the risk of a slide towards protectionism.

The Commission of the European Communities (1985a) estimated the cumulative effect over three years of a number of different possible developments in the world economy – US budget cuts of 1 per cent a year, US dollar depreciation of 20 per cent, a 20 per cent fall in the oil prices and a 2 per cent fall in real interest rates. The results varied considerably, as might be expected, with output growth and inflation rates having ranges of about 3 per cent in their predicted outcomes. This underscores the uncertainty that must prevail.

Panel 1.4 presents evidence that, in Britain, uncertainty has indeed risen in respect of aggregate consumer spending and fixed investment.

Panel 1.4 Indices of uncertainty with respect to investment (UI) and consumer spending (UC)

Period	UI	UC
1969–74	1.65	2.40
1975–80	1.87	3.60
1981–86	2.12	5.42

The index is constructed as a six-year average of the standard deviation of the three main forecasts for which a long run of data is available (National Institute for Economic and Social Research, Treasury and OECD).

Llewellyn *et al.* (1985) have pointed to the increased accuracy with which output and inflation are now forecast in OECD countries compared with the 1960s. However, this appears to be due to the lessening of systematic error, while the variance of forecast error across the years has actually increased over time, indicating greater uncertainty.[13] The adverse effect of this increased uncertainty on expansion is confirmed for several OECD countries by Batchelor (1982) and Faxen (1983). Given the increased uncertainty detailed above, it is hardly surprising that no rapid and sustained private-sector growth has emerged, sufficient to allow a significant reduction in unemployment.

The relevance of the structural view

The structural view focuses on heightened uncertainty at a time of increased structural change and on the effect that this has on future commitments, in particular on fixed investment. Fear of inflexibility causes cautious expansionary investment at times of increased uncertainty. The greatest uncertainty exists when unusual opportunities exist for profitable change in techniques and products. So it is that price signals are least effective when they are most needed. As long as change is incremental and does not suddenly alter traditional market structures, industrial boundaries, or the world pattern of production, it can be accommodated. But if change is not incremental the opportunities for growth are counterbalanced by macroeconomic uncertainty in relation to virtually all economic variables.

The transition from a regime of incremental to major change and the converse has been studied elsewhere (Abernathy, 1978; Perez, 1985). It will only be stated here that major change will involve the organisation and process of production as well as the composition and growth of output. The response to the first challenge is met by firms cutting costs and introducing new technology; in some ways, though not all, this direct task is efficiently signalled through the market. But the second problem, involving decisions on the composition and growth of output, is not amenable to clear or decisive action by individual firms, in part because the future output composition consequent on industrial restructuring depends on the evolution of incomes and cultures – patterns that only become clear when the dust has settled. Uncertainty over new-product demand thus remains high and economic development becomes distorted, with an unbalanced preoccupation with cost-cutting to the detriment of expansionary investment.

The structural view incorporates elements of both classical and Keynesian positions. In particular, it accepts that low profitability characterised the onset of stagnation, while also stressing market failure and the importance of institutional intervention as a necessary condition for renewed growth.

The differences between the broad views just outlined are important for policy formation. If the economy is merely off track due to temporary shocks, it can still be expected to behave according to known and calibrated rules. If, on the contrary, the future development of the economy is likely to entail major changes in competitive conditions, legal and social controls, consumer expenditure patterns, new technology, hours and patterns of work, international trading relations and many other factors, there can then be no guarantee that either traditional macroeconomic approaches or indeed unaided market forces can be relied upon to sustain growth and employment. An interventionist approach is needed, not to block evolving changes but to guide their evolution towards a new period of stable growth.

It may be instructive to look at an example of contrasting policy implications of the orthodox and the structural approaches. In the orthodox 'labour-market' approach, well captured by the Layard and Nickell (1985b) synthesis of classical and Keynesian views, unemployment would be made worse, not better, by worksharing. It would simply add to existing real wage pressure through one mechanism or another.[14] In the structural view, by contrast – and this case is expanded on in Chapter 8 – the transition to fuller employment may require a shift in consumption and production patterns which could be eased by a reduction in working time. The differences between these broad views arise because the orthodox approach regards all determinants of behaviour outside narrowly-defined economic variables to be given exogenously.

The structural view and the trend fall in profitability

Having set out the structural view, it is of interest to examine the reasons why the economy has now become characterised by increased structural change, cost-cutting and greater uncertainty. The long-run trend of falling profitability in OECD countries is important here. Without straying too far from the subject in hand, it is possible to sketch the relevant developments in a way that illuminates differences in the Keynesian, classical and structural approaches.

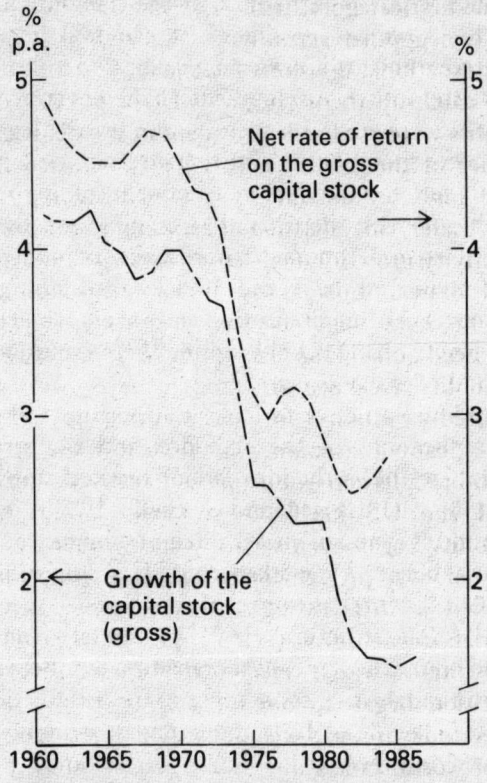

Figure 1.2 Rates of return and growth of the capital stock, at constant prices – UK, France, W. Germany and Italy. Three-year moving average. *Source*: Commission of the European Communities (1985a).

Figure 1.2 shows the long-run trend in profitability in European economies and the corresponding trend in fixed investment.[15]

Reasons for the profits squeeze may conveniently be categorised into three important effects. The first two constitute the twin blades of a scissors – competitive pressure working to keep prices down and inflationary pressure working to keep costs up. The third reason concerns the structure of production and is important in so far as the other reasons do not seem to account adequately for the secular fall in profitability in recent years.

In the first category, that of competitive pressure, are to be found two popular accounts – the catch-up theory, and the new international division of labour.

The catch-up theory argues that favourable opportunities for profits were especially prevalent in war-damaged European countries of the 1950s. Technology borrowed from the US yielded high profits due to restrictions on the mobility of capital. Later, liberalisation of capital movements implied that productivity growth rates would converge towards that of the United States, causing the erosion of excess profits. The argument here suggests that the early high profit-rates experienced outside the US may have been historically specific and should have been expected to be transitory. This view undoubtedly contains some truth but it does not explain all the facts. It cannot account, for instance, for the pattern of profitability falls across European countries. And how can the case of the US itself be explained, where the slide in profitability began even earlier than in other countries?

Another way in which competitive pressure may have intensified is through heightened competition from newly industrialising countries (NICs). Certainly, profitability in the United States was eroded in the mid-1960s as Japanese competition began to bite. But is the same pattern being repeated today in the developed world as a whole, with a rising share of world trade going to the NICs? These economies do seem to have been impervious to the problems which were evident in OECD countries in the 1970s. Unlike the OECD, productivity and output did not decelerate in the NICs in the 1960s and 1970s. It is still the case of course that the total value of trade between the NICs and OECD countries is relatively small. For the UK, at the end of the 1970s, the figure was less than a fifth of trade with EEC countries for a narrow group of NICs, or 30 per cent for a broader set which includes more developed economies such as Israel and Iran.[16] However the size of the trade flows does not in itself represent an indicator of the associated effect on profitability. The effect is more properly gauged by assessing any correlation between the strength of NICs competition in home and export markets of the developed economies and the corresponding falls in profitability. A sensible, if imperfect, measure of competitive pressure is the level or rate of change of import penetration, and it has been shown that these are not correlated across countries with change in profitability (Chan-Lee and Sutch, 1985). Furthermore, when sectoral rates of profit within countries are analysed, it is clear that the problem of profitability is not located simply in vulnerable industries such as steel, footwear, clothing, textiles and electronics.[17] Thus it would appear that if competition from the NICs is a factor, it has not been the overriding one.

The second blade of the scissors concerns rising production costs, in particular labour and raw materials costs. A rise in real wages above productivity will tend to increase the wage share and reduce the profit share if substitution is limited between labour and capital.

The rate of profit depends inversely on the labour share and directly on the productivity of capital – output per unit of capital. An inspection of the data for OECD countries shows that, in most countries, falling profitability was accounted for not only by a rise in labour share but also by a fall in capital productivity.[18] This is important because it could be argued that the rise in labour's share is a statistical artifact, caused by a failure to measure properly the quality of labour input. Indeed, in Britain, the share of wage income has trended upwards for more than a century. Statistical work for Britain also suggests that the trend fall in profitability since 1960 cannot be adequately explained by input-cost pressure alone (Williams, 1981).

The structural explanation for falling profitability

The fall in capital productivity can partly be explained by the exhaustion of organisational improvements of an incremental kind within existing industry. New technology which could significantly raise the rate of profit is available, but its deployment will devalue much of existing capital and cause great disturbance to the macroeconomy, which in turn will lower the return on existing capital in the transition period. But even new investments may not show much of an improvement in profitability in the short run. This is partly because output per unit of capital will continue to be depressed, even for new additions to capacity, given that the full return can only be realised after a period of learning and integration, which occurs only as the technological systems diffuse more widely.[19] The non-incremental nature of technical progress thus lowers profitability simultaneously with increases in structural dislocation. It has an effect also on research and development commitments, particularly for new products.

R&D expenditure and associated patent applications faltered in all major countries except Japan in the late 1960s or early 1970s. In the United States 'company financed R&D which had been growing at 6.4% a year in real terms during the 1960s peaked in 1969 and then declined for two years – an event unprecedented in post-World War II history' (Scherer, 1984). In all major countries except Japan, non-defence expenditure on R&D as a percentage of GDP remained fairly constant between the years 1970 and 1980, whereas the ratio had climbed sharply from the early 1960s. In the late 1970s there was a slight rise in the US and West Germany and a rather sharper fall in the UK and France (Mayes, 1985). However a further slowdown took place in the early 1980s; between 1981 and 1983, gross expenditure on R&D grew even slower than in the previous decade. R&D expenditure of the EEC countries declined relative to other OECD countries in this period, largely due to the UK, where such expenditure actually fell in constant prices (OECD, 1985b).

These trends in R&D expenditure reflect the profitability of undertaking R&D, which suffered a squeeze in the early to mid-1970s. The reasons for this fall in R&D profitability are, however, imperfectly understood. One reason, advanced by Scherer, seems plausible, though it seems more descriptive than analytical. He argues that by the beginning of the 1970s the pool of technological opportunities had, apart from specific sectors, been 'fished out' more rapidly than it could be replenished through advances in science and new technical breakthroughs. This explanation would clearly apply with most force to the 'frontier' country, the US, but it might also have some relevance to imitator countries in so far as basic or original research is concerned.

It is possible to examine more closely the proposition that the pool of technical opportunities has been partially exhausted. Kleinknecht (1984) has jointly analysed data on industrial patterns of innovations and West German production growth in the same sectors. He found fairly high correlations between the relative innovativeness of sectors and sectoral growth rates for periods up to 1970, when the correlations began to weaken:

> With the increasing maturity of new products, the tendency to standardisation and a higher degree of mechanisation in the production process, it is increasingly difficult to realise further radical improvements. Therefore we should expect a lessening impact of innovation on output growth, owing to a diminution in the degree of radicalness of innovations and a shift in emphasis from product to process change. (p. 259)

The argument that the degree of radicalness of innovations has declined can only be supported with imperfect evidence, and further investigation is required. Nevertheless, when account is taken of the importance or radicalness of innovations as judged by firms, there does appear to have been a decline in such innovations. Furthermore, there is stronger evidence to support the proposition that there has been a shift of emphasis within manufacturing from product innovation to process innovation (Kleinknecht, 1984, p. 259). It is not always possible to distinguish between these two innovation types, and some activities such as food preserving or insurance services defy classification. Nevertheless, a rough correspondence can be made between product innovation and expansionary activity and between process innovation and cost cutting.

It is of course true that one industry's new product may be another industry's process, but in so far as consumer demand is concerned, product innovation helps to create new consumer demand. Process innovation can also facilitate new demand, but its unplanned development can depress employment, at least initially (Katsoulakis, 1986). As the balance changes between product and process innovation it destabilises the relationship between industrial output and employment, leading to job losses that are not compensated by new growth. This is the structural view: it is distinct from the classical one, not only in terms of the originating impulses but also in so far as it draws attention to the difficulty of achieving a transition to a new path of expansionary investment.

The macroeconomic context of policy debates

The economic problems of the developed world did not begin with the oil shock in 1973. By the late 1960s, profitability had been falling in a number of major countries. The sharp reflation in OECD countries in 1972–3, the devaluation of the dollar in which primary commodities were priced, the speculative forces unleashed by easy credit and the Arab–Israeli war all help to explain the first oil and commodity price shock. The consequences were predictable. Capacity utilisation fell sharply, especially in energy- and capital-intensive industries. Investment growth rates suffered everywhere except the US, with a marked fall-off in expansionary investment. Despite an increase of modernisation investment, productivity growth rates declined due to excess capacity and problems of restructuring.

It was widely expected that the shock would only have temporary effects, as had been the case with the only serious previous commodity price hike at the time of the Korean war. Macroeconomic policies in the OECD did not reinforce the external contractionary forces – fiscal stance being broadly neutral – while world interest rates remained fairly stable in this period. A recovery was evident between 1975 and 1979, but it masked serious problems. For these four years, productivity growth averaged 2½ per cent, compared with nearly 4 per cent from 1960 to 1973.[20] It is perhaps surprising that in the event a 4 per cent output growth figure was achieved, not far from historical rates.

Taken together, the above figures for output and productivity growth imply a positive growth in employment. It seems clear, however, that the medium-term prospects for unemployment were not good in Europe, even if the growth had been sustained. There was severe imbalance between the OECD countries. The US showed a productivity growth of less than 1 per cent, but output there grew six times faster than productivity during the recovery period. In Europe, on the other hand, output and productivity rates of growth were close, so that employment hardly grew at all and, with rising participation rates, unemployment increased.

A further round of OPEC price increases occurred in 1979 as OECD capacity utilisation rates were approaching previous peak, or at least normal, levels. This time, governments responded differently:

> Rather than seeking to support demand in the short term, the overriding concern . . . was to prevent wages rising at the expense of profits . . . in order to lay the foundations for a high and sustained level of investment, needed if the upswing (when it came) was to prove sustaining. (Llewellyn et al., 1985, p. 38)

Restrictive fiscal and monetary policies were applied from 1979. Firms now faced a business climate of high real-interest rates, higher energy prices and a fiscal squeeze. Government economic strategy was to restore profitability by a combination of recession-induced closures and restructuring, while maintaining pressure on labour costs through high unemployment. Public-sector employment failed to play a counter-cyclical role, given the tight fiscal stance. It can fairly be said that a commitment to a high unemployment policy was standard throughout these years. Even Edmond Malinvaud (no enthusiast of the classical view) could not summon up much serious hope for a successful Keynesian incomes policy: 'the immediate and temporary unemployment may be viewed as being the price to pay for reaching a level of real wage that would be appropriate in the long run for full employment' (1982, p. 10).

The effect of these policies in Europe was particularly devastating, coming on top of the previous steady rise during the 1970s. In the United States, by contrast, the cyclically-adjusted budget deficit increased each year from 1982, fuelling the strongest recovery since the Korean war and bringing about some fall in unemployment.

It is of interest to sketch the experience of the British economy in these years under the hypothesis that the structural view is correct. At the cost of some simplification, the matrix in Table 1.1 shows the approach followed by British governments before and after the late 1970s (top left and bottom right respectively). If the structural approach were correct, the appropriate response would have been an interventionist approach to restructuring. Yet certainly in Britain, and to a certain extent in the rest of Europe, the relevant box (top right) is an empty one.

Table 1.1

	Little restructuring	Much restructuring
Interventionist approach	Up to the late 1970s	Never attempted
Market approach	Not applicable	After the late 1970s

The macroeconomic debate in Europe

The agenda for economic debate in Europe has not included the structural case as a main issue. This is partly because for most of the 1970s there was little recognition that anything other than a temporary hiccup had occurred. The subsequent period has seen a preoccupation by macroeconomists with questions of the labour market, to the neglect of the more fundamental issues of investment and technology.

The recent performance of European economies tends to be viewed from either classical or Keynesian perspectives. Neither of these basic stances should be regarded as adequate; they are simply benchmark hypotheses. This section shows that neither view offers a realistic hope that unemployment will come down sharply in the near future.

Common to both understandings is the belief that a 'real wage gap', already evident in most European countries by the start of the 1970s, had been greatly amplified by the external price shocks that followed. The 'wage-gap' concept can be expressed in different ways, but it always measures the extent to which wages and productivity diverge from some base year; it thus gives an index of a real wage or a productivity problem.

The classical position is that wages may well have to grow more slowly than productivity; the existence of any involuntary unemployment implies either an excessive general level of wages, an inappropriate wage structure, or obstacles to labour mobility. Policymakers of this persuasion believe that a natural rate of unemployment (NRU) exists, corresponding to a stable rate of inflation. Government action can only reduce actual unemployment by reducing the natural rate, which in turn can be achieved by supply-side measures such as reducing trade union power, eliminating skill shortages and improving competitiveness. Since most of these supply-side measures are rather difficult to implement, the prospects for employment are, by implication, rather better in the longer run than in the immediate future. Indeed it is a dedicated concern with the long run that now, as ever, separates the classical from the Keynesian school.

It would be wrong to say that there is no long-run Keynesian theory, but it is certainly true that its main policy prescriptions can best be understood in the context of its critique of the classical approach, held by Keynesians to be ineffective and even counterproductive. Most Keynesians argue that the theory of the natural rate and that of policy ineffectiveness is flawed, though generally it is not rejected outright. It is rather argued:

1 that the natural rate can be affected by different variables from those stressed in the classical account
2 that the natural rate may track actual unemployment and
3 that the economy may get stuck in an unemployment state above the natural rate.

The first of the above criticisms concerns additional variables that might help determine the price or wage equations. Since any such variable will help to determine the natural rate, there is a wide menu to choose from and consequent scope for divergent views. Gavyn Davies has sensibly pointed out that it is 'really absurd to use the term "natural rate" since it can change for institutional reasons such as an increased or reduced desire by unions to cooperate with an incomes policy' (Davies, 1985, p. 73).

The second criticism is that wage inflation (and price inflation) responds not so much to the level but more to the *rate of change* of unemployment. This will evidently be so if the fear of unemployment is better measured by the likelihood of becoming unemployed rather than by the length of the existing dole queue. The implication of adding the rate of change of unemployment to a wage equation is that the NRU will track actual unemployment as long as unemployment is rising; this could signal governments to pursue even more restrictive policies, which in turn keep unemployment rising.[21]

The final point is, perhaps, the most important one and links with the structural view. If markets, and particularly future markets or money markets, function imperfectly there will only be weak tendencies pushing the economy towards full resource use. It is thus likely that unemployment will exceed the 'natural' rate for significant periods of time. There are now a battery of models in the literature showing how unemployment can persist indefinitely, with a lively controversy between proponents of models based on inflexible prices under monopolistic competition and those based on more traditional Keynesian concerns.[22]

The theoretical positions described above have their counterpart in more pragmatic policy debates. As long as the wage gap was high and rising, classical and Keynesian views coincided on the need for wage restraint, however implemented. With the gradual erosion of the wage gap, the Keynesian emphasis swung once more towards reflation. As long as profits are not actually being eroded by a widening wage gap, Keynesians see the possibility of absorbing unemployment through faster growth. The financing problem is answered by reference to the endogeneity of profits or by reference to the argument that previous levels of profitability may not be appropriate to the current context.

It is extremely difficult to assess in advance the viability of a reflationary approach; to do so implies, at minimum, a forecast of the paths for both wages and productivity as the economy expands. Normally, in the past, productivity has risen in expansion due to the presence of hoarded labour and a pool of marginally uneconomic spare capacity. Given that the productivity gains of the early 1980s were obtained by a massive shedding of labour and permanent withdrawal of capacity, the normal pattern of events cannot be expected with any certainty.

This difficulty with predicting an expansion path for productivity is paralleled by a similar difficulty in predicting a path for real wages. Apart from cyclical considerations, it is likely that the composition of demand, and consequently of labour skill, would influence the outcome, which is therefore not independent of what happens to productivity. Given these uncertainties, it is not surprising that the Keynesian case is most plausible under an assumption of social accord. However a major difficulty in reaching such consensus lies in the fact that no strong indisputable evidence exists in support of any particular level of profitability as the appropriate one.

The prospect for unemployment: simulation results for classical and Keynesian views

No credible quick route to full employment by means of wage cuts has been offered by those of a classical persuasion. Even if the possible short-term contractionary effects of lower wages are completely discounted, the putative medium-term gains appear to be rather modest. This is so even on the most favourable assumptions – those chosen by the UK Treasury to argue the case for wage moderation. The first row of Table 1.2 presents some of the results of the Treasury simulation on this question. It is important to realise that a large part of the gain in employment comes from increased competitiveness *vis-à-vis* other countries. Clearly, not all countries can simultaneously pursue such parasitical policies, so the effect of a generalised wage cut would be different. Another feature of the simulation is that it contains no explicit allowance for any unfavourable effect on investor confidence due to a lower wage path. This unfavourable reaction would certainly be expected in sectors producing primarily for domestic wage-

Table 1.2 Simulation results: changes relative to base after four years

	Unemployment	Real GDP growth (%)	Consumer prices (%)
1 HM Treasury	−300,000	0.9	−1.8
2 NEDO/Warwick	−102,000	0.5	0.8
3 NEDO/Warwick	−74,000	0.5	0.7
4 CAMBRIDGE (1985)	−700,000	0.1	0.0
5 CAMBRIDGE (1985)	−180,000	0.5	−0.1
6 CAMBRIDGE (1986)	−430,000	2.46	4.15
7 CAMBRIDGE (1986)	−510,000	2.13	−2.1
8 NIESR (1986)	−819,000	3.3	0.9

Notes to the numbered simulations:

1. Real wage reduction of 2 per cent with unchanged nominal targets for financial strategy. Competitiveness improved by 3 per cent. A quarter of the job gain is by factor substitution.
2. Expansion of government current expenditure by £1bn; money supply accommodating (average of HM Treasury, London Business School, National Institute of Economic and Social Research). PSBR rises by about £1.5bn; current balance deteriorates by about £1bn.
3. Expansion of government capital expenditure by £1bn, money supply accommodating; as 2, except current balance deteriorates by £1.5bn.
4. This is the Charter for Jobs package. Expansion of Community Programme by half a million jobs; rise of 20 per cent in government expenditure; cut of 50 per cent in employers' national insurance. PSBR rises by about £4bn; current balance deteriorates by about £1.5bn.
5. Government expenditure boost of £1.6bn at 1980 prices; wages and exchange rate held to base. Results do not alter radically if wages and exchange rate are endogenous.
6. Construction Programme; a balanced injection on public capital infrastructure spending, rising to £4bn extra (1980) prices by 1990. PSBR as a ratio of GDP rises by 2.8 per cent; balance of payments as a ratio of GDP falls by 2.9 per cent.
7. As 6, but with an assumed incomes policy. PSBR ratio rises by 2.5 per cent; balance of payments ratio falls by 2.2 per cent.
8. Illustrative combination of virtual elimination of employers' national insurance contributions, increase in income tax and small increase in public spending. Real interest rates are held constant. PSBR rises by £0.8bn; current balance deteriorates by £5.4bn.

Sources: *The Relationship Between Employment and Wages*, HM Treasury, 1985; Cambridge Econometrics Conference on Industry and the Economy, Selwyn College, Cambridge, June, 1985; Cambridge Econometrics Conference on Industry and Services, Robinson College, Cambridge, June, 1986; *National Institute Economic Review*, February, 1986; Davies, Kilpatrick and Mayes (1986).

earner consumption and it might well outweigh favourable expectations elsewhere.

The Keynesian view, at first sight, appears to offer greater promise for reducing unemployment. If wage growth could be held broadly in line with trend productivity growth and if expansionary policies were not simply to lead to sourcing from stock, a rise in employment should result. The questions are by how much and for how long? This will depend partly on the state of world trade and on the investment response of companies to a demand boost.

A selection of simulation results for the Keynesian case is presented in rows 2 to 8 of Table 1.2. It is clear that the employment effects are greatest when the expansion is accompanied by measures to contain labour cost. Provided that the demand expansion is sufficient, such wage moderation does not in general work by exporting unemployment. It is notable, however, that the size of the job gain is generally disappointing. The Charter for Jobs simulation achieves a significant reduction, but a large part of this is based on the assumption that three-quarters of a million people can be employed in the Community Programme at extremely low wages. The National Institute package involves a large increase in the current account deficit.

Despite the inadequacy of the employment gains, it does appear as if some progress is possible along the lines of a managed expansion. It may even be possible to do significantly better by means of an expansion targeted in specific areas, as discussed in Chapter 7. Why then do governments seem reluctant to go down this particular road? Ignorance and mendacity apart, it may be assumed that some rational basis exists for caution.

Malinvaud (1982) has attempted an answer of sorts to this question, arguing that problems are likely to be experienced on the balance of payments front and in obtaining sufficient public funding. Both of these problems do in fact arise in the case of the Charter for Jobs simulation, the NIESR package and that of the Construction Programme; nevertheless, the underlying argument seems weak. Firstly, the balance of payments consideration would not prove a real constraint if a block of countries were to reflate simultaneously, but this is also resisted. Secondly, there is no proven link between government borrowing requirements and interest rates, so that concern on this issue can only be justified by the preference in financial circles for tight public accounting.[23]

A second reason why governments may be reluctant to reflate concerns the extent and type of spare capacity in the economy. In some sectors substantial fixed capital has been scrapped in the recessions of the last decade and, consequently, inflationary forces will set in quickly if the economy is stimulated. In other sectors, especially those areas of excess capacity most in need of restructuring, inefficient plant would be pressed into service. While this might be good for employment in the short run, it would interrupt the forces of rationalisation which are working only slowly.[24] Investment would accordingly be slow to respond under either of these scenarios, either because of anticipated inflation, on the one hand, or because the demand pattern would be concentrated in sectors of over-capacity.

Both of these arguments have a certain force. It has been argued earlier that recent investment has been labour-saving and it can also be established that some accelerated scrapping has occurred. There are also industries where the presence of sunk costs act as exit barriers and these have prevented rationalisation by market forces. It is somewhat paradoxical, however, that some efficient industries are currently denied a demand stimulus because of the belief that demand restriction will, ultimately, allow restructuring of excess capacity elsewhere. It is hard to avoid the conclusion that the reluctance of some governments to reflate is correlated with a strong desire to avoid the process developing into a state-directed set of industrial planning measures and directives. In eschewing this route it becomes imperative for them to argue that governments have only a limited ability to influence growth.[25]

The structural critique of Keynesianism

A distinctive feature of the structural argument is that restructuring and planned expansion need to go together. There is no particular Keynesian view on restructuring. It is questionable, however, whether a serious rebuttal of the classical case can rest solely on macroeconomic considerations. Indeed it could be said that the Keynesian case has sometimes been undermined by a denial of any validity in the classical preoccupation with trend profitability and structural change.

In particular, the much-quoted work of Layard and Nickell (1985a, 1985b) and publications by the Employment Institute (1985) take a stand against the notion of structural or technological unemployment, preferring to focus on existing possibilities for increased employment: 'the level of capacity utilisation in Britain over the period of high unemployment since 1974 has been below its historic average in every year except 1979 and 1984' (Layard and Nickell, 1985a, p. 81).

This argument seems less than convincing. The really extraordinary fact is that capacity utilisation (on CBI figures) could be at similar levels both in 1979 and 1985, with a difference of two million unemployed to account for.

The truth is that there has been an unusual dispersion of capacity utilisation rates, as shown in Fig. 1.3. This dispersion is partly due to differing rates of restructuring and rationalisation and partly due to different rates of output growth, one cause of which is undoubtedly the knock-on effects of low public investment in infrastructure. There is a degree of slack in the system, but much of it is concentrated in particular sectors. Capital scrapping has risen sharply so that only part of the unemployed could be immediately reabsorbed, even at full capacity. It appears, therefore, that any solution to the problem of unemployment will require a sustained rise in investment and targeted growth.

These critical and cautionary remarks are not intended to undermine the case for traditional reflation. Keynesian policies have been pursued with some success, notably in the US and in France under the Mitterand government where the results compare favourably with the UK, as shown in Table 1.3

It is important, nevertheless, to be clear about the prospects for this course of action for the UK. There is evidently room for targeted reflation where industries have spare capacity that can be utilised viably. The criterion of viability – if not commercial – should be some clear social cost-benefit, rather than flexible special pleading. The case for reflation has

No future?

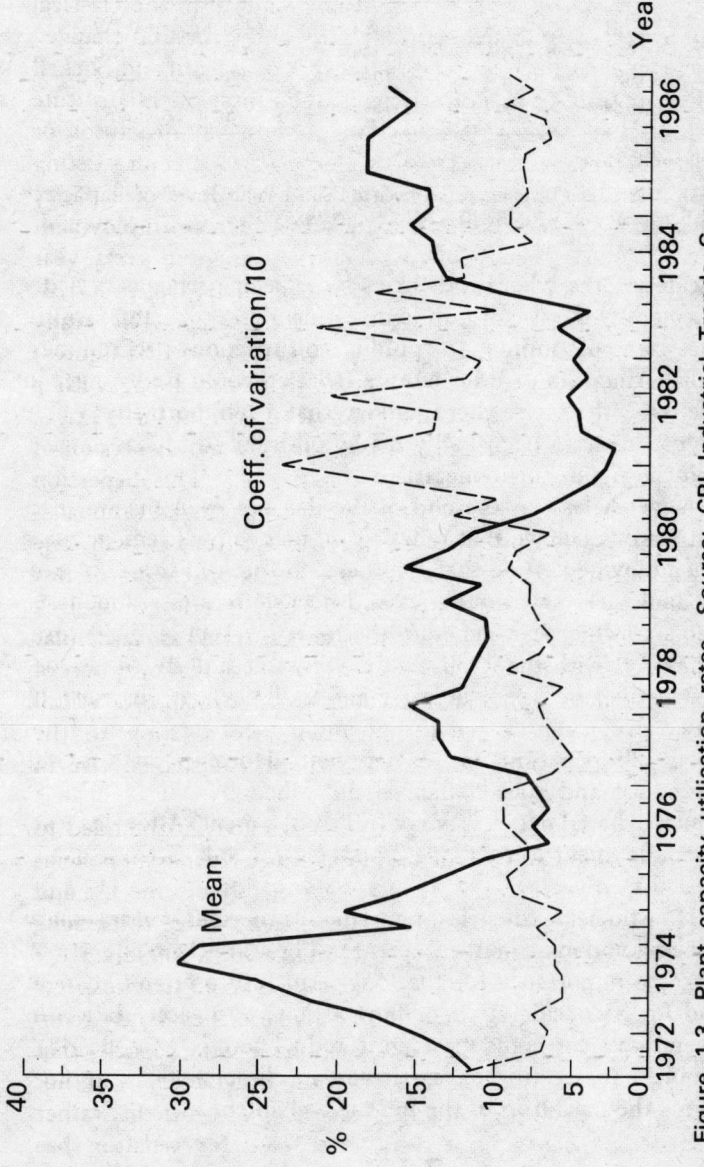

Figure 1.3 Plant capacity utilisation rates. *Source*: CBI Industrial Trends Survey, question 14, author's calculations.

Table 1.3

	Unemployment rate		Inflation rate	
	France	UK	France	UK
1981	7.4	9.9	11.8	11.9
1982	8.1	11.5	12.6	8.6
1983	8.3	12.3	9.5	4.6
1984	9.7	13.5[a]	7.3	5.0

a Ignoring change to counting procedure.

Source: Sachs and Wyplosz, paper given to London Policy Panel, CEPR (Centre for Economic Policy Research), 11 November 1985.

greatest force where industries have been particularly badly affected by the use of public investment as a regulator, e.g. in the case of inputs to public construction programmes. Furthermore, a case for simple reflation could be stronger in the UK than elsewhere, given that even normally viable industries have been badly hit by oil-induced exchange rates and the rigours of monetarism.

Nevertheless, at the end of the day not even the warmest enthusiasts believe that reflation on its own will remove mass unemployment. For that, we need to think in terms of new technologies, new industries and new sources of autonomous demand which can generate the mass markets of the future. Analogies with the 1930s are never exact but are sometimes instructive. Between the early and mid-1930s a construction-based expansion caused the unemployment rate to fall from about 20 per cent to 15 per cent. However, it was the structural and social changes unleashed by World War II which ushered in a new era of full employment. After the War, unemployment went above 2 per cent for only five out of the next fifteen years.

How do new industries, new labour processes, expansionary climates and mass markets emerge? These are clearly questions of some importance for the long-term future of employment and for a consideration of how a downward acceleration in unemployment could be engineered. There is now clearly a problem in creating an expansionary climate. This problem forms the backdrop to the next five chapters.

2 Workshop and the world

This chapter is mainly concerned with manufacturing. The structural view, introduced in Chapter 1, suggests that when technology and lifestyles are changing rapidly, the economy will tend to get stuck in a cost-cutting mode rather than balance this with new-product development and expansion of new-product areas. One implication of this is that industrial policies to encourage new areas of production should go hand in hand with those aimed at industrial restructuring, and that a key aim of policy should be to minimise uncertainty over future demand.

Four key issues

Industrial policy is notoriously difficult to get right. It involves steering the industrial structure in a particular direction, which requires a strategic overview of all the important currents affecting the evolution of technology, consumption patterns and trade. This chapter investigates four key issues in British manufacturing in order to provide a sound background for the discussion of industrial policy in later chapters. These issues are as follows:

1. Deindustrialisation – is manufacturing still important?
2. The new technologies – can Europe compete?
3. Manufacturing in Britain – how competitive are different sectors?

4   Alternative policies for manufacturing – do they mean more jobs?

Deindustrialisation

A considerable degree of confusion appears to exist as to whether the UK economy is undergoing a process of evolution normal to advanced economies, whereby the service component increases over time, or whether a more fundamental and dangerous type of deindustrialisation has been occurring. The latter view has been advanced most forcibly by the House of Lords (1985) Select Committee on Overseas Trade, which concluded that a failure to arrest the decline in manufacturing would have:

> a devastating effect on the future economic and political stability of the nation ... in most other major economies, services have increased their share of output while that of manufacturing has fallen. But in those countries, manufacturing has continued to grow in absolute terms. (pp. 42, 48)

As against this, the Treasury view has been that it is not unusual for energy-producing nations to experience a more rapid switch from manufacturing.[1]

It is necessary to have some concept of 'normal' deindustrialisation before these competing views can be assessed. Beyond a certain low level of development, the share of money-GDP accounted for by services tends to rise with national income.[2] This tends to happen even if the share of real GDP, i.e. the volume of services in relation to the volume of total output, actually falls. In recent decades the price of many services has tended to rise in relation to goods, with the result that services output is valued at higher prices and accounts for a higher proportion of nominal GDP.[3] Some particular examples for the British case are striking. In the twenty years to 1983 the relative price of having a meal out rose by 30 per cent while durable household goods and clothing fell in relative price by about 40 per cent.

Provided that the share of service output in volume terms

holds up reasonably well in the face of higher relative prices – which it appears to do – the share of service employment must rise. With lower relative productivity in services it takes an increasingly larger share of the workforce to produce the same share of output.[4]

Because of measurement problems, it is easiest to track the path of services bought by individuals – consumer services. The share of services by volume in consumer expenditure is shown in Fig. 2.1. It is roughly constant across OECD countries, regardless of their level of affluence.[5]

It is also possible to examine for various countries the time-path of the share of services in consumer expenditure. It is

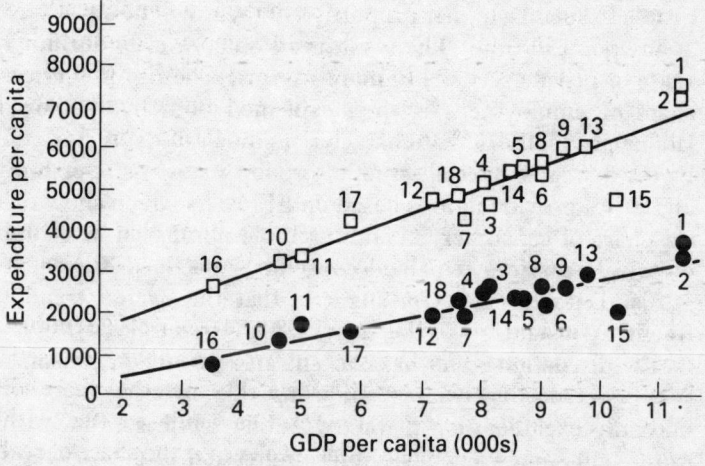

Figure 2.1 The relationship between real expenditure per capita and GDP per capita. Key: 1, USA; 2, Canada; 3, Japan; 4, Austria; 5, Belgium; 6, Denmark; 7, Finland; 8, France; 9, Germany; 10, Greece; 11, Ireland; 12, Italy; 13, Luxembourg; 14, the Netherlands; 15, Norway; 16, Portugal; 17, Spain; 18, UK.
a) At average international prices using purchasing power parities and denominated in US dollars.
b) Medical care, transport and communication, recreation and education, and miscellaneous goods and services.
Source: OECD Economic and Statistics Department Working Paper no. 17, December, 1984, Paris, Organisation of Economic Cooperation and Development.

widely believed that services are similar to luxury goods, in that a higher proportion of expenditure is allocated to services over time as societies increase their income levels. This view has been challenged for the case of private services by Gershuny (1978) and Gershuny and Miles (1983). They argue that in many countries the share of consumer expenditure devoted to marketed services has not risen over time. Rather, consumers have tended to substitute durable goods and their own labour for purchased services. Examples of this are the replacement of live entertainment and personal service by domestic electrical appliances, and private motor cars for public transport. The widespread diffusion of home computers may extend the range into medical advice and education. This substitution occurs mainly because of the relative price rise in services. It tends to cancel the opposing tendency for richer people to spend a higher proportion of their income on services at any point in time. The result is a stable, or even declining, share of private services in money terms. The rise in services' share of employment is then explained both by the lower labour productivity that characterises much of the sector, and by the increased specialisation of producer services. Gershuny and Miles provide figures based on EEC data which show that the share of consumer expenditure on a number of categories of private services remained constant or declined during the 1970s. Data for the UK suggests that the overall trend is roughly constant up to the early 1980s (Driver, 1984).

The discussion so far has concentrated mainly on consumer services. One disadvantage of using this category is that it normally excludes non-marketed public services.[6] Since this can give a somewhat misleading impression of growth rates, the share of total services in GDP over three decades is presented in Table 2.1. It is clear from these figures that the share of services' volume in GDP has risen by only a small amount in recent decades in most countries.

One of the main reasons why the volume share of services has been constant is that low productivity growth has prevented the price of services from falling rapidly. Much of the sector has been unaffected by new technology, at least until recently. Baumol *et al.* (1985) have shown that in such 'stagnant' activities (repairs, insurance, professional services,

Table 2.1 Output shares of services in GDP

	GDP value %	GDP volume %
United Kingdom		
1954	44.5	47.9
1963	46.2	47.6
1973	47.8	46.9
1983	50.5	50.3
United States		
1953	44.5	50.4
1963	47.5	51.4
1973	51.5	51.9
1983	54.1	54.6
Japan		
1964	43	51.7
1972	50	50.3
1982	53.9	48.8
Germany		
1964	39.6	45.2
1972	44.4	45.9
1981	50.3	49.7
France		
1964	47.2	51.6
1972	49.9	49.7
1981	46.7	53.7
Italy		
1964	45.5	48.2
1972	49.7	48.6
1982	51.4	49.6

Source: Bank of England (1985), p. 408.

and parts of health, education and leisure), volume shares in the United States remained constant for thirty years up to the late 1970s. Increasingly, however, technology will affect a number of these stagnant sectors as much as the existing 'progressive' sectors such as communications, where productivity already matches that in manufacturing. Expert systems may soon virtually replace some professional services; the thinning out of support staff has already occurred. Gershuny (1982) has pointed to similar possibilities in non-marketed services. Repairs can also now be minimised by adjusting design at the manufacturing stage. Even in the classic case of live entertainment, in so far as it is not displaced by broadcast forms, it is possible to envisage new forms of social innovation.[7]

The discussion so far suggest that, if past trends are repeated, services are unlikely to see any great increase in their share of the volume of output in the forseeable future. Of course, the past is not necessarily a good pointer to the future and a major source of uncertainty is the extent to which new technology and social innovation will be diffused through public and private sectors as well as households. This is paralleled by a further uncertainty in regard to the response of users to large price (or cost) reductions. The fact that services' share of expenditure has held up well in the face of persistently-rising relative prices suggests either an insensitivity to prices or a strong desire for services growth. If the latter were paramount, a fall in relative prices could give a significant boost to consumer services. Even on this projection, however, the *share* of services' output would not necessarily increase greatly, since inputs from manufacturing would be required. On the basis of the latest input–output tables, these are of a significant magnitude in many service industries (Driver, 1987).

To sum up, the demand for manufacturing in relation to services depends on a number of uncertain outcomes; none of these outcomes, however, would render manufacturing unimportant. Even with a fast rate of technological diffusion and high growth in service activities, manufacturing would still provide a significant proportion in real terms (and probably a rising level) of consumer demand. This may occur either through an expansion in domestic manufacturing capacity or through a greater reliance on imports, the balance being largely determined by domestic performance in the manufacturing sector.

Can Europe compete in high technology?

Accepting that manufacturing is important, are there particular sectors of it which matter more than others? Two popular views are often expressed in respect of this question. The first is that Europe is now so far behind the US and Japan in high-technology industries that it is almost impossible for it to catch up in these fields; rather, it is relegated to competing on cost grounds with low-income countries. The second view is that only high-technology industries matter and that the traditional industries will eventually succumb to low-cost competition. Neither of these views can be wholly accepted.

Certainly it is true that the US and Japan have been increasing their lead in high technology, as defined by the ratio of research-and-development expenditure to sales. Japan has also been increasing its lead over Europe and the USA in medium technology. Table 2.2 summarises some recent trends.

Table 2.2 Change between 1962 and 1982 in the percentage trade balance of GDP by sector and country

	High technology[a]	Medium technology[b]	Low technology[c]
Japan v. Europe	+4%	+5%	−1.5%
USA v. Europe	+0.5%	−1.5%	−1.5%

a Aerospace, office machines, electronics and components, pharmaceuticals, instruments and electrical machinery.
b Cars, chemicals, other manufactures, non-electrical machinery, rubber, plastics and non-ferrous metals.
c All other manufacturing.

Source: OECD (1985a).

In the field of high technology, European producers have relatively high shares in pharmaceuticals but only in one part of information technology – telecommunications. In mainframe computers, the indigenous European share of the world market is less than 5 per cent, compared with 70 per cent for IBM alone. In semiconductors, European-owned companies again account for less than 5 per cent of the world market and this share has been falling. Between 1975 and 1983, total electronics production grew in real terms by 10 per cent in Japan, 5 per cent in the US and only 2 per cent in Europe. The EEC sells to Japan and the US one-fifth and one-third respectively of computers and electrical goods imported by the EEC from these countries.[8]

Europe's strongest areas are in the medium-technology fields of classical engineering, in sectors such as engines and construction equipment, but Japan has now taken the lead in many of these products. In machine tools, which increasingly incorporate high-technology products, Japan now produces 50 per cent more than the next-largest producer – West Germany.

Two reasons appear to command broad support in explaining Europe's poor performance in high technology. One is that European markets are fragmented, with consequent difficulties in achieving scale economies. This applies with extra force to products with short lives, in that this makes developmental projects risky and a large market base is needed to encourage innovation.[9]

A second plausible reason advanced for Europe's failure in high technology centres on the extent of resources allocated to education and high-technology research outside defence. The contrast in education is particularly marked, as shown in Table 2.3. Not only are proportionately fewer people in third-level education, but the expenditure per student and researcher is much less in the EEC than in Japan or the US.

Table 2.3 Degree-level and postgraduate qualifications as a percentage of labour force

Country	Qualifications as % of labour force
UK	7
Germany	8
USA	19
Japan	13

Source: British Industrial Performance, 1985.

There are some tentative grounds for optimism in expecting a rebound in European competitiveness in high technology. Increasing reliance on custom-made computer chips will tend to lessen the advantages of technical economies of scale; new ways of joint European research and collaboration are being explored; joint ventures with Japan and the US, where they do not undermine European production, may also help. On the medium- to high-technology front, all countries seem to be experiencing common difficulties in breaking into the new important area of flexible manufacturing. Nevertheless, the scale of the problem in information technology should not be underestimated. The very process of custom-made chips which lessens advantages of scale also demand close cooperation between those who design chips and those who use them in computer manufacture.

It is sometimes argued that Europe does not need to compete in high-tech areas. The approach suggested is to buy in components or know-how from Japan or the US. Behind this view lies the observation that the US, with a high-tech lead in the postwar period, did not grow particularly fast. Furthermore, diffusion of technology is now more rapid than in the past, so it is more difficult to extract long-term technological rents from research. A sensible strategy would certainly include buying in technology under licence, since no country can be self-sufficient in all high-technology areas. This approach, after all, characterised recent Japanese growth, where technology has been imported and re-exported on a larger scale than many European countries. Indeed, Japan still has a negative technological balance of payments as defined by the net payment for royalties, licences, etc., for high-technology products. Japan, nevertheless, has been moving rapidly towards a position of net export of technological know-how, a role traditionally played by the US (see Table 2.4).

Table 2.4 Technological balance by country: million national currency (1975 prices) divided by purchasing-power parities, 1975

	Receipts (1983)	Balance (1983)	Growth of receipts (%) (1972–83)
UK	651	140	16
Germany	365	−364	36
France	558	−60	85
Japan	646	−103	201
US	4329	4196	35
Italy	120	−366	48

Source: OECD STIU databank

Whatever the necessity to import licensed technology in some sectors, there are dangers in a country becoming too reliant on this route. Firstly, there is generally a system of fund transfer within large corporations from mature products to innovative ones (Knight, 1980). This process, which operates by overpricing mature products and subsidising research on new ones, will apply whether or not a company's high technology is located in a particular country; in other words an outflow of funds to subsidise high technology elsewhere will occur in countries that are deficient in new-product development.

Secondly, there are long lead-times, often eight–ten years, in developing new products, but short sales-lives. This means that development costs have to be extracted in periods as short as two years. Producers are accordingly less willing to license the technology immediately. Furthermore, without early or prior exposure to the technology it is hard for those who get the licenses to use it to full advantage before it is outmoded. Indeed, some companies sustain upstream component- or materials-divisions precisely for this reason. All of this is a source of concern for European countries. It is a special problem for Britain, where the technological balance has deteriorated faster than in any other major European country.

The Advisory Council for Advanced Research and Development (ACARD, 1986a) has drawn attention to ways in which a high-tech advantage can be used to secure economic or political domination. Companies may decide to make sophisticated software available only in binary rather than source language; similarly, new advanced hardware may be restricted, as in the recent US technology embargo. English (1984) has instanced a case where access to modern US machines was denied to French scientists for political reasons, and the former permanent UK representative to the European Commission, Michael Butler, has warned that if Boeing in aircraft or IBM in information technology become any bigger 'the temptation to behave like monopolists will be great. European industry in other fields will suffer' (*Financial Times*, 5 February 1986).

The position of Europe in the high-technology stakes remains in doubt and must hinge to a large degree on the extent of collaboration that can be obtained between the major economies. The ESPRIT programme brought together 300 firms and 200 research institutions for basic research, but doubts about continued funding were expressed by the British government in 1986. It is, in any event, more important to get collaboration in the area of commercial applications; the Eureka programme will attempt this in high technology, but it has no central funds and is biased towards smaller firms.

British manufacturing

The European-wide problems of market share and competitiveness in high-tech areas are evident in Britain to an even greater extent than elsewhere. The British share of the IT (information-technology) market is about a third of the combined German and French share, while the UK growth rate has been about two-thirds of the average of these countries since the early 1970s. The Ashworth report on the industry (NEDO, 1984a) concluded that 'on present trends, the UK will not have an independent broad-based IT industry by the end of the decade' (p. 9). Market share is only likely to be regained by focusing research on new products and areas of applications. This the Alvey programme has attempted to do, but its research money (public and private) is small relative to what comparable countries are spending and it is not yet clear whether the follow-on programme recommended by industrialists in 1986 will be accepted by government. The scale of the problem is illustrated by the fact that the entire revenue of the UK industry is equivalent to what the US spends on IT research. The British government has declined to endorse the Ashworth strategy of more directed support and restructuring of the industry using government purchasing power and selective assistance. Since that report, the situation has deteriorated further. In software, also, a government-sponsored report (ACARD, 1986a) has been extraordinarily hard-hitting, suggesting that within ten years on present policies only those firms supported for defence reasons would survive:

> The UK is likely to underinvest in R&D, underinvest in capital equipment, underinvest in staff retraining and

underinvest in development and marketing. There are too many small companies which cannot afford this investment and too many large companies which will not make the investment unless forced to by public purchasing or government subsidy. (p. 15)

In other areas of high technology, the picture is mixed but not, on the whole, encouraging. The ratio of exports to imports fell, in varying degrees, in all high-technology product-groups except aircraft between 1979 and 1984.[10]

In the UK case the industrial problem is not confined to poor performance in high-technology areas; a question mark hangs over the whole pattern of development of its competitive advantage. A recent National Economic Development Council report (NEDC 84(21)) showed that the UK had held on relatively better than elsewhere in:

several traditional industries, usually characterised by relatively standardised and price-sensitive products, often now the subject of major expansion by newly industrialising countries . . . conversely, the UK's trade has generally fared less well than abroad in higher value-added, more skill and innovation intensive products. (p. 1)

The analysis here referred to change in trade performance *vis-à-vis* European competitors between 1972 and 1978. However an updating of the data to 1981 shows a similar pattern.

The poor performance in medium-technology areas such as engineering is a disturbing development, since the fortunes of the basic consumer industries such as textiles and clothing are highly dependent on innovative machinery-design involving the application of electronics to classical engineering. Knitting machinery, for instance, has been transformed from standard equipment into machines that can be set up from kits and that are programmed via computers to produce any particular design. Failure to keep up with such developments has meant the demise of knitting-machinery manufacture in the UK. A similar story can be told in respect of many sectors of mechanical engineering. The decline of some engineering sectors has also had a recursive effect on high-technology industries. The collapse of the typewriter industry and other precision mechanical-engineering activities did not enhance the chance of entering the growing electronic-typewriter and word-processing market. Import penetration here is 90 per cent and many other areas of office machinery such as microcomputers and micrographics are similarly placed.

The National Institute for Economic and Social Research (NIESR) estimated in their *Review* that, even by 1990, mechanical engineering will be operating below its 1980 level of output (November 1985, p. 50); motor vehicles and metal manufacture as well as parts of electrical engineering have also seen large declines in output. Part of this deterioration is due to the manner in which the government responded to the rise in oil production, but part is also due to long-term trends in competitiveness.

Reasons for poor performance in the engineering industries have been investigated by NIESR using matched samples of companies (Daly *et al.*, 1985). The UK firms seemed inferior in quality of machinery, but the major differences were in the technical competence of supervisory management and in the technical ability to cope with production difficulties or to get the best from complex machinery. This underscores the general point that British employers have traditionally paid scant attention to training (MSC/NEDO, 1985).

In one way this information is encouraging, in that there seems to be a readily identifiable problem with a solution which, however difficult to resolve in practice, can at least be made a focus for policy—technical education of an appropriate calibre. In effect, however, the NIESR and other studies are profoundly discouraging. The problem of technical education has been identified repeatedly in the past by other researchers, without producing an adequate response. Far from the training record of companies improving, it has got steadily worse in recent years as the number of apprentices has dropped and as government efforts have focused on low-skill alternatives such as the Youth Training Scheme (YTS).[11]

Not all of the long-run deterioration of UK manufacturing is attributable to the poor state of production management and technical competence. Industry has also had a poor record of research, innovation, product design and patenting. Researchers have shown that a low level of product patenting has contributed to a loss in trade, particularly so in metals and engineering (Pavitt, 1983; NEDC, 84(21)). A recent report by the Advisory Board for the Research Councils (1986) shows that Britain spends less per head of population on academic research than any of the other European countries studied, with the Netherlands spending twice as much as Britain. Other research by the ABRC confirms that the relative decline in funding has had a serious effect on research output.

New breakthroughs in production technology – advanced manufacturing technology – are now becoming commercially viable. These techniques consist of an amalgam of older methods such as numerically-controlled machinery, computer-aided design and operating (production engineering, planning, storage and transport) and flexible manufacturing systems (FMS, which involves computer-controlled interaction between two or more sets of machines and a conveying system). In 1984 there were only twenty-five FMS plants in Europe, of which four were in the UK, but the number is growing rapidly. Even if the diffusion of FMS is slower than expected, the widespread adoption of computer-aided design and manufacturing will transform existing methods of production in a short time.

Given the poor skill record of supervisory management revealed in the NIESR and other studies, it seems questionable whether such technology will be adequately exploited in Britain. The Policy Studies Institute (Northcott *et al.*, 1986) state that not enough production engineers have the skills to cope with robots and many need to rely on suppliers to get the equipment operational.[12]

The opportunities that the technology offers could compensate, however, for many of the existing failings. Japanese success in achieving greater organisation in production was by and large achieved before any advanced automation was prevalent. FMS technology now gives the opportunity of achieving similar and even greater gains in productivity. By allocating work flexibly between workstations and increasing speed of design changes, FMS can achieve better utilisation of equipment and materials, lower stocks, higher quality and shorter delivery times.

Batch production will no longer entail such high set-up costs and unit costs of small runs will be cheaper. Although FMS has so far been mainly applied to heavy engineering such as manufacture of trucks, machine tools, construction equipment and in the aerospace industry, it will increasingly be used for other applications. Some companies may wish to reverse their retreat into speciality production given that FMS offers the opportunity of cheaply producing a mix of products; the constraint will be on sales and marketing ability. 'The traditional response by companies to increasing competition, that is to maximise volume and minimise variety in order to reduce conventional production costs may no longer be an adequate option' (NEDO, 1984b, p. 2).

The previous discussion has highlighted problems for virtually all areas of British manufacturing: high technology, which has problems similar to those of other European countries though on a greater scale; engineering sectors, which have declined unusually rapidly in the UK for a variety of long- and short-term reasons; and low-technology industries, some of which have performed well, but not absolutely, only in relation to the loss in market share common to all advanced countries. On the whole the picture is not encouraging; long-term decline has been exacerbated by the punitive stance of government to manufacturing industry, especially in the early 1980s – in 1986, manufacturing output was still well below its 1973 level.

Employment prospects for manufacturing

The prospects for manufacturing employment on current trends are not encouraging either. Table 2.5 gives broad sectoral forecasts to 1990 based on work done by the Warwick Institute for Employment Research. These figures suggest that, on present policies, all manufacturing sectors will contribute to a continuing fall in employment.

One alternative approach would be to produce higher-quality products which would increase demand and value-added without necessarily involving job losses. This was part of the rhetoric of the 1975–9 industrial strategy, though in practice it proved hard to increase quality without rationalis-

Table 2.5 Employment forecasts in manufacturing

Industry	Employment change, 1984–90
Food, drink, tobacco	−51.5
Chemicals, oil refining	−28.9
Metal manufacture	−23.7
Mechanical engineering	−104.0
Other engineering, vehicles, Shipbuilding and metal goods	−160.4
Textiles	−49.3
Leather, clothing, etc.	−57.5
All other manufacturing	−54.2

Source: *Review of the Economy and Employment*, Institute for Employment Research, 1985.

ations which entailed redundancies. Nevertheless, moving up-market in quality and type of goods produced is a classic way of achieving gains in market share and jobs.[13]

It is also possible that increased exports could bring more jobs, even if there was a corresponding increase in imports. This would happen, for instance, if the associated change in trade patterns resulted either in increased labour intensity or in higher value-added production with consequent multiplier effects. Increased trade with advanced countries might stimulate labour-intensive production while trade with less-developed countries might stimulate demand for higher value-added goods such as construction machinery.

Conceptual exercises along these lines have been investigated using simulation techniques by Driver, Kilpatrick and Naisbitt (1985, 1986). Five different experiments were attempted, each involving a change in the pattern of traded goods or an expansion of exports (with balanced imports) to various trade blocs. In each case input–output tables were used to assess not only the effects in the industries concerned, but also the indirect effects in supplier industries. The experiments are described below.

Experiment 1 – Adopting the West German trade structure

This involved a consideration of the employment changes that would occur if the UK had a similar trade structure to West Germany, but without changing the magnitude of the overall trade balance in manufacturing. It has been argued (e.g. Pavitt, 1983) that the imperial orientation of British trade reduced the pressure on British firms to adjust and may be the reason that British trade remained more oriented than others towards slow-growing markets and product areas. While there are problems in imposing the German pattern of trade on the UK industrial structure, the two countries are known not to differ very markedly in respect of the latter (Panic, 1978).

The employment implications of the changed trade pattern – which involve increased specialisation in vehicles and engineering, and less export activity in textiles and clothing – are not obvious *a priori*. The overall employment effect is the sum of the sectoral changes and the effect on supplier industries also needs to be calculated.

Experiment 2 – Convergence towards West German productivity

This was identical to experiment 1, except that the adoption of the German trade pattern was paralleled by a closing – by 25 per cent – of the gaps between labour-productivity levels in the two countries. This was thought to make the first experiment somewhat more realistic.

Experiment 3 – Magnification of existing trade specialisation

As with the previous cases, this involved a change in trade patterns. Instead of imposing the German pattern, a new one was simulated by increasing by 10 per cent the trade balances that were positive and decreasing by 10 per cent those that were negative. The total trade balance change was again arranged to be zero.

Experiment 4 – Balanced trade expansion with the EEC

This involved an expansion of trade with the EEC of £1bn in 1979 prices. The assumption here was that extra imports would balance extra exports and that the composition of the extra trade would mirror the existing pattern with the EEC.

Experiment 5 – Balanced trade expansion with the NICs

This was identical to experiment 4, except that the country-bloc considered was not the EEC but a broad group of newly industrialising countries (NICs). This experiment is of considerable interest in view of the recent tendency of the NICs to cut back on imports in response to recession, high interest rates and the problem of debt finance. While the growth of imports relative to GDP actually increased in advanced countries in the 1980s compared to the previous years, the growth of developing-country imports relative to GDP was more than halved. If, as seems likely, this situation is at least partially reversed over the rest of this decade, the experiment of increased balanced trade with the NICs could correspond to a real development.

Conclusions

In the case of each of these experiments, the employment effects in the traded industries were added together and the totals are presented in Table 2.6

Table 2.6 Results of trade experiments

Number	Net employment change	Change in value added[a]
1	229,800	£1,352m
2	−727,800	£1,352m
3	−4,900	£177m
4	−2,230	£−17m
5	10,130	£28m

a The further employment effects of these changes are not analysed.

It seems clear from Table 2.6 that the results of these experiments do not provide any hope that British manufacturing employment could increase significantly. The first experiment showed a total gain of over 200,000 jobs, but this was converted to a loss of 700,000 when the productivity gap between West Germany and the UK was closed by a quarter, as in experiment 2. It is true that even in the second case there was an increase in UK national income which would ultimately represent a compensating increase, but this offset would not amount to much more than 150,000 jobs initially. The case of simply increasing trade specialisation, as in experiment 3, resulted in a net employment change of virtually zero.

In the balanced trade expansions, there are only small changes in UK employment in the case of trade both with the EEC and the NICs. These small totals mask considerable change between sectors, with mechanical engineering gaining and textiles and clothing losing in trade with the NICs: motor vehicles lose ground in trade with the EEC and the gains are more evenly spread. In the case of EEC trade, the direct gains are actually positive but are outweighed by the indirect effects.

The results of these experiments are only indicative. The analysis was carried out in 1984 on the latest available input–output tables, which were for 1979. Extensive changes may have occurred in the structure of production since then, but the broad conclusion will not have been affected; no easy route exists via changed patterns of trade or increased balanced trade which would lead to an expansion of UK manufacturing employment. An expansion of demand coupled with policies to control inflation and increase customer satisfaction with domestically-produced goods might increase manufacturing employment, but the results of the macroeconomic simulations presented in Chapter 1 did not indicate that large job gains would accrue through reflation alone. This applies with even greater force to manufacturing, where a target of even sustaining present employment levels seems optimistic.[14]

The experiments above have confirmed that a switch of production between sub-sectors of manufacturing has only small employment effects.[15] However disappointing this may be for employment hopes, it also implies that industrial restructuring, achieved through promoting some sectors rather than others, would not have any adverse impact on employment, though of course there would be gainers and losers. This question of industrial restructuring is examined below.

Industrial policy

The UK manufacturing sector has been in long-term decline. Nevertheless, much of the recent loss in output and employment is attributable to the high value of the exchange rate since 1980, brought about by a combination of government policy and North Sea oil. In 1985–6, policy was explicitly aimed at maintaining upward pressure on the nominal exchange rate, in order to squeeze firms' liquidity and thus control wage costs.

The government view has been that future opportunities for manufacturing would emerge if wages remained under control while the exchange rate depreciated with the peaking of oil revenues (Department of Trade and Industry, 1985). The assumption here is that industry will prepare in advance for a favourable export environment.

This seems an extraordinarily relaxed view. Even before the fall in oil prices in early 1986, the view was that the UK's oil surplus would have disappeared by 1990. This period may now have shortened. In contrast, the length of time required to break into new markets or regain old ones is lengthening as products become more sophisticated and greater learning problems arise. In vehicle manufacture, for instance, producers moving into new market segments typically require three product generations to catch up with the market leaders (Jones, 1985a).[16] If companies are now expecting an export boom, it is inconceivable why manufacturing investment should now be so low; preparation for the boom should already be in hand.

The argument in favour of a coordinated industrial policy to help arrest the present decline in manufacturing now seems irresistible. The non-interventionist approach to industrial priorities involves at least two dangers. Firstly, nearly all firms except the 'megacorps' have short-term horizons. Not many such companies think further ahead than two years in so far as investment payback is concerned. This approach is necessitated by pressure on share prices whenever a serious investment or research commitment threatens a regular income-stream or whenever a takeover is announced. Even where institutions exist to channel funds into long-term, high-risk areas, the results are not predictable. Most UK venture capital raised in the early 1980s went to the US. And even in the US, where growth conditions were favourable, the role of venture capital in long-term restructuring is questionable and there has been intense interest in industrial policy of the European variety (Reich, 1982). New industries were for a while stimulated by large flows of venture capital in the US, but speculative support ebbed in the mid-1980s in favour of takeovers and management buyouts; pension funds reduced their new investments in venture capital by nearly half.[17]

A second reason for market inadequacy is the policies of multinationals, who often seek to destroy rivals by cross-subsidy and predatory pricing. It has now been well established that there is a direct correlation between market share and profitability (Shepherd, 1975). The largest companies are aware of this and are prepared to spend large amounts in order to undermine competitors. They may also be using a 'Trojan horse' policy in their foreign investment (Dunning, 1985). The losers in this process are likely to be technological laggards, even where the performance gap is temporary and where a viable recovery path exists. A case in point is the experience of the UK car industry, where Austin Rover has suffered in the attempt of General Motors to use the surplus liquidity from its North American sales to buy market shares in Europe (Jones, 1985b).

The dangers alluded to above are accentuated during a period of rapid structural change such as the major economies are now experiencing. The strategy of pursuing short-term gain is more attractive under heightened uncertainty. Furthermore the opportunity for predatory behaviour is greatest when a company or industry is preoccupied with the problems of restructuring. For these reasons, and because of the arguments inherent in the structural view as set out in Chapter 1, governments need to be involved in choosing industries for priority support and in identifying future viable production opportunities which are ignored by private business. This corrective to market failure is appropriate, given the possible benefits, external to companies' balance sheets, of a coordinated approach. If targeting of potential growth sectors is properly done in the sense of focusing on industries with a future, it will minimise the opposition of industrialists.[18] It will also provide a clear rationale for any temporary selective-management of market trade. To the extent that the industrial targeting works with, rather than against, the grain of desired structural change, it would be most likely to succeed.

It must be said, however, that it is rather difficult to arrive at clear principles in targeting industrial areas for expansion and support. This is especially true if it is also desired to maintain the maximum consensus. The industrial strategy of the Labour government 1975–9 had mixed success, but one of its chief failings was the inadequate basis on which decisions for industrial priorities were based. Firstly, the areas covered by the strategy – about 60 per cent of manufacturing – had not been carefully chosen according to any rationale. Secondly it must be doubted whether the powers of selective intervention under section 8 of the Industry Act were used to maximum effect. For instance, a lot of aid was initially directed towards ferrous foundries without insisting on rationalisation to ensure a viable industry.[19] There was much emphasis on diffusing best practice throughout an industry but little idea of how to do it, given that direct intervention in rationalising production within sectors was ruled out. The confused objectives of that period are exemplified by the potentially conflicting criteria for choosing priority industries: '(i) the large industries . . . (ii) industries where there is scope for . . . the application of modern technology, and (iii) industries where our relative performance has most severely deteriorated' (NEDC 75(69) p. 10).

The failure to plan properly in the 1970s and to separate clearly industrial and employment objectives is not an argument for abandoning the process of targeting. The resources exist for developing a successful prioritisation. There is now a number of major institutions in Britain researching into technological change; these include units at the universities of Sussex, Aston and Manchester and the Technical Change Centre. There are also merchant banks with experience of restructuring and marketing, and economic research institutes that could contribute, along with the Department of Trade and Industry team. Companies themselves can help to prioritise areas, as has been done on a European scale with the ESPRIT programme.

Employment policy

Manufacturing will continue to be important in terms of output share in the foreseeable future. Any deterioration in a country's manufacturing growth rate should therefore be viewed with concern, as it could affect living standards and employment prospects. A loss of manufacturing potential is not, however, to be confused with necessary restructuring. It is inevitable that whole areas of industry will, periodically, shift regionally or internationally, in accordance with development patterns. The employment losses occasioned in this way could, theoretically, be compensated within manufacturing by newly-emerging sectors, but in practice these new sectors are unlikely to be labour intensive. Employment is likely to contract within manufacturing, even at historically rapid growth rates of output, as confirmed earlier. Even in the US, where 14 million net new jobs are forecast between 1984 and 1995, only 1.4 million will be in manufacturing.[20] Job losses in manufacturing must be compensated by jobs in other sectors, in particular those stimulated by the high-income growth that restructuring manufacturing will make possible. If other job-creating strategies exist, it would be short-sighted to insist on maintaining labour in sectors where cheaper imports will inevitably mean ultimate job losses.

It is suggested in the House of Lords Report (1985) that industrial policy should combine 'careful planning of long-term industrial priorities' with 'consensus and commitment at national and company level' (p. 51). But this imperative fails to clarify how these principles can be combined, since any prioritisation requires gainers and losers and people made redundant may face a life on the dole.

Opposition to change by industrialists will be minimised by targeting areas with a viable future, but what of those whose jobs may be threatened? Trade unions will not expect a direct or immediate benefit from rationalisation and targeting growth areas may mean little extra in the way of direct employment in the short run.

The only way to square the circle and achieve both restructuring and full employment is to pursue a policy of guaranteeing low unemployment. This requires generating enough jobs to accommodate the unemployed and those threatened by rationalisation. Quite apart from the question of its social cost, the fear of unemployment must not act as a constraint on targeting growth sectors within manufacturing. The following chapters will examine how such an approach to employment could be made consistent with a long-term industrial strategy.

3 High road or low road?

One approach to unemployment is special measures to subsidise people into work. The skills and aptitudes of the unemployed are assessed and jobs matching this potential are created. Many existing schemes, such as the Community Programme, or measures to induce employers or employees to accept low-paid work are in this mould. The House of Commons (1986) Select Committee on Employment and the CBI (1985) have both suggested further measures such as construction schemes to help create jobs; these are discussed further in Chapter 7. The argument for such low-tech or 'no-tech' jobs are that they can offer a swift response, even where the capital stock and the stock of skills are too low to support the creation of many 'real jobs'.

It should be evident, however, that such schemes cannot of themselves solve unemployment. The work offered has to be permanently subsidised; cost per job is an important consideration and the work is generally low-skill in consequence. But Chapter 2 has argued that the general level of skills and training is one of the factors responsible for low productivity and decline. In any case, low-skill job creation just postpones the problem. Only a certain proportion of people are in circumstances where a low-paid job is a reasonable alternative to the dole. The existence of many low-paid jobs is therefore conditional on unemployment remaining large enough to feed the pool of marginally-attractive jobs.

The temptation to pursue a policy of low-skill job creation is increased by the concentration of less-skilled people among the unemployed. Labour force surveys show that less than 10 per cent of the unemployed with a previous job were managers or professionals, but these categories cover about one-third of the workforce. In contrast, manual workers are more heavily represented. The unemployment rate is four times higher for those with no qualifications as it is for those with degrees. One study of a cohort of unemployed showed that 50 per cent had earnings in their last job in the bottom fifth of the earnings distribution (Moylan and Davies, 1980).[1]

There is an alternative approach to matching new job creation to the attributes of the unemployed. Many people in existing low-paid jobs are potentially 'over-qualified' given the lack of opportunities for using their aptitudes or upgrading their skills. It is of course difficult to prove this conclusively, but consider the opinion of one person who is in a position to know.

> At least four-fifths of the population could do anything we asked of them and I venture to suggest that even in the best run industries and in many other aspects of our national life we grossly underestimate and underuse the potential of our people. For example, so many people spread the story that people over a certain age cannot cope with computers and high technology. This is simply not true. All through its history my own company has found that men from the farms, the mines, the shipyards have adapted perfectly readily to the needs of a high technology business. The introduction of information technology into our offices causes no real problems to men and women of all ages. Please do not fall into the trap of regarding whole generations of our people as obsolete. (Harvey-Jones, 1986)

The expansion of opportunity at the upper end of the skills range could involve a general rise in skills and, eventually, draw at least an equivalent number of presently unemployed into work as existing jobs fell vacant in the process of mobility. Arguably, it is only in so far as this process works too slowly, say because of specific regional problems, that the targeting of job creation to the unemployed should be considered at all. Consideration will be given to this in Chapter 7.

Some of those who argue in favour of an expansion of low-skill labour-intensive activities do so out of conviction that it minimises the danger of an upsurge in labour market wage pressure (Layard, 1985). Others argue that not enough fixed capacity exists to sustain any expansion except one directed towards labour-intensive areas where capital use is insignificant (Robinson and Wade, 1985). The first point has been questioned and qualified in the discussion of the 'natural' rate of unemployment in Chapter 1. The second view amounts to an empirical judgment, but the evidence offered in its defence is highly questionable. The authors argue that about £25bn or 13 per cent of the manufacturing capital stock was scrapped in the 1980 recession. This is based on the unsupported assumption that the capital–labour ratio remained on its previous trend. The only other evidence offered is the fact that the CBI index of capacity-utilisation reached its previous peak level in 1985, indicating that capital shortage might be a problem. This notion of a capacity ceiling has been used to argue that new jobs can only come in areas 'where capital labour ratios are both lower and more flexible than they are in manufacturing' (Robinson and Wade, 1985, p. 4). This argument that the economy is at full capacity is refuted in Panel 3.1. This also shows that the least constrained set of manufacturing activities are those that enter into investment expenditure. Consequently, if final demand were to be biased towards investment, this would not only lessen current constraints but future ones as well.

The negative arguments against a policy of expanding along a medium- to high-skill path can be shown to be spurious. But are there positive reasons to believe that new jobs can be other than low skill? One indication may be found in a consideration of existing tendencies in job creation, both in terms of industrial and occupational change. These questions are investigated below.

Industrial structure and skill

We have already observed in Chapter 1 that industrial change is currently at an unusual level. But which industries are

Panel 3.1

The argument that the economy is at full capacity is not soundly based. The estimate by Robinson and Wade (1985) of capacity loss in the early 1980s was obtained by fitting a linear trend to the capital–labour ratio and using this to assess the true capital stock. This amounts to a belief that the official figure on the capital stock suddenly became unreliable at this date; otherwise the authors would have to justify fitting a line to suspect data. No evidence is offered for the prior assumption. Arguments based on the CBI index of capacity-utilisation are also dubious. Not only do the questionnaires tend to cover only those plants currently operating, but they take no account of shift work. More importantly, the index quoted is not an index of capacity use but of the proportion of firms working below satisfactory capacity. The statistical relationship between these two concepts is likely to change over time and in recent years this has biased the CBI index upwards: 'a given percentage recorded as working below capacity in the CBI series may correspond to an increasingly lower true index of capacity utilisation' (Driver, 1986a, p. 50). A further point is that capacity constraints appear to be lowest in those industries that feed directly and indirectly into investment goods. Using input–output analysis, it is possible to derive an index of the capacity constraint on increasing manufacturing by one unit as part of various types of demand expansion. The indices obtained for consumer spending, government spending and exports were all approximately 15 per cent higher than for fixed investment (Driver, 1986b). This suggests that the constraint on investment is not as serious as average figures might imply and that accordingly future constraints would be lower as well. A similar, though more equivocal, conclusion can be drawn in relation to skill shortages.

tending to grow and which are declining? Panel 3.2 shows how industries can be categorised into various growth patterns. The areas of accelerating growth are business services, education, health, banking and other professional services. The areas showing exponential decline are timber, clothing and metal goods. While the latter categories require specific skills, they do not on average compare in complexity with the new fast-growing activities, as argued in the panel.

Another feature of current industrial change merits comment. Skill shortages are again beginning to emerge in some industries, though with mass unemployment the level is not as high as previous peaks. It is not the level, however, but the dispersion of skill shortages between industries that gives grounds for comment. The coefficient of variation of skill constraints across industries is shown in Fig. 3.2 to have risen sharply since 1980, suggesting a marked contrast between different sectors, with job opportunities emerging mainly at the high-skill end.[2]

The Manpower Services Commission (MSC, 1986) has identified constraints mainly in the area of 'higher-level skills' – professional engineers, computer and management services, general management, financial personnel, accountants, marketing managers, industrial designers, technicians, multiskilled craft occupations, secretaries trained in new office skills and sales personnel trained in foreign languages. The process of accelerating structural change would create more such jobs. Those who argue this case stress the necessity for more training, institutional reforms and increased investment in new-product areas to speed the pace of change. This is in contrast to the alternative policy of directly subsidising workers into jobs. That policy tends to be most effective in creating low-skill jobs as the subsidy cost is thereby minimised; it is also likely that the elasticity of substitution with capital is higher for unskilled labour so that, again, it is the least-skilled jobs that are created by programmes of wage subsidies.

Occupational structure and skill

There is now a range of studies examining the tendencies in

Panel 3.2

Different patterns may be distinguished for the trends in the employment proportions of various industries. Stylised trends are shown for some industry groups 1948–85 in Fig. 3.1. The patterns were identified by regressing employment proportions on time, time squared, and a cyclical indicator.

The allocation of industries to the patterns shown in Fig. 3.1 is given below.

Pattern	Industry
a	Professional services, financial services, distribution, miscellaneous services, public services
b	Food, paper, other manufacturing, construction, gas and energy, engineering, vehicles, pottery, chemicals, metal manufacture
c	Timber, textiles, clothing, metal goods, leather
d	Mining, transport, agriculture

At the end of the data period (1985) over half of employment was concentrated in group a, over a quarter in group b, while c and d had 5 per cent and 10 per cent respectively. The groups showing accelerated growth – the service industries in group a – are not only more numerous but they also contain a higher proportion of skilled workers. For instance, in the economy as a whole, the top two social-class groups, which are a rough proxy for skill (managers and professionals such as teachers, nurses, senior administrators) constitute less than 30 per cent of male workers. By contrast, in the service industries the figure is about 40 per cent. The position for women is a little more mixed. In the total female workforce, the top two classes constitute just over 20 per cent, whereas in the private services sector the figure is less than 15 per cent. However, in public services, where a far higher number of women are employed, nearly 40 per cent are in the top two groups, well ahead of the overall percentage.

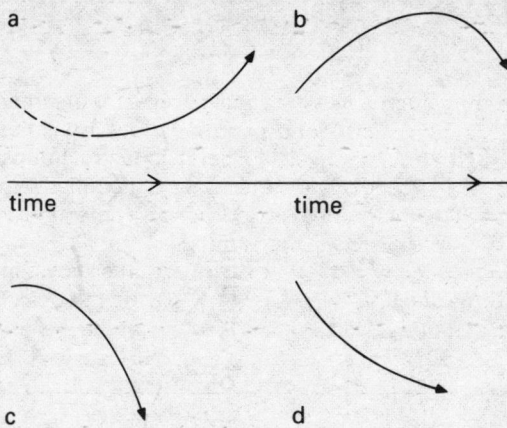

Figure 3.1 Trends in employment proportions of various industries. See Panel 3.2 for key.

occupational change within market economies. The general conclusion appears to be that occupational change results in job creation at upper-skill levels with some, but perhaps minor, deskilling and some polarisation between medium- and high-skill workers. White (1985) has confirmed that the long-run shift towards the upper occupations, observed in the postwar boom, continued right through the periods of recession from the early 1970s (p. 5). This is not of course the only tendency; there has also been an increase in temporary, casual and self-employed labour, much of it unskilled. Some research evidence on these questions is examined below.

The experience of the United States may offer a guide. Despite claims to the contrary, the pattern of job creation in the US has largely been one of growth in medium- to high-skill occupations. Between 1960 and 1982, civilian employment rose by a surprising 51 per cent or nearly 34 million jobs. A continuing high rate of growth, if somewhat less than the historical one, is forecast by the Bureau of Labour Statistics. The situation is of course not directly comparable with Europe or Britain since population growth has been very rapid in the US. Nevertheless it is instructive to observe the skill pattern. Rowthorn (1984) has assessed the growth of different skill categories over the 1970s, as shown in Table 3.1.

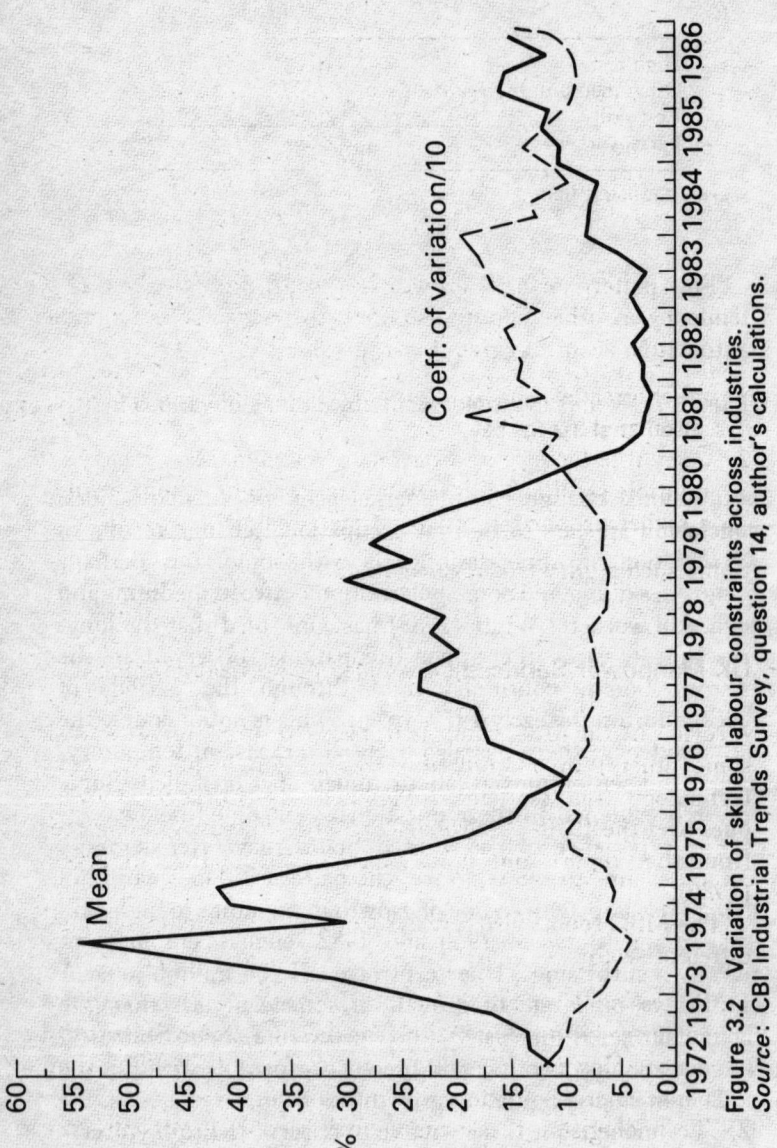

Figure 3.2 Variation of skilled labour constraints across industries.
Source: CBI Industrial Trends Survey, question 14, author's calculations.

Table 3.1 Change in US employment, 1972–82

	Thousands	Per cent
High-tech	1,704	58.2
Other medium–high skill	12,020	29.2
Low skill	2,892	9.1
Farm workers	4,001	11.4

Source: Rowthorn (1984)

This pattern of skill growth has also been observed as a tendency in other country studies. In particular, studies of automation seem to agree that it involves:

1. much greater skills in designing, managing and operating automated systems;
2. a key role for high-skill technical maintenance;
3. multiple skilling, with training and retraining constituting a higher proportion of work time.

Some such studies are reviewed below.

UK Manpower Services Commission, Burgess (1985)

A review by the MSC confirmed the above characteristics (and some others) in a study of the skill implications of new technology. The tendency for higher skills to displace lower ones over the 1970s is fairly evident from Table 3.2, extracted from that report and updated from information in MSC (1986).

The MSC report also forecast various skill developments in different sectors.

1. Professionals – here the tendency is for new technology to enhance skill; routine tasks have become and will be automated. However there may be a tendency for polarisation between professionals and support staff.
2. Technologists – these workers will need multiple skills and upgrading in areas such as software writing, systems analysis and electronics.

Table 3.2 Occupational change 1971–84

	Total 1981 (000s)	1971–81 Annual % change	1981–4 Annual % change
Managerial and administrative			
1 Managers and administrators	706	+2.7	+0.4
10 Sales representatives	365	−1.2	+1.2
20 Skilled personal service	2,128	+0.4	+0.6
Higher-level service			
2 Education professions	863	+2.3	+1.2
3 Health and welfare	955	+4.6	+3.0
4 Other professions	977	+2.0	+2.7
5 Literary, artistic, sports	179	+1.9	+5.0
Higher-level industrial			
6 Engineers, scientists	578	+2.8	+2.3
7 Technicians, draughtsmen	543	+0.6	+3.5
Lower-level service and supervisory			
8 Clerical occupations	2,538	−0.2	−0.9
9 Secretarial occupations	877	+0.5	−0.8
11 Other sales occupations	1,034	−0.5	+2.5
12 Supervisors	295	+3.9	−2.0
21 Other personal services	1,779	0	+0.8
Craft/foremen			
13 Foremen	544	−0.1	−5.9
14 Engineering craft occupations	1,724	−1.0	−2.4
15 Construction craft occupations	762	−0.6	+3.6
16 Other craft occupations	282	−2.8	−6.5
Lower-level industrial and others			
17 Skilled operatives	643	−2.4	−4.1
18 Other operatives	5,782	−2.1	−3.5
19 Security occupations	283	+2.3	−1.3
22 Other occupations	603	−3.6	−0.9
All in employment	22,460		

Sources: Burgess (1985); MSC (1986).

3 Technicians – the need here also is for multiple skilling and ability to contribute diagnostic skills within a design-and-development team. Polarisation is evident between higher- and lower-technician roles.

4 Operators – here many simple tasks have been automated. There is polarisation between machine minders and

operators who can intervene in the highly-skilled task of control and diagnosis.

5 Office workers – some skills for clerks and secretaries have been upgraded. Redundancy is most prevalent in less skilled, clerical, keyboard and administrative work. Greater polarisation between a secretarial hierarchy and a marginalised group with easily replaceable skills may emerge.

Overall, new technology is argued to have 'undermined traditional skills at the lower end of the occupational hierarchy, while sometimes enhancing those at intermediate and higher levels' (p. 402). A two-tier skill structure may be emerging, with highly-skilled technical and professional staff coexisting with a mass of workers with more basic skills, though it is argued that there is some scope for choice in regard to the pattern that emerges.

NEDO case studies

The emphasis given to polarisation in the MSC study contrasts somewhat with the conclusions of a NEDO report of fifteen case studies on the employment effects of information technology: 'the jobs that remain . . . require a greater use of discretion, initiative, understanding and creativity' (NEDO, 1983, p. 24). Jobs that were completely lost were mainly clerk/typists, data-processing operators or machine operators. Jobs created involved management, communications and advisory skills. Secretarial and supervisory roles were widened; technical, professional and management roles were generally enhanced, with a decrease in routine work. However, the NEDO study was fairly narrowly-defined and did not look at the question of polarisation external to the firm. There is now considerable evidence that UK industry is becoming more polarised into a core of key workers with secure conditions, and a periphery of insecure and sometimes low-paid workers (Atkinson, 1984). However it has also been argued that this development is a response to the present high level of unemployment and favourable political conditions rather than inherent in the general tendency of occupational change.

Leontief and Duchin (1985)

The studies so far cited are all based on observations from a particular set of industries or enterprises introducing new technology, and it is somewhat unsafe to draw inferences from them concerning the whole economy. However, more complete studies that have looked at interactions between sectors have come to similar conclusions. Leontief and Duchin (1985) have authored one such study – an input–output analysis of occupational change in the US economy to the year 2000. Their work suggests that the diffusion of computer technology will, depending on its speed, increase employment of technical professionals to between 17 per cent and 20 per cent of employment from the 15 per cent observed at the end of the 1970s. A reduction in clerical workers from 18 per cent to between 15 per cent and 11 per cent is also expected. These percentage figures conceal the extent of relative change in two ways. Firstly, the percentages are stabilised by a near constancy in the proportion of service workers and labourers.[3] Secondly, the occupational categories themselves will change in skill content so that clerical jobs, for instance, will become more skilled than at present.

Conclusion on occupational change

All the studies cited seem to point in the same general direction – towards an economy with an increased use for more capable, flexible and skilled personnel as structural change proceeds. An apparent exception to the view that the skill structure is likely to shift towards the upper end is the study by Rajan and Pearson (1986). They accept that this is true for manufacturing, but argue that in the service industries the occupational structure is likely to 'shift in favour of less skill-intensive personnel and support services' (p. 187). Three observations seem in order here. First, this view does not appear evident from the data provided by the authors themselves, which is reproduced as Table 3.3. Secondly, in so far as the remark is inferred from the tendency of large firms to economise on labour while small or medium firms lag behind,

Table 3.3 Service industries: occupational changes in period 1985–90[a]

	Likely to:		
	Increase (%)	Remain static (%)	Decrease (%)
Managers and administrators	39 (Small)	54 (Small/medium)	7 (All)
All professions	47 (Small/medium)	48 (All)	5 (Large)
Support services	45 (Small/medium)	39 (Small/medium)	16 (Large)
Personal services	28 (Small/medium)	63 (All)	9 (Large)
Technicians, Craftsmen and operatives	48 (All)	39 (All)	13 (All)
Others	43 (Small/medium)	42 (All)	15 (Large)

a Under each percentage is given the type of employers dominating the result. Four employer-types have been designated for this purpose: large (over 500); medium (200–499); small (under 200); All (no dominance by size).

Source: Rajan and Pearson (1986), Table 16.9.

this may be seen as a temporary development. Thirdly, the authors themselves recognise that even the lower-skill categories will be enhanced in future: 'innate attributes, social skills and work experience were increasingly regarded as vital for these hitherto less skill-intensive occupations (support staff and personal services such as cashiers, receptionists, waiters)' (p. 199).

Some will wish to argue that the trends noted above are themselves the result of current wage structures and that a sufficiently flexible wage structure can provide for as many jobs at the low-skill end as are needed. Certainly, it is unwise to assume that skill structure and employment content follow directly from technology. But the point of observing the tendency of occupational change was to see whether it indicated the possibility of a different approach which accelerated existing trends; this it appears to do.

Training

The preceding discussion points to the need for more and better training.

Enhanced skills are needed at all levels of work. This has been demonstrated in the discussion of craft and management skills (Daly *et al.*, 1985), in general comparisons of education levels with other countries (NEDC, 1984), in the documentation of changing job patterns (Atkinson and Meager, 1985) and in reports of existing and impending skills shortages (MSC, 1986). The necessity for greater training was graphically illustrated by the fall in the purchase of office machinery in Britain in 1986 due to a lack of fully-trained staff to utilise existing equipment properly.

The increased structural change in recent years might have been expected to lead to an equivalent increase in training. This has not happened: rather the reverse. Apprenticeships have fallen in recent years from 100,000 to 40,000. The proportion of employees in manufacturing receiving training has dropped from 5.5 per cent in 1967 to 3.2 per cent in 1982 and 2 per cent in 1985 (Davis, 1986). The Youth Training Scheme is of course now two years long and it has the critical support of the TUC, but in so far as it has been practised to date, 'this contains little in the way of specific vocational skills' (Prais, 1986). In the economy as a whole the percentage of full-time workers receiving formal training (including YTS) fell from about 7 per cent in 1974 to about 5 per cent in 1984 (Davis, 1986, pp. 84, 85). In adult training and education it might have been expected that the fall in 16–19-year-olds (from 3.7 million in 1982 to a projected 2.6 million in 1994) would have offered an opportunity to divert resources towards adult provision. This has not happened; the government's attitude here has been that 'in training and retraining of adults, Government's direct contribution through its own programmes is at the margin. The centre ground belongs to employers' (NEDC 83(54)). This might be acceptable if employers were prepared to give training top priority, but the MSC's own research shows the opposite; many employers are not even aware how much they spend in this area. The resources of the MSC itself are also far from adequate. Its budget was reduced in the early 1980s and staffing reduced by 13 per cent. According to the House of Commons Employment Committee in 1986, the MSC is 'strapped for cash' and expenditure on adult retraining is less now than in 1979–80.[4]

To return to the questions posed at the outset of this section – what kind of training and for whom? – it is important to note that the unemployed are not a homogeneous group. Some would clearly be unsuited for an early transfer to high-skill training. One-quarter of the unemployed were previously in an unskilled or semi-skilled job; a further third have never had a job or have been unemployed for more than three years. But on the other hand, one-third of the unemployed and a quarter of the long-term unemployed are under twenty-five and they will need serious training if they are not to spend the rest of their lives at the margin of unemployment. The conclusion appears to be that some of the unemployed – perhaps a third – should go on to training schemes and attempts should be made to shift upwards the skill distribution of the entire workforce, generating in the process a set of lower-paid jobs to be filled by those unemployed who are unlikely to benefit from immediate training. If this process is to work properly it is important that access to training should be offered to all who could benefit from it, including women and ethnic minorities who are presently disadvantaged in terms of access and who consequently occupy jobs which do not fulfill their potential. Rather than arguing that women should be discouraged from entering the labour market (Hart and Trinder, 1986), the argument should be in favour of more training opportunities.[5]

The value of the enhanced training route is underscored by studies on the effects of company training.[6] But, quite apart from this, labour shortages in many high-skill areas are now emerging, even with over 3 million unemployed. In spite of many warnings – at least three major reports since 1980 – skill shortages continue in electronics and information technology. There is also an increasing shortage of management skills and technicians, as well as marketing, accountancy and financial skills.

One way of encouraging more training is the idea of an

individual training credit, which would entitle everyone from school-leaving age to a minimum amount of training, which could be cashed in at any stage during an individual's career (MSC/NEDO, 1985). Davis (1986) suggests that each member of the working population would accumulate an entitlement to a month's training for each year of work, funded by employers, employees and government in a way similar to pension entitlements.

Another approach would be to combine training with short-time working. Metcalf (1985a) has proposed a self-financing short-time-working scheme, with contributions from employers, employees and government. It should be possible to modify this proposal, reducing the non-government contributions where retraining is carried out in the days off work. Where occupations or industries were experiencing falls in employment, much of the training would be conversion training. However the scheme could also work in areas of expanding employment; a phased programme of training in these areas could enhance the skills of existing workers while allowing many jobs to be filled by those currently unemployed.

Unemployed adults need a proper large-scale training programme with at least as high a profile as that of youth training. Often it will make sense for this to be work-related training involving employers (MSC/NEDO, 1985). This would mean expanding the existing Job Training Scheme, perhaps with an in-company component. It may be expected that this will meet with stiff opposition, and perhaps not only from management, since a large influx of trainees can be disruptive of established customs. The public sector will also have a role here; and the training element of the Community Programme, which at present is virtually non-existent, could also be made substantial.

Finally, it may be noted that the latent demand for training is very high, especially for marketable skills. This was revealed in a Gallup poll in 1985.[7] Nine per cent indicated that they would wish to pursue a course in computer training and a further 9 per cent in other vocational areas, but were inhibited by cost or availability. In nearly half of these cases the chief reason was availability rather than cost.

4 New jobs and old

White (1985) has noted that one cannot create a full-employment economy simply by a higher level of human capital investment: 'all that is being claimed is that if we could get there, an economy with these characteristics would be more likely than the present one to have low unemployment levels' (p. 11). This prompts the question of what policies could precipitate movement along a high-skill path?

Structural change in the economy does appear to be at an unusually high level, but it is taking place without the necessary growth in jobs and so must be considered distorted. The continued existence of mass unemployment suggests that there is either a wage problem or an investment problem, solutions to these problems roughly corresponding to less and more structural change, respectively. This book leans towards the latter view, that investment and structural change have not proceeded fast enough to create sufficient new employment opportunities. If a faster rate of investment were possible and if the structure of production could be changed in a manner compatible with higher skills and real wages, it would be reactionary to preserve the existing structure, whether by protection or by 'flexible wages'. And, since the evolution of the industrial structure is not efficiently arranged by market forces (of which more below), there is no unique appropriate wage level.

This argument operates against two distinct viewpoints. The first is that unemployment is a result of wages being 'too high', an argument which is at best unproven, especially if investment is, for other reasons, 'too low'. The argument also works against those who use 'shadow wage' arguments to imply that production of declining industries should be subsidised on the grounds that the opportunity cost is very low. The opportunity cost may not of course be low if the misallocation of subsidies and investment is preventing restructuring. None of this means that real wages cannot be too high – only that an exclusive preoccupation with wages as the cause of economic difficulties is misplaced.

The defence of this line of argument requires an identification of the forces blocking structural change. Answers need to be given in respect both of the adjustment of mature industries and the expansion of new ones.

The importance of the distinction between mature and new industries may not be immediately obvious but it is in fact crucial. Industries tend to progress from a fluid stage of combined product and process innovation to a more mature phase where the standard form of product has more or less fully evolved (Abernathy, 1978). There is a balance to strike between minimising production costs and reaping the benefits of innovative change. In the earlier or fluid stage, an industry not only engages in product development but at the same time experiments with different forms of process and organisation. However, at a later stage the emphasis turns to cost reduction; now there is a necessity for stability in the process – change here tends to originate with suppliers – and for only limited or periodic product improvements. It is inevitable and indeed desirable that industries settle into a mode where cost reductions are the norm; mass consumption would otherwise be impossible. However the pace of innovation depends on the continual emergence of new industries which are the source of new technologies and ways of working. Eventually, of course, the new techniques and work patterns affect established industries as well; it has been shown that in Britain from the 1930s the old staple industries contributed as much to increased labour productivity as the newer industries did (Tunzelmann, 1982). Nevertheless, the source of technical improvements is often the newer industries.

The previous discussion has concerned technological differences between new and older industries. However there is an even more important distinction to be made in respect of differences in market demand – a distinction of some importance for employment. Beyond a certain stage of maturity, process innovations may not feed through to higher demand, which can only be stimulated by new products. There are two reasons for this: substitution effects may be weaker than income effects; and prices may not fall in line with costs for some commodities. In the latter case, any rise in employment would depend on the reinvestment of profits and on the efficacy of financial intermediation. Product innovation, on the other hand, could be expected to lead to a higher propensity to consume and an increase in the demand for labour. These intuitive notions have been confirmed, within certain restrictive assumptions, by Katsoulakis (1986). It is of interest also that employment in Britain in the 1930s was strongly stimulated by the new industries and in particular by their backward linkages with the old staple industries. Employment in seven new industries rose by 170,000 in the first half of the decade, or over 80 per cent of all secondary-sector employment. However, when linkages are accounted for, the employment created may have been as high as half a million (Tunzelmann, 1982). It is of course not yet clear how strong the backward linkages are from today's equivalents of 'plastics and automobiles'. It may transpire that forward linkages out of incomes are now of equal importance. But whether or not this turns out to be true, the over-cautious approach to new-industry expansion and slow adjustment of older ones will retard the path of job creation. Table 4.1 shows that in recent years in Britain, employment has been falling even in the new high-tech manufacturing industries; it is shown later, in Chapter 7, that service-sector growth is also slower than might be expected.

The mature industries

One problem with mature industries is that no effective mechanism exists to effect rationalisation at a reasonable pace or to effect the transfer of resources from old to new markets. Excess capacity can remain for years, or even decades, in some

Table 4.1 Growth of output and jobs in high-technology sectors

Year	Employees (000s)	Index of production
1975	702.1	85.8
1977	661.8	86.5
1979	678.0	96.2
1981	651.5	101.0
1983	610.9	114.2
1985	612.1	142.6

Sources: Dept of Trade and Industry; Dept of Employment.

High technology industries are defined as the ten with the highest ratio of intramural R&D to value added in the UK (see McKay, 1985).

industries. Part of the reason is that exit-costs are high in the case of capital-intensive or vertically-integrated industries and diversification into entirely new areas is difficult because of entry barriers. Product diversification in industry tends to take place in small steps; it is generally based on links with suppliers or with firms who have similar marketing or technical interests (MacDonald, 1985). It is not altogether surprising that mature industries are cautious over investing in new industries. Biggadike (1979) undertook a study of major new-product launches and concluded that a long-term perspective was needed for survival. Heavy losses tended to be incurred in the first four years while the average break-even period was eight years; ten to twelve years were needed to match the performance of mature products. It is therefore quite tempting for the profitable mature-industry companies to sit on their cash or at best to pursue narrow product-differentiation within their own industry. Indeed, management strategists advise this because it is the path pursued by the most successful of such companies (Ergas, 1984). Such advice may be right for individual firms but not for the industry as a whole. Some firms also need to exit; from the perspective of overall growth it might be better if some of the more dynamic firms left the industry and diversified. To a certain extent this may be prompted by market forces. The large firms that dominate W. Germany's older industries are now said to be moving over into newer markets, though not without difficulty.[1] This process requires acceleration and merits government support since there are positive social gains from a form of restructuring that is less anarchic and brutal than recession.

Of course market rationalisation works some changes and forces weak firms out of business, but this is problematical in that it can involve the elimination of the wrong firms. Diversified multi-plant firms or those with fully-depreciated assets are less likely to liquidate. There seems to be no close correlation in some industries between the productivity-level of firms and the likelihood of closure, a fact clearly brought out by a case study of the UK cutlery industry (Grant, 1986). Not only was the pace of adjustment very slow, but every failure in the industry 'was followed by caution towards the whole industry on the part of banks and suppliers'. The clear message here is that unaided market forces may work slowly and inefficiently in industrial restructuring.

The reluctance of established industries to engage in new-product development has been noted by a number of researchers. Karlsson (1986), in a study of five Swedish companies, noted their reluctance to use internal product-development as a way of changing their structure; acquisitions were preferred as a quicker route and this led to low receptiveness for new ideas within firms. Freeman *et al.* (1982) have also noted that 'while the large, multi-product firm will no doubt diversify into new areas, most of its output will be into relatively mature industries or products' (p. 143). The actual position, at least in Britain, seems to be worse than implied by these authors. Not only is fixed investment for any given level of profitability lower for mature industries, as shown in Panel 4.1, but the same pattern emerges when acquisition expenditure is added in.[2]

The finding that mature industries invest less for a given profitability would be of less concern if holdings of liquid assets were efficiently recycled by financial intermediaries or if the funds not used for investment were put to other productive use. If this is not the case there may be grounds for state intervention with discriminatory rules aimed at encouraging diversification and new-product development by mature sectors. One approach would be to make it mandatory for firms to create new capacity to match that scrapped or disposed of. It

Panel 4.1

Results of cross-section regressions

	1984	1983	1982	1981
Dependent variable	(I/K) 1984	(I/K) 1983	(I/K) 1982	(I/K) 1981
C	0.037 (1.63)	0.076 (4.11)	0.078 (4.95)	0.101 (6.19)
(P/K) − 1	0.010 (5.72)	0.006 (3.21)	0.007 (3.93)	0.003 (1.58)
DUM	−0.018 (0.90)	−0.048 (2.45)	−0.031 (1.88)	−0.037 (2.12)
R^2	0.62	0.49	0.50	0.24
	N = 23	N = 24	N = 24	N = 24

where I is assets purchased net of acquisitions, K is net capital stock, P is profits before tax, N is the number of observations.
Shipping and transport is excluded for 1984 due to missing data.
DUM is a Dummy Variable = 0 for product innovation industries; 1 for mature industries.
Mature industries are defined as drink, building, contracting, food manufacturing, food retailing, metals, motors, newspapers, oil, packaging, shipping and transport, stores, textiles and tobacco.

Source: Datastream.

has proved possible for British Steel to do this reasonably effectively, and similar progress should also be expected from other companies. Encouragement might also be given – though not in a rigid way – to promote internal developments rather than acquisitions as a way of reorientation for mature industries.

Newer industries

The arguments above concern the failure of mature industries, but this is at most only half the story; indeed, quite a lot of process improvements and labour-saving investments have taken place in mature industries, even if the rate of capacity adjustment has sometimes been slow. The parallel problem is that the potentially dynamic sectors producing new products are less than fully committed to exploiting new opportunities.

Reasons for the slow pace of new-product development are examined later, but it is of interest to recall that in some specific instances the rate of development has been breathtakingly fast. The developments in semiconductors from the 1960s onwards is a case in point. The US pioneered this rapid change and it is instructive to see how it happened. The structure of demand was important; public procurement for computer use in military and space programmes led the way in the US, while in Europe the emphasis was on less-advanced products aimed at existing consumer-durable products. Between 1962 and 1964 the US government purchased over 70 per cent of the integrated-circuit output of American firms (Malerba, 1985). The technological head-start was important in securing a cumulative advantage, reinforced by the role of public policy in fostering the rapid growth of computer output, pulling many new producers into the industry. This process encouraged innovation, leading to the digital integrated-circuit and eventually the microprocessor. Firms in Europe focused on the largest domestic-demand segment – consumer electronics – where the technology was less dynamic.

Part of the reason why each bloc concentrated on its home-market opportunities was the existence of trade barriers, but it also resulted from the need for continuous and direct interaction between consumers and producers, as originally argued by Vernon (1966). This author has since qualified his own theory and argued that the development of multinationals and the convergence of national markets towards similar patterns weaken the importance of the home-market impulse. However he adds that 'strong traces of the sequence are likely to remain . . . the specification of new products are usually in such a state of flux that it is infeasible for a time to fix on a least cost location' (Vernon, 1979). The exploitation of home-market opportunities is of course especially important when technology is fluid; transitional advantages so gained can be built into cumulative advantage. However it is precisely in such a period when product development is most risky. An example is the medical equipment industry in Britain. ACARD (1986b) has warned that failure to pursue a policy of encouraging general practitioners and the health service generally to purchase innovative equipment – creating a strong domestic-market pull – has resulted in a pessimistic outlook for the industry.

The constraint of uncertainty

One reason for the slow rate and narrow base of new-product development is uncertainty over the direction of consumer choice and over technological developments. Little research has been done in this area, but the adverse effect of risk on investment and production, beyond that captured by the interest rate, has been confirmed (Ben Zion and Mehra, 1980; Batchelor, 1982).

Yet another reason for the hesitancy of expansionary investment is that new forms of consumer expenditure tend to be bound up with new social conditions, such as patterns of work, legal arrangements, acceptance of technology, changes in the education system and so on. In other words, a social infrastructure is needed to harmonise commercial possibilities with areas of life not subject to market infuences. Aglietta (1979) has drawn attention to this in the context of the postwar boom in the US and it has also been stressed by Perez (1985) and Soete and Freeman (1982).

It is also plausible to argue that uncertainty will rise when the outcome of any one company's project depends on favourable responses from others, i.e. when product interdependence is high. This will be particularly so for new products where networks of suppliers are not in place. This type of uncertainty will have most force in a period of large potential change, when markets and technical advances are still volatile and when, in consequence, project success is dependent on a constellation of responses by a number of companies, perhaps in more than one sector.

An example of this is the introduction of teletext in the UK. The television-broadcasting companies made technical advances which made teletext possible and an electronics company began production of the integrated circuits. However the set manufacturers were reluctant to invest in an uncertain market, resulting in a high price for equipped sets and low growth for the entire project. It required an interventionist approach, with fiscal measures, before the market was encouraged sufficiently to move towards self-sustaining growth.

That example illustrates the inhibiting force of uncertainty which is further examined below in its technological and market aspects.

Technological uncertainty

Even in times of settled continuous growth it is unlikely that decentralised investment decision-making is efficient. As Leontief (1985) has argued, decisions are generally based only on a company's knowledge of the technologies employed in its main processes, rather than on likely technological developments in supplier- or downstream-industries. Furthermore, there is nearly always a failure to model the likely evolution of prices and wages in the whole economy, partly because it makes formal investment appraisal very complex (Harcourt, 1972). In settled times these problems are minimised by the incremental nature of the investment undertaken. They are magnified, however, in a period of structural change when the likelihood arises that an investment will be relegated to second best before the first sale has been completed, and where the relationship between product price and input costs is more volatile than normal. It is true that this instability creates new opportunities and offers the incentive of high but risky return to new venture capital. In this respect, technological uncertainty is double edged. However, as long as industries are characterised by entry barriers and powerful firms, the positive effects of uncertainty are probably minimised. Uncertainty may have a stimulating effect on lower-level management, but this is unlikely to be a dominant factor. In relatively fast-growing innovative sectors, firms often tend to have decentralised management structures in view of the complex nature of product development. This causes company boards to exercise caution, both in respect of external financing and in terms of the returns and payback periods expected of projects.

Companies may fail to pursue such worthwhile projects unless they can share risk with the major customers, i.e. unless they can compensate technological risk by hedging on market outcomes.

Market uncertainty

There are at least two sources of market uncertainty – future income distribution and future consumption patterns conditional on any particular distribution. Income distribution, of course, is influenced by technological trends. The upgrading of skills that is now occurring in many occupations is leading to enhanced pay for those in work, in marked contrast to those who have been dispossessed of jobs. The distributional consequences have been regressive. In Britain the income share of the bottom 40 per cent of households fell from 19.45 per cent to 17.5 per cent between 1976 and 1985 and is forecast to fall to 16.3 per cent by 1990 (Henley Centre, 1985). The share of the top 10 per cent shows a symmetrically opposite pattern. However, future political intervention might alter these trends and this is a major source of uncertainty, given that patterns of consumer demand depend on the income and proportions of various types of income recipients. Manual-worker households, for instance, spend a far higher proportion of income on non-durables, while non-manual households consume more durables and services in proportion to income; it can be expected that marginal propensities to spend differ also (*Family Expenditure Survey*, 1983).

A second source of uncertainty concerns the pattern of demand that will be chosen, even for a known income-distribution. Market forecasters see factors such as the cultural climate, e.g. whether it favours autonomy or self expression or whether it is more of the 'aggressive materialist' variety, as being important in this respect, but there is no consensus of views. Steindl (1985) has commented:

> When a high standard of life is reached, the structure of demand is bound to change dramatically. As long as you can copy existing models, for example, the American way of life, you are able to follow a given pattern. But once you have

yourself reached a high standard of national income you have to become a pioneer in consumption. (p. 226)[3]

The uncertainty inherent in this pioneering or learning process is commented on in Pasinetti (1981) and in Stanback *et al.* (1981), where it is reported that people have poorly-developed preferences for things they have not tried (p. 33).

The discussion above has shown how uncertainty tends to inhibit market forces, especially at times of structural change. Industries which should have contracted or diversified have not done so successfully and investment in the fastest-growing sectors has not been especially high – certainly not adequate to pull the economy towards full employment. This 'investment-gap' argument is a controversial one, but it has support from technologists (Soete and Freeman, 1985) and even within mainstream economics (Klau, 1984). It appears to have found some support in official circles in Britain (Bank of England, 1986). The investment-gap argument is also supported by the Swedish Industrial Institute for Economic and Social Research; its position is that unemployment is due in large measure to the effect of non-calculable risk on investment (Eliasson and Fries, 1983).

Certainly in Britain it is clear that fixed investment has responded only cautiously to the upward movement in profit rates, as is clear from Fig. 4.1, which shows a widening gap between investment and profits. Statistical relationships also show that investment is under-performing relative to what would have been expected by model predictions.

The constraining role of uncertainty applies not only to fixed investment but to training and R&D as well. A recent survey of company training (MSC/NEDO, 1985) concluded that 'uncertainty was the reason most commonly cited by the companies we interviewed for not doing more training . . . sometimes there was a concern about the future economic climate . . . sometimes a reaction to the uncertain impact of rapidly changing technology' (p. 10).

Solutions to uncertainty

Solutions to the problem of uncertainty are hard to devise.

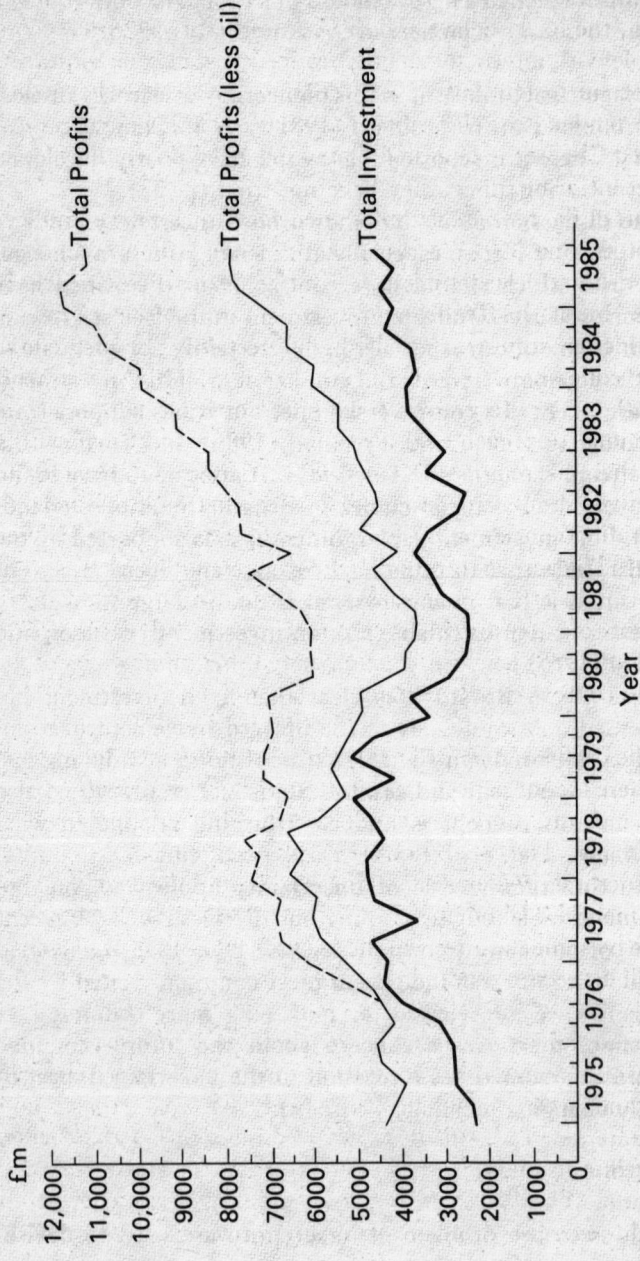

Figure 4.1 UK gross trading profits, net of stock appreciation, and gross fixed investment: industrial and commercial companies, £m at 1980 prices. *Source:* CSO.

Attempts at international cooperation are obviously crucial but, given, the likely delays and difficulties, national policies compatible with international cooperation must also be found. An important insight is that low inflation is not, as policymakers have tended to believe, synonymous with low uncertainty; indeed Chapter 1 suggested that unpredictability has increased in recent years.

Part of the recent concern with 'flexibility' in wages and with profit-sharing (e.g. Weitzman, 1985) stems from a recognition that risk and uncertainty may have increased. There may be some merit in these proposals but there has been no convincing argument to date that transferring income-risk from companies to workers is a feasible strategy for faster growth.[4] An alternative strategy for countering risk is the traditional approach of subsidising R&D or fixed investment, but there is reason to believe that this is only marginally effective. For one thing, the cost of capital is not the overriding consideration for most major companies (Eichner, 1986). The accelerator model, modified in various ways, is still superior to other models, showing that the important determinant of investment is product demand (Clark, 1979). Britton (1985) has lucidly summarised the implications of this in the context of the demand for labour:

> The problem remains that the market itself does not know where the jobs are coming from, so future employers have no incentive to recruit or to train labour in anticipation of demand. The conclusion seems inescapable that the structural problems cannot be solved until the overall demand for labour is in fact increased or potential employers are by some means given the assurance that full employment will indeed be restored. (p. 39)

Demand, however, cannot be increased indiscriminately, since this would not generate confidence that it would be sustainable. Demand would have to be focused on areas that would generate new investment, facilitate desired structural change, as well as avoiding production bottlenecks and a surge in imports. The question arises whether government can or should exercise control over final expenditure, including consumer expenditure-choices. If the aim were to reduce uncertainty the category of private consumer-demand would also have to be subject to infuence, since it is a sizeable part of final demand and an even higher proportion of the independent element of this. But some welfare loss would be occasioned by consumers if they were persuaded by price, quantity or income controls to alter their patterns of expenditure. Clearly this potential welfare-loss requires some justification.

If all that were involved were general uncertainty in all consumer markets, it might be resolved in indicative planning, with no welfare loss at all, but part of the case that has been made above is that uncertainty is particularly high in the case of novel products and services, where consumer demand is often only latent. There is no evidence that the variability in the structure of broad consumer-expenditure categories has increased in recent years. Rather it appears to be remarkably stable, as shown in the analysis in Panel 4.2. The full story may, however, be rather complex. The stability in consumer-expenditure changes, despite important changes in technology, is evidence of the slow pace of product development and take-up. Welfare losses may accrue to some individuals if the state intervenes to try to force the pace of these developments.

Major breaks in consumer patterns are difficult to forecast. Social attitudes seem to be fairly important. For instance, if the 'aggressive materialist' culture were to dominate, it might imply an increase in expenditure on comestibles, clothing and household goods, with little increase in private or public services except defence and public order. The 'autonomous' culture, on the other hand, might lead to an increase in home-based activities, recreation and education, as well as health and health products.

Consumer-spending patterns are, of course, centrally influenced at present, not only by taxation but by policies such as those which encourage home ownership. It is unlikely that a programme of overall coordinated approach would have to increase the level of intervention very much, but it would be planned to some single end rather than attempting to meet a multiplicity of goals. The major justification for such an explicit programme of influence would be if it could boost development of new products and services. Many of these are

Panel 4.2

The stability of the rate of change in consumer expenditure patterns may be tested in the same manner as the analysis of employment change in Panel 1.3. Data on eight broad commodity groups is available at constant prices over a long run of years. These groups are food, fuel, clothing and footwear, motor vehicles, other consumer durables, housing, housing operation, and other services. Expenditure data of these groups at constant prices were converted to proportions and differenced over five-year periods from 1950. The pattern of stability was judged, as before, by calculating $\Sigma \,|\, \Delta x_i \,|$ where Δx_i is the five-yearly difference in the proportionate consumption of group i. There was no significant trend in this indicator; rather, it appeared to be remarkably constant over time.

held back, not only through normal risk aversion but by the high degree of interdependence that characterises new products, especially when they are grouped around a single technology. The purchase of one new commodity – say a cable subscription – may be heavily correlated with others such as the purchase of an expert system for health screening. These interconnections will be evident to companies *ex-post* but will not favour initial investments, given that the products are made by different firms and possibly in different sectors and coordination across these boundaries carries extra risk.

Although initial welfare losses will be incurred as a result of influencing consumer-spending patterns, it needs to be said that individual choice is not always in itself a viable method of maximising consumer welfare – railway would have been late in coming if passenger subscriptions had to be first collected. Often there are indivisibles or interdependences not taken account of in product-launch decisions and in such cases the market price will bear little relation to the price that would prevail with different take-up rates. The development of a mass market may be inhibited by the lack of an adequate physical, legal or social infrastructure (Perez, 1985). An example of such constraints on market growth, and hence the ability of consumer choice to determine production, is the early period of the development of mass-production goods; Aglietta (1979), reviewed in Driver (1981), describes the facilitating infrastructures that were necessary – roads, collective bargaining, guaranteed incomes via social insurance, hire purchase, etc.

The view that non-incremental technical developments may be slow to emerge, especially where incremental technical change is increasingly unprofitable, has been advanced in a slightly different context by Stoneman (1985). Stoneman suggests that certain technologies, especially in the information field, only give high returns when in wide usage. Thus the linkage of word processors in networks may be necessary in order to obtain major benefits. The possibility of market specialisation may also only emerge above a certain threshold-level of sales.

Left to its own devices, the market does of course make some progress. The experimental emergence of home shopping and banking in some parts of the country are cases in point. However it is important to be able to see these limited developments in the context of what is technically feasible. Not only were these projects delayed substantially, but they are still quite modest developments compared with what is technically feasible, a point that is discussed further in Chapter 5.

The pattern of domestic expenditure that would best facilitate a transition to higher employment is difficult to divine. There is a short-run answer as well as a longer-term perspective. For the short-run case it is relatively easy to experiment using differential taxes or other incentives so as to weight expenditure more heavily towards areas that generate high employment. The results of a simulation along these lines are reported below. However the thrust of the policy must be sustainable and directed towards products and services with a strong latent demand and good supply-side potential. A long-run policy needs to take into account the interrelationships between technology, income distribution and new patterns of living such as work times and consumer culture.

The most promising constellation of activities that merit government support – on grounds of employment implications, structural change and latent consumer-demand – are those information services and associated hardware that are embryonic in existing public and private services. An important set of these activities concern the development of home information or entertainment services – interactive home systems. This development has implications for electrical, electronic and computing appliances, monitoring, metering and telecommunication services, as well as architecture, construction, entertainment, education advice and management. Many information technology experts now believe that the next major competitive battle in IT will centre on the domestic environment and consumer electronics; Japanese work on fifth-generation computing will produce enabling-technologies with applications in a large number of new products for home use. Italian companies are using Eureka research funds to develop these products. In public services, too, information constitutes a major activity and innovative services will have wide appeal. The exact balance between public and private services will reflect in part the political disposition towards redistribution. However, many services such as advice functions or energy conservation are most appropriately performed in the public sector because of complications over property rights. The challenge here will be to make an extension of public services politically acceptable by significant improvements in organisational efficiency and accountability.

Expenditure switching

One way to speed up job creation is to alter the pattern of demand towards labour-intensive activities. The kind of switch envisaged here involves a redistribution of consumer expenditure, keeping the total spent constant. Of course it is quite possible that such a shift would simply promote low-paid dead-end jobs, but labour-intensive activities are not necessarily like that and it should be possible to favour areas which

Table 4.2 Industries ranked by employment income per unit of final output[a]

Ranking	Industry
1	Banking, finance, insurance, professional and business services, hiring
2	Other services[b]
3	Public administration[c]
4	Transport services
5	Postal services and telecommunications
6	Distribution, etc., and repairs
7	Hotels, catering, public houses, etc.
8	Road and other inland transport
9	Construction
10	Manufacturing
11	Owning and dealing in real estate
12	Air transport
13	Agriculture, forestry, mining and utilities
14	Sea transport

a Railway transport is omitted from the table, despite its high labour intensity, as its ranking is distorted by an unusual level of subsidy.
b This includes cleaning services, artistic enterprise, R&D and various other activities.
c This category includes most of health and education expenditure.

make use of skills and where a career structure is possible.

Labour intensity may conveniently be defined in terms of the direct and indirect employment-income generated per unit of final output. A ranking of industries by this measure is shown in Table 4.2, with the most labour-intensive at the top. It can be seen that most service industries and construction are more labour-intensive than manufacturing, agriculture and utilities, although there are some other service industries – air and sea transport, owning and dealing in real estate – which are not very labour-intensive. It is of course difficult to be precise since the categories are rather broad; construction, for instance, spans a range of distinct activities.

An expenditure switch of consumer expenditure towards the more labour-intensive goods and services was simulated for the author by Cambridge Econometrics in 1984. The labour-intensive activities identified amount to about 20 per cent of total consumer spending. The simulated changes in the pattern of expenditure in the two following years are shown in Table 4.3. The changes are equivalent to a 10 per cent increase on items 15, 34–42 and 46, spread over two years, with corresponding falls spread over other items in proportion to spending (3.8 per cent on average). The effect on jobs builds up slowly, contributing to the generation of less than 100,000 jobs by year four. However inflation and disposable income are hardly affected and the PSBR improves by over £500 million. This would appear to indicate that if the simulation were run with nominal government expenditure fixed, the effect on jobs could be quite substantial in the medium term. Table 4.4 summarises the simulation results.

Table 4.3 Consumers' expenditure: changes from base run (£m) 1975 prices

		1985	1986 and subsequent years
1	Bread and cereals	−30	−60
2	Meat and bacon	−73	−145
3	Fish	−7	−14
4	Oils and fats	−10	−20
5	Sugar, etc.	−23	−47
6	Dairy products	−32	−63
7	Fruit	−15	−30
8	Potatoes and vegetables	−30	−61
9	Beverages	−19	−38
10	Other menu food	−8	−15
11	Beer	−62	−124
12	Wines and spirits	−52	−104
13	Tobacco	−48	−96
14	Rent, rates, etc.	−214	−427
15	Maintenance, etc.	+105	+210
16	Coal and coke	−6	−11
17	Electricity	−33	−66
18	Gas	−19	−37
19	Other fuel	−3	−7
20	Footwear	−17	−35
21	Other clothing	−86	−172

Table 4.3 *continued*

22	Motor cars, etc.	−70	−139
23	Furniture, etc.	−32	−63
24	Other durables	−55	−109
25	Household textiles	−11	−22
26	Hardware	−12	−23
27	Matches, soap, etc.	−9	−17
28	Books	−4	−8
29	Newspapers	−11	−21
30	Magazines	−3	−7
31	Chemists' goods	−24	−47
32	Misc. recreational goods	−41	−81
33	Other misc. goods	−28	−56
34	Running costs of MVs	+322	+644
35	Rail travel	+20	+41
36	Bus	+25	+50
37	Other travel	+47	+93
38	Postal services	+8	+17
39	Telephone	+44	+88
40	Entertainment	+98	+195
41	Domestic service	+14	+28
42	Catering	+212	+414
43	Other services	+203	+407
44	Balancing items	−11	−22
	Total	0	0

Planning

There is still little consensus on the merit of centrally-directed change. Because of past failures in planning, any attempt to offer a measure of central coordination must start from a premise of supporting existing tendencies in the economy. But even with such a cautious stance, the question arises whether it is possible to identify any basic thrusts of development which can be facilitated or strengthened in a desired way. Put differently, if companies are unsure of future patterns of technology, income distribution, consumer preferences and occupational changes, is not the same true of governments? The question is a good one but it is too sharply posed. Companies' uncertainty reflects, in large part, the timing of developments that they are fairly sure will eventually happen. Governments, if they correctly identify and accept these

Table 4.4 Results of a simulation involving expenditure switching to labour-intensive services[a]

	After 4 years	After 8 years
Absolute change in private employment (thousands)	91.4	165.3
% change in real personal disposable income	−0.38	−0.65
Absolute change in PSBR (£ million)	−560	−2034
Absolute change in consumer price index	−0.04	−0.22

Source: Cambridge Econometrics

a Service industries representing the most labour-intensive (direct and indirect) parts of consumer expenditure were identified. They accounted for about 20 per cent of consumer expenditure. A rise of 5 per cent in each of the first and second years was simulated, with other categories of consumer expenditure being proportionally adjusted downwards to keep the total unchanged.

developments, can have some control over timing and stability of the changes involved and, in some limited circumstances, over the direction of change. Governments are also in a position to arrange institutional reforms in order to accelerate developments that otherwise would be impossible and they can, through the tax system, overcome the problem of threshold effects where the cost to a pioneering consumer is very high.

It is of course true that the recent history of western industrial policy is dotted with errors. Some observers suggest that the prospects for the future are no better.

> Central government agencies will never be as informed about commercial and technological frontiers as the advanced companies actively operating in the field . . . success may have as much or more to do with non-technical matters like marketing . . . a government push to get domestic firms into very large-scale, very sophisticated, heavy-investment hardware production in microelectronics . . . may easily get its industries stuck with producing the previous generation of technology products. (Eliasson, 1984, pp. 313, 314).

But Eliasson also makes another important point, namely that so-called market solutions face exactly the same problem as the planning approach. Since some distortion exists in prices – which it is desired to eliminate so as to permit efficient micro-level allocation – it is necessary to know what the appropriate price structure is; that in turn demands as detailed an understanding of the economy as the interventionist approach.

It appears therefore that neither solution is unproblematic. Policymakers must intervene, but they will minimise errors only if there is a good control system to avoid over-commitment to clear failures at an early stage.

Whatever the verdict on the merits of intervention, there seems broad support for the idea that governments should at least share the risks that firms carry in sophisticated new-product development (Eliasson, 1984). Recently the Advisory Council for Applied Research and Development (ACARD, 1986c) called for procedures to identify exploitable scientific areas. This would require identifying technological developments likely to be economically important over a ten-to-twenty-year period and allocating scientific resources accordingly. The CBI too has launched a forecasting programme – Vision 2010 – to work on a blueprint for the future of industry: 'much of their [Japanese] success can be attributed at least in part to their development of visions of the future and of strategies to achieve these goals'.[5] These proposals signify an important shift towards a belief in planning the development of the industrial base. They complement an equally important but less-remarked-upon shift by the Manpower Services Commission towards the notion of long-term skills-planning (MSC, 1986). Nevertheless, it must be doubted if the ACARD proposals go far enough. The pooling of expert advice on future markets and the use of this information to influence science policy will not have a major impact for at least a decade. On the other hand, the rate of new-product development could and should be speeded up immediately. One way to do this is to foster market growth at planned rates for particular services and products. As was noted earlier, many advanced developments are best pioneered in the home market where there is constant interaction between customers and producers. The planning of home-market consumption would not merely reduce market uncertainty but it would stimulate advanced-product development which would later feed through to export growth.

Planning consumption to conform with eventual expectations will never be entirely accurate. Coordinated attempts are most likely to be valid where large interdependent changes are anticipated, as is the case where rapid diffusion of technical change is possible. The gain to the economy arises from the potential output-gain as market-risk is reduced for producers. A planning framework could involve announcements of expected paths for indirect taxation, an integration and revision of market forecasts, plans for public consumption and infrastructure provision.

Conclusions

This chapter has suggested that employment-creation based on the further development and acceleration of existing or potential developments offers the best long-term hope for moving towards full employment. Alternative policies which hold back structural change or which rely exclusively on low-skill job subsidies are likely to make little long-term contribution. Uncertainty in its various aspects is a major constraint on increased private-sector investment in new products. The solution to these problems requires an element of planning in the future evolution of consumer patterns. Any short-term welfare loss entailed in this should be set against the context of the present challenge of job creation.

5   Ways and means

The last chapter has suggested the need for an interventionist approach to final expenditure in order to accelerate out of the low-growth trap. However although this discussion pointed in general terms to future shifts in consumption patterns and skills, it did not identify policies or target areas for growth; this chapter attempts to do that in broad terms.

It is convenient to begin by saying what will not be attempted. There is no intention here to spell out the exact industrial composition of new jobs. Such an exercise – identifying areas such as crafts, leisure, security, new forms of retail, personal care, agriculture, communications or energy conservation – is useful in that some people appear to believe that consumer wants are satiated.[1] However such forecasting is always speculative and, in any case, the listing of possible output-patterns does not illuminate how effective demand will arise. This requires an economic analysis.

It is possible conceptually to draw one important distinction between different types of economic activity. There are those where labour productivity can rise fast and those where this is more difficult. The sectors most susceptible to productivity improvement are those where the process is standardised, i.e. exactly repeatable; all of manufacturing except craft activities is of this sort, though many functions classified within manufacturing which require one-off decisions or interpretative judgment can be regarded as non-standardised and atypical of manufacturing. Many of the judgmental or interpersonal roles, such as professional and social services, cannot be readily or fully standardised. In these activities there is less recourse to automation and labour-productivity growth is slow.[2] The importance of this distinction lies in the fact that jobs will occur in a high productivity-growth area, chiefly when the price elasticity is high, and in a low productivity-growth area when income elasticity is high.

The above discussion is relevant to the question of whether service activities can be considered 'engines of growth'. This term is usually employed to assert the priority of manufacturing. The supporting arguments for this focus on the possibility of raising productivity via faster output growth, on the linkages between manufacturing and the rest of the economy; and sometimes on the supposed higher skill-levels in manufacturing. Whatever the merits of this view of growth, it cannot now be claimed to support a privileged status for manufacturing, given the recent 'industrialisation' of many services and consequent high productivity-growth. True, manufacturing has in the past exhibited higher earnings per head – about 7 per cent higher than the rest of the economy – but the comparison is complicated by the higher proportion of part-time and of female workers in services, as well as low pay in the public sector. It is clear from Table 5.1 that the services categories are, on average, broadly similar in skill content to the rest of the economy, however heterogeneous their composition.

Some services at least are now akin to manufacturing in many respects, though others such as professional, personal or social services remain highly non-standardised. Where will the growth in employment come, if at all? There does seem to be a tendency for employment in non-standardised services to rise faster than manufacturing. This is because, despite rising relative prices for these services caused by lower productivity, consumers have demonstrated a fairly high income-elasticity for them. In this sense, these services have not been 'engines of growth'; rather their fortunes have depended on the general rise in incomes. But perhaps the reverse causation, whereby higher productivity induces faster output-growth through price reductions, has operated as an alternative 'engine of growth' for some services? If this were the case, services would

Table 5.1 Occupation groups (% across)

	Managers of large establishments	Supervisors and other managers	Trainees	Professional employees	Other employees and self-employed
Private services	4.9	14	1.4	1.1	78.6
Public services	4.8	6.5	2.4	4.4	81.9
All industries and services	4.6	10	2.6	3.2	79.6

Source: Economic activity tables, 1981 census.

be expected to have a combination of high productivity-growth and high price-elasticity.

Estimates of price- and income-elasticities for some service categories are reported in Table 5.2.

Services productivity is more difficult to measure due to the well-known problems of measuring output, but estimates of services productivity based on different assumptions have been calculated by Barras (1984). Table 5.3 shows labour productivity-growth in services 1960–79, obtained as a weighted average of the two measurements given by Barras and correcting for part-time work.

Putting together Tables 5.2 and 5.3 is problematic because the categories do not fully correspond. The most that can be said is that no single category stands out as an engine of growth on the criteria of high price-elasticity and high productivity-growth. Miscellaneous services, with the highest price-elasticity, could generate growth if productivity rose rapidly, but investment in that sector has risen much less slowly than in private services generally (Barras, 1984). Transport is similarly placed, and public services, whatever their 'price elasticity', have not performed well in the productivity stakes and are under-capitalised.

Given these observations, it would not be surprising if two patterns tended to dominate future trends – jobless growth in high productivity-growth areas and slowly increasing employment in the low productivity-growth areas. This pessimistic conclusion appears to be borne out by the disaggregated forecasts of the Institute for Employment Research.

Can anything be done about this? We have seen in Chapter 2 that manufacturing is unlikely to be the source of new jobs, but what of services? The message from Tables 5.2 and 5.3 is not encouraging. Nevertheless, it must be remembered that there are other determinants of services-growth apart from domestic incomes and prices. Optimism turns on whether faster autonomous growth in services can be facilitated, i.e. growth that is independent of the general level of domestic incomes. Some conditioning factors in services growth are listed below, with an indication of the service sectors that they are most relevant to.

If policy were focused on facilitating and accelerating these

Table 5.2

	Price elasticity[a]	Income elasticity	Expenditure share, 1981
Transport	−0.47	0.78	11.6
Communications	−0.08	0.75	1.5
Housing[b]	−0.36	0.55	14.7
Miscellaneous[c]	−0.61	1.01	20.8
Manufacturing[d]	−0.36	0.99	45.1

a Compensated price elasticity.
b Rent, rates, water.
c Recreational (including hotels and catering), cultural, cleaning, personal, professional services and some luxury goods such as jewellery and perfumes.
d Weighted average of food, drink, tobacco, clothing, durables and household goods.

Source: Borooah (1986)

Table 5.3 Labour productivity-growth 1960–79[a,b]

Sector	Growth (%)
Transport and communications	(3.2)
Distribution	2.4
Financial services	1.0
Professional and scientific	(0.5)
Miscellaneous services	1.5
Public services	(0.6)
Manufacturing[c]	(2.7)

a Obtained by weighting the quantity and the value measures in Barras (1984) by two-thirds and one-third respectively (reflecting my judgment) and using a correction factor for part-time work based on his results. Figures in brackets have *not* been corrected for part-time work.
b These figures are historical averages and it is likely that productivity-growth in some services is now potentially higher. True, capital-per-worker has been lower than manufacturing in all public and private services except transport and communications, but growth in capital-per-worker in private services has been about the same as in manufacturing and has been faster in recent years. In public services and transport, on the other hand, the growth of capital-per-worker has been only half that of manufacturing.
c Quantity measure only; manufacturing output statistics are quality-corrected.

conditioning factors, it might provide some prospect of faster growth.

1 Provision of infrastructure – software and information services, transport and communications.
2 Redistributive policies – most private-sector services.
3 Slackening of public expenditure constraints – health, education, transport, recreation.
4 Growth of export markets – tradeable services such as financial and advisory services; health and education.
5 Quality improvement and availability – domestic and repair services, catering, leisure.
6 Reduction in working time – leisure services, transport, education, entertainment.

Most of these conditioning-influences on spending-patterns are obvious, though the extent of their impact is difficult to judge. The next sections take a closer look at:

1 infrastructure provision;
2 redistributive policies;

3   public service constraints; and
4   export markets, including liberalisation of trade.

Other topics are dealt with elsewhere – quality improvement in Chapter 7 and working time in Chapter 8.

Infrastructure

Infrastructure is used here in the loose sense of an environment which is a pre-condition for other activities – not just the physical installations, but the management and information systems that go with them. The focus here will be on electronic communications. There is little doubt that many services other than this also need improvement and expansion; services such as transport are referred to later under the heading 'redistribution'.

A big gap in communications is the lack of a modern system of two-way cable which would not only allow a greater variety of entertainment and information channels but would also allow a range of 'interactive services' such as home shopping to be carried out efficiently.

Some believe that information provided to consumers, whether free or purchased, is now at saturation point. On this view, there is little prospect of increased autonomous demand in this area; the impact of information technology will rather be felt in different ways – in the choice of goods opened up by new production-and-distribution methods (Petit, 1986).

Doubts have also been expressed about the likely speed or extent to which such interactive services will become popular and whether they will constitute the basis for a new mode of consumption.

> At present all we have are rather unconvincing examples . . . home shopping and other Prestel-type applications . . . there is nothing here to parallel the fundamental socio-economic impact of new technology systems embodied in TV or the motor car . . . This is a challenge that the literature has yet to meet; the specification in some detail of plausible new chains of production for human needs. (Gershuny, 1985, p. 83)

One attempt to answer this challenge has been made by the NEDO Long-Term Perspectives Group (1985). It has pointed not only to the wide range of functions which can be accommodated by information technology (IT), but to the possibilities of integrating several functions around composite units; examples here are home entertainment, education and interactive services (centred on the computer and audio-visual unit), home security (fire and theft) and home-energy management (conservation, metering, remote control). A set of potential applications for IT which are feasible at present is shown in Table 5.4. It may be of interest to expand on just a couple of these applications. In transport, IT applications include not only information and booking, but route-planning for cars, for delivery vehicles and for buses, where routes can be varied depending on destinations and pick-up points of assigned passengers. In teleshopping, it will be possible to check stocks and/or delivery times; eventually good-resolution simulations will be possible to demonstrate goods. Existing systems of home shopping in Britain are fairly primitive, with poor resolution, little information and reliance in some cases on printed catalogues.

There are also many potential applications of interactive services in health, education, government and community services. In health care, for instance, meters have been developed for use in the home which can monitor blood disorders or cholesterol levels. The increased use of self-diagnosis will lead to increased demand for information on health and this could be supplied from databanks accessible from the home; expert systems to diagnose complaints could also be accessed. In education there is an enormous potential market for specialised services. Most education is free, but consumers still spend £1.5bn a year on extra services. Experiments in the use of interactive services in increasing participation in government have been made in the US and France. It is possible to simulate conferences or meetings with two-way communications.

The proliferation of IT in the home is not just a futurist dream; 10 per cent of British homes now have a personal computer, and the rapid take-up of new products in the past shows that quick diffusion is possible. For instance, only 30

Table 5.4 Potential applications of information technology in household activities

Household activities	Illustrative potential applications of advanced information technology
Formal work	
Employment	Telework
Banking and tax	Telebanking, computer-aided tax form-filling
Personal care	
Nutrition	Monitoring nutritional standards, diets
Sleep	Relaxation, alarms
Childcare	Monitoring infant well-being, alarms
Dressing	Aiding choice of cloths
Washing	(Improved energy efficiency)
Housework	
Cleaning	(Improved energy efficiency in washing and drying machines)
Cooking	Menu assistance, automated ovens
Gardening	Garden-planning aids
Household maintenance	Monitoring heat loss, damp, etc.
Decoration	Computer-aided design
Maintenance of equipment	Fault-finding with sophisticated goods
Routine shopping	Teleshopping
Non-routine shopping	Teleshopping, consumer information
Communications	
Transport	Travel booking and route planning
Telecommunications	Electronic mail, interactive services
Entertainment	
Spectator sport	Booking seats, delivering video recordings
Participator sport	Booking facilities, locating partners
Games	Video games, computer-assisted games
Performance art	Delivering recorded performances, reviews
Cultural facilities	Electronic libraries and newspapers
Education	
Basic education	Instructional programmes
Higher education	Teleducation, teleconferencing
Specialised skills	Access to online databanks
Vocational training	Computer-aided instruction, simulations, teleducation
Health	
Health maintenance	Programmes for lifestyle planning and monitoring
Curative medicine	Diagnostic programmes, remote counselling
Emergency care	Emergency alarms, improved equipment and communication in ambulances
Social relations	
Friendship and kinship	Improved telephony
Political participation	Telecommunication aids to community association
Legal authorities	Online access to legal advice
Voluntary associations	Telecommunication between voluntary workers, clients, coordinators
Security	Fire and intruder alarms

Source: NEDO Long-Term Perspectives Group

per cent of houses had central heating in 1970 but this more than doubled in ten years. The same is true of telephones. An even more powerful diffusion was evident in the case of the motor car – the percentage of households with a car increased more than tenfold to 50 per cent in the two decades to 1970.

Survey information also suggests that there is a possibility for diffusion to be relatively rapid. A survey of expert opinion carried out by the NEDO Long-Term Perspectives Group (1986) resulted in an average projection that a quarter of households would be making use of interactive services by the year 1995. This is contingent, however, on infrastructure developments; over 60 per cent of respondents listed both telecommunications and cable as most likely to be the main technological factors affecting progress in this area.

Cable has a broader bandwidth than ordinary communications links and can carry more information, with better resolution and faster response time. However some interactive services are already available in many countries through telephone links. In Britain services such as travel booking is available through the British Telecom service Prestel, but there are less than 100,000 terminals, mainly for business use. Although the take-up is expected to be boosted by an increase in services such as electronic yellow pages and new software for home computers, the contrast with earlier hopes or with progress elsewhere in Europe is dramatic. France, for instance, came late but enthusiastically to the videotext concept, with the setting up of its Teletel system in 1981. By 1985 1½ million subscribers had been found, expected to grow to 3 million by 1987. The take-up was boosted by the free handout of terminals, but even the number of sophisticated bought-terminals exceeds the total British number of Prestel terminals by a factor of three.

The French telecommunications authority, the DGT, is also pursuing the most ambitious cabling programme in Western Europe, passing 1 million homes a year with advanced fibre-optic cables at a cost of about £0.5bn a year. The DGT recognises that the system will not cover costs on entertainment alone and is aiming to provide extensive interactive srvices. These will be better-quality than can be offered with telecommunications and will free the telephone for voice communication.

The contrast with Britain is again striking. There are only about 150,000 cable subscribers connected, many to the older-type systems that were put in place because of poor TV reception. Forecasts for cable growth in Britain have been revised downwards. In 1982 the independent consultancy research firm CIT thought that 36 per cent of homes would have access to cable by the mid 1990s. British Telecom later suggested a figure of 50 per cent, which was the datum taken by the Information Technology Advisory Panel (ITAP) in 1982. But a more recent report by CIT put the likely figure at only 20 per cent. Of the eleven franchises granted to cable companies in 1983, only seven had come into operation three years later. Some have been withdrawn; most are behind schedule. Because of this slowdown several electronics companies have mothballed switching equipment or withdrawn from projects completely.

The slowdown is entirely due to the failure of government to prioritise or even encourage cabling. The attitude has been that 'it is not for government to dictate the speed at which cable will develop or even to guarantee its success' (NEDC 84(36), p. 5). But the success of a venture like cabling is dependent on government help. It is a high-risk project where most of the costs come early and the profits late. The future supply of programme material is uncertain and also needs encouraging. Programme-makers and software-developers face a double uncertainty of the market, for their own product and for cable generally, and the small companies involved often have trouble raising finance due to their lack of a fixed-asset collateral. For the cable companies themselves there is little hope of profit in the first five years, so the government system of capital allowances was particularly important: however these were phased out completely between 1984 and 1987. Many of these points were reported to have been made in an unpublished report by the ITAP (Information Technology Advisory Panel), which saw its original optimistic projections coming to nothing. ITAP is also said to have suggested that British Telecom should make its own underground ducting available to cut the cost of cabling. Certainly the earlier report by ITAP considered that subsidies were essential; it referred to the paradox where cable was an:

> essential component of future communications systems, offering great opportunities for new forms of entre-preneurial activity . . . however, the initial financing of cable systems will depend upon none of these things, but upon estimates of the revenue from additional popular programming channels. (p. 48)

There are of course risks with rapid development of cable, as with any high-technology venture. Some argue that advances in cable design will make even current best-practice-technology outdated within a decade. Certainly in order to carry a large volume of high-capacity interactive-services, better techniques in network design will be needed. But even if these cautions merit being taken seriously, it is still inexplicable why the same degree of special support as is given to the computer industry in Britain is not afforded to cable.

The privatisation of BT has also stymied radical proposals for furthering cable. It has prevented any possible merger between the major television companies and BT to provide common carriers for telecommunications, broadcast and cable television. The legislative framework for BT now means that it can no longer operate as other European telecommunications authorities in cross-subsidising long-term developments. It is forced by competition and law into more short-term considerations; indeed it appears that it may even be prevented in law from giving away free terminals for Prestel as the French have done with Teletel.

The implications for jobs

Several estimates explicit or implicit have been made of the jobs potential of interactive services for the home. ITAP estimated in 1982 that cable could generate an extra billion pounds of business, though not all of this would be interactive services; the result would be tens of thousands of jobs, although short of the optimistic numbers sometimes quoted. Lord Orr-Ewing of the Telecommunications Users' Assocation has been quoted as suggesting a figure of 20,000 jobs from cable.[3] British Telecom took a much more cautious view, even on the assumption that half the country would be cabled within ten years. The building and installation of cable would generate only 6,000 permanent jobs, while the increase in programming staffs was discussed in terms of hundreds rather than thousands, partly because competition from the existing telephone network was predicted to prevent any big take-up of non-entertainment services. Imported American products would be largely used for entertainment because cable audiences would not be big enough to support programme-making. There was said to be no evidence of demand for new television sets equipped with stereo sound or high definition. And finally, the overall impact on jobs in services such as home banking and shopping was thought to be broadly neutral (NEDC 84(34)). This pessimistic view was echoed in a report on cable by the Greater London Council (GLC, 1982, 1985). Assuming over 3 million homes eventually connected to cable, it estimated that net job gains would be zero in view of a likely loss of 25,000 jobs in live entertainment and other areas.

It is hard to take the British Telecom or GLC projections seriously. Although job growth has been minimal in recent years, this is entirely due to the failure of cable or interactive services to develop rapidly. It is puzzling why the GLC should regard the slow development of Prestel as an argument that there is little demand for new information services (GLC, 1985, p. 402). It can certainly be agreed that few jobs will be provided in the construction or manufacturing of the systems or sets, but the services provided are labour-intensive activities. The crucial question is whether consumer-use of these services will mean displacement of existing jobs, and there has been little serious thought given to this. Displacement can occur either where a service such as home shopping displaces jobs in the existing non-electronic service or where a new service such as home gambling displaces expenditure on other forms of consumption. The first point is an empirical one, but it has been noted that there is a tendency for service companies to respond to new technology by differentiating their service and increasing quality rather than by shedding staff. This has been noted in office and bank automation for instance. The second point is more difficult to assess. In so far as the services are novel, they will probably lead to an increase in borrowing and reduced saving rather than to crowding out existing expenditure. This is because most of existing expenditure will have assumed the status of 'necessity' due to habit. It also seems likely that many interactive services such as information retrieval, payments and booking will save considerable amounts of search and administration time in the home. This is likely to free people for leisure activities in and out of the home. The notion of leisure activities suffering as everyone retreats behind a video screen is implausible and is not borne out by recent developments. The 1985 Henley Survey on Leisure Futures showed that leisure expenditure outside the home was again beginning to increase in relative importance.

These thoughts on future job implications are somewhat speculative but it is possible to get a further insight by looking at the pattern that is emerging in France, where interactive services are more advanced. With the Teletel system, each terminal is used for about one-and-a-half hours a month, adding up to a yearly communications bill of less than £50 on average for the 1½ million subscribers. This will not generate many extra jobs in communications, but it is interesting that there has been an explosion in the number of new services offered and used. There are now several thousand services offered by hundreds of companies. About half have been set up by professional bodies for the use of doctors, lawyers and accountants. But consumer services such as messaging, dating systems, software downloading, home shopping and banking are also available. The charges for these may be overt or hidden, but many extra jobs will have been generated. In Britain, services such as Ceefax and Oracle employ between fifty and a hundred people each. A thousand services the size of these would make a substantial contribution to jobs. Furthermore, the French system is still growing rapidly, with a million new subscribers every year. Presumably the average connection time of about five minutes per day will also rise as the variety of services offered increases.

The job potential of these services will also be boosted by export markets and by the help to the computer industry of having French computers equipped with circuitry enabling access to Teletel. Export markets exist for the hardware and the software elements of interactive services. Prestel, for instance, has obtained a contract to set up an ambitious videotext system in Singapore. Countries to the forefront of these developments in their home markets – as Britain was in the late 1970s – will undoubtedly be able to sell their software routines and programmes. This consideration is especially important in the case of European countries, whose software industries cannot compete in most of the areas linked with standard computer operations (operating systems, compilers, etc.); the markets for these are dominated by the computer giants, in particular IBM. However European countries do perform well in customised and innovative software. There is clearly potential for growth in these areas. The British computer services industry employs a much smaller proportion of the workforce than that in the US. Interactive services is a good example of the type of innovative software market that could be opened up. The software industry is unusual in combining labour intensity with high labour-productivity. This means that it can grow fast and create jobs. However, despite government support for developing innovative software, growth has not been rapid in Britain – 20 per cent a year, as compared with a world rate of nearly twice this. A report by ACARD (1986a) has warned that slow growth in software will bring about a 'major new source of balance of payments deficit' (p. 2). One route to avoiding this is to generate areas of high-demand growth for innovative software. Chances have clearly been missed to date in respect of interactive services and the contribution it could make to growth and jobs.

Redistribution

It has often been argued that new spurts of demand originate with the better-off – they engage in purchases, often of new products, which eventually lead to extra employment either directly (consumer services) or indirectly (manufacturing), thus generating additional incomes which sustain the demand process. But does the initial stimulus from the better-off depend simply on their higher incomes or on their having a higher marginal propensity to consume than others? Some recent studies have established that the marginal propensity to consume declines with income class (Borooah and Sharpe, 1984; Arestis and Driver, 1984). It seems that a redistribution towards lower-income groups, or away from non-earned income, would tend to increase consumer expenditure, at given average income levels. However it also appears that redistribution of this sort would lead to an increased tendency to import consumer goods (Arestis and Driver, 1987). The process would therefore only be sustainable for a country like Britain if the resultant influx of imports could be moderated. Explicit import controls would set a dangerous precedent under present trading conditions and might, in any event, exacerbate long-term problems by promoting inefficiency. It would be preferable to channel redistributed incomes towards labour- and skill-intensive services. This would amount to a boost to domestic producers and it would not favour domestic producers of traded goods over imports. The practice suggested is in fact commonly employed – it is achieved by boosting public services. The subject is dealt with in the next section; here it is sufficient to note that other methods are available for channelling redistributed incomes towards privately-produced services. Such a programme may be acceptable to those who favour redistribution but are distrustful of public enterprise on efficiency grounds or because of its arbitrary redistributive effects, as when the poor make less use of some services than the middle classes. A redistributive programme could be arranged to encourage expansion of many privately-provided services in a way which would satisfy consumer demand.

There is some evidence that there is latent demand for many services which would be stimulated by redistribution. This can be illustrated by reference to a recent Gallup poll on consumer services.[4] Table 5.5, extracted from that survey, shows the extent to which various services are currently used, broken down by social class; those for which there is latent demand for extra provision and those where the constraining factor is affordability or price. The table shows that for many services the latent demand is not expressed because of price or affordability. In some cases it is quality or availability which constrains demand, and this is dealt with in Chapter 7. But it

Table 5.5

Service	% who ever use	By social class AB/C1	Rest	Wish to use more (%)	Of which 'too expensive/can't afford'
Holidays	55	61	51	25	22
Eating out	72	88	62	26	23
Cinema/theatre	4	5	3	3	2
Music lessons	5	8	4	6	2
Sports lessons	12	14	11	8	5
Other tuition	5	8	4	4	2
Open University	4	6	3	4	2
Computer course	4	6	3	9	3
Vocational	8	10	7	9	2
Taxis	49	56	45	19	18
Buses	68	61	72	18	8
Trains	55	67	47	25	16
Libraries, etc.	67	77	61	4	0
Private sport	47	59	39	16	8
Legal services	34	45	26	5	5
Other professional services	89	97	85	12	11
Electrical repairs	50	60	45	8	7
Car repairs	50	70	29	10	8
House repairs	27	39	20	17	14
Decorating	12	17	9	18	14
Gardening	6	10	4	9	6
Dependent care	6	6	6	6	3
Domestic help	3	6	1	7	5

Source: Gallup.

is clear that in many major areas – catering, holidays, repairs, sport and travel – that expenditure is almost wholly constrained by cost and affordability. This opens up two possible strategies for redistribution. It is possible to pursue the approach adopted by government since 1979 to reduce the cost of such services by reducing wages. The removal of wage-council protection from some workers and the operation of various special schemes has put pressure on wages in many of these service sectors. However it also appears that another strategy is possible. Greater markets for these services could be generated by a redistributive programme which made them accessible to a wider range of people. The latent demand is certainly in evidence, even though it may not be as strong as for imported consumer-durables. While it is not certain that the marginal propensities to spend on services is higher for lower-income groups, the differential-usage figures and the fact that the propensity is higher in so far as total expenditure is concerned makes this a plausible proposition.

One method for combining a redistributive programme with the expansion of such services would be the use of a voucher system. Companies could be encouraged to pay a fixed component of income in the form of tax-free vouchers. These would be usable for a range of services, acceptable at a conversion rate decided by the company offering the service. The vouchers would not be transferable but could be redeemed by individuals on payment of a standard tax. If such a scheme proved too complicated or unacceptable, alternative methods could be devised such as price subsidies to producers, or differential rates of VAT.

The redistributive approach has one other merit, dealt with in more detail in Chapter 8. This is that progressive redistribution should reduce the number of hours offered by workers and lead to increased worksharing. This is because the longest hours are worked by those on low incomes and, as incomes rise, fewer hours tend to be worked.

Public services

The number of full-time equivalent workers in various public services is shown in Table 5.6.

Table 5.6 Public-sector employment (full time equivalents; thousands)

	Total	Central government	Local government
1978	6526	2140	2325
1980	6512	2161	2343
1982	6158	2158	2274
1984	5978	2114	2275

Source: Economic Trends, March 1985.

It appears from these figures that employment in general government has been relatively stable. The greatest reduction in public-service employment has been outside the general-government sector, in public corporations and nationalised industries, partly due to privatisation. This is interesting as it reveals how difficult it has been for a government committed to reducing public-sector employment to effect it in practice. This reflects a strong tendency for public employment to grow for reasons other than political preference.

Public-sector employment can of course only be a partial answer to the employment problem. It constitutes only 30 per cent of total employment and cannot be expanded indefinitely. It is however a valid means of employment creation as long as there is demand which can best be satisfied by public-sector growth. There is no basis for the claim that has sometimes been put forward that the public sector is somehow less worthwhile or less productive than the private sector.[5] The absurdity of the view that public-sector or non-marketed production is unproductive can be seen by considering countries where most output is administered in non-market forms. It can hardly be the case that these economies are almost totally unproductive. The notion of the public sector as unproductive is sustainable only in so far as some public-sector expenditure constitutes immediate consumption and in that sense is a drain on the capacity to produce for the future. But a country can 'consume' too much by over-eating, as it can through the excessive provision of health care. The arbiter of productiveness is of course the taxpayer; if he or she refuses to foot the bill for public services or fails to take account of the social wage in pay bargaining, then public services can be considered unproductive. But the claim would only be unambiguously true if this were the case for every possible distribution of the tax burden.

Public expenditure in Britain has been unnecessarily constrained on many fronts in recent years. The case of health care is a clear example. Figure 5.1 shows a comparison between expenditure per head on health in OECD countries. It is apparent that UK expenditure is approximately 25 per cent lower than would be expected if it were in line with countries of comparable national income. This has important implications for employment. If the UK were in line with other countries it would mean an extra 300,000 employed directly in health, with a large extra indirect effect in other industries. There are certain *caveats* to be noted here – the measure used is a cost one and it is possible that the NHS is more cost-effective than other health services. In particular the mix of nurses and doctors is different, with the NHS having a higher relative input from nurses who are of course less-highly paid. Nevertheless, the contrast with the rest of the OECD is not to be doubted. Not only is the level of expenditure per head lower than for comparable countries, but the rate of growth of real health expenditure in Britain between 1960 and 1983 was approximately a quarter less than the average of the major seven OECD countries (OECD, 1985c).

It is sometimes argued that there is no economic rationale for speaking of suppressed demand for health care, in that it is available privately. But the marginal or incremental cost for private health-care is very high, given that free health-care, whatever its inadequacies, is financed out of taxation. And there is evidence from a number of sample surveys that the public is prepared to finance more health care provision in the NHS out of taxation. Table 5.7 shows the response from the Gallup survey mentioned earlier.

It sometimes seems implicit in writings on the public sector that any increase in its value or volume-share of total output is to be deplored. But just as with private services, there are legitimate conditions where demand justifies increased provision. In the case of a marketed service, falling costs and prices, coupled with a high price-elasticity, would encourage greater

Ways and means

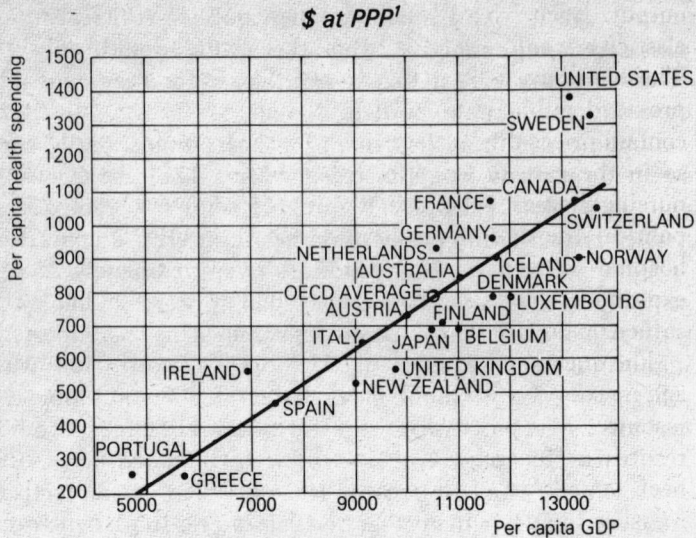

Figure 5.1 Per capita health spending, per capita GDP, 1982
23 countries
1. Converted into dollars from local currencies, using GDP purchasing power parities.
Source: The Financing and Delivery of Health Care in OECD Countries: Past, Present and Future, available from OECD's Social Affairs, Manpower and Education Directorate. Taken from OECD Observer, November 1985, p.14, table A.

Table 5.7 Which would you like to see improved or expanded by the NHS even if it meant higher taxation?

	Social class	
	AB/C1	Rest
Hospital facilities	53	55
Dental treatment	19	19
Nursing homes	17	22
Home nursing	18	18
Health clinics	26	29
Ambulances	19	16
Homeopathy/osteopathy	18	12
Psychiatric services	16	12
Screening	36	23
None	18	26

Source: Gallup.

output. Even where prices rose moderately, a high income-elasticity would lead to increased output and expenditure. These principles do not change just because a service is provided publicly. Of course, in some cases it is difficult to contain prices due to stagnant productivity; this is particularly so in the case of services with a high care-content such as nursing homes – the extent of provision here is largely a political question. However in other areas, such as acute hospital services, where there is no evidence of a cost explosion, the existence of a strong and rising demand is sufficient justification for greater provision.

The question is somewhat more complex where cost savings and increased efficiency depend on increased expenditure. For instance, it is possible for a modest sum to computerise the records of general practitioners, though this has only rarely been done. Part of the reason for this is that it is difficult to measure the gains in efficiency, but it is also the result of the general squeeze on public expenditure.

While the provision for social consumption (pensions, benefits, remedial health-care, recreation, etc.) is largely a political choice, it is unlikely that the pressure for growth and expansion will lessen in the future. The main reasons for this lie in the expected increase in the proportion of older people and changes in family structure. Health expenditure and pensions rise with the proportion of elderly and greater life-expectancy; the disappearance of the extended family, more single-parent families and greater equality of treatment for women will also add to the pressures for higher social spending. It is important that efforts to prioritise social consumption do not degenerate into irrational programmes of budget cuts which indiscriminately lower social investment in the process.

It is possible to argue about the scope for increased public spending and borrowing, but very little sensible discussion is possible until public-sector accounting is reformed so as to take account of the difference between consumption and investment, i.e. provision for the future. The latter is not at all the same as the present category of capital expenditure, which merely includes fixed investment in buildings, plant and vehicles. The way in which public-expenditure control is maintained at present results in constraints on investment and consumption so that projects such as preventative health or many forms of education are constrained unnecessarily. It must be an urgent priority to set up a commission of experts – including sympathetic City figures – to reform the public accounts so as to make this distinction explicit. Without such measurement it is quite senseless to engage in debate on the 'optimal level of public-sector debt'.

One of the advantages of making this distinction between consumption and investment explicit is that it offers incentives to those in the public sector to increase efficiency and accept restructuring. The classification of a project as an investment could be expected to lead to an increase in funding.

The public sector needs such rational planning no less than private companies. No well-planned private firm would starve of resources a division that was set to continue all its activities and even increase in importance; the aim would rather be to provide assistance for reorganisation. It has to be assumed either that governments are not committed to maintaining public services at previous levels or that short-term thinking is governing policy. Consider the amount of resources committed to research and development in public services. Such research includes evaluation of different methods of delivering services, whether via computer-aided learning or expert medical systems, or the use of information technology for health screening or appointments. The available data is somewhat old, but if official sources are to be believed the numbers employed in research in the entire area of services and utilities is less than 2 per cent of the numbers employed in research elsewhere in the economy, mostly in manufacturing.[6] OECD figures suggest that public-services research is particularly low in the UK. Government funding on R&D in health, environment and social welfare is a half that of France, a quarter that of Germany, and one-thirtieth that of the US.[7] Further details are shown in Table 5.8.

The low level of research is not however confined to the UK. The OECD has pointed out that by the end of the 1970s between a quarter and a half of all government outlays were spent on social security and welfare: 'However, governments seem to feel that R&D has only a small part to play in coping

Table 5.8 R&D expenditure as a percentage of government outlays in health and social security

	US	Germany	France	UK
Health	7.5	2.4	2.1	1.5
Social security	0.25	0.28	0.09	0.1

Source: OECD.

with the problems involved' (OECD, 1986b, p. 101). The implicit criticism in that remark echoes an earlier OECD report (1980) by a group of experts commenting on technical change and economic policy. A recommendation of this report was for more resources for 'social technologies, by which was meant the design and diffusion of both hardware technologies and modes of organisation, communication and participation. In particular the fields of public transport, health services, urban amenities, education, cultural provision and care for the elderly were mentioned as areas for social innovation. Research into new modes of providing services in these areas is most likely to be successful in a context of expanding rather than contracting services, since management resources will not then be concentrated on coping with the negative aspects of cost containment.

The lack of research in areas of social provision is disturbing because it will perpetuate dissatisfaction with these services despite a strong latent demand for improvements. Public provision is often not offered in an imaginative and differentiated way that increases choice. If this were done it might simultaneously increase support for public spending and increase the use made of the services. Examples here might be the availability of credits in education, which could be used for any module, and the availability of a wider range of medical advice on the NHS. Such a transformation of the public-services sector would require a reasonable input of surveys, research, experimentation and evaluation, all of which is precluded by present spending-limits.

One important example of a public-service innovation which is clearly a social investment is the provision of computer-aided learning in schools and further and higher education. If this could be justified on rational social-accounting terms the resultant boost to jobs would be very significant – certainly enough to halt the expected decline in teacher numbers over the next decade.

The potential of this form of learning is immense; an OECD view is that the whole education sector ought to be placed in 'semi-permanent retraining' (OECD, 1986). The same report recognises, however, that constraints such as the lack of trained teachers, finance, and insufficiently clear agreement on future directions make this 'wildly impracticable' (p. 73). Certainly the lack of skills and software-development would be a constraint, even if finance were available. White (1985) states that remarkably little has been done in Britain to develop the role of information technology in education or even seriously to assess its potential.

> The computer industry has conspicuously failed to develop methods and standards for its own professionals. Software costs remain high, quality is much more variable than in the case of hardware . . . in this economic chain reaction therefore, it is the training of IT software professionals which has the key position. (p. 33)

It will be very costly to overcome these skill- and software-shortages in the application of information technology in education, but the opportunities are substantial. A London headmaster has commented on the gains:

> It frees children from the slavery of data acquisition which so often they were unable to relate to meaningful programming. It frees them to test and try and discover the essential modes of thinking: how to be logical, how to sift evidence . . . it frees teachers to organise learning effectively in all ability situations, to team teach, to coordinate resources. (Chambers, 1982, p. 150)

These possibilities are far from being fulfilled. Despite the presence of computers in most schools, they are grossly under-utilised. Most staff have only a few days' training, except for the small number who are able to be replaced for the half-year courses that a proper training demands. If public resources were allocated rationally, the expected loss of teachers – at a rate of 1 per cent a year – over the next decade would be halted in favour of a phased programme of half-year replacements for teachers on training.[8]

The huge scale of public funds required to introduce a comprehensive and effective programme of computer-aided education requires some hard justification. It is probably impossible to make more than a plausible case; none of the many research projects in recent decades has been able to establish without doubt that education favours growth (Peston, 1985). However it is in such matters that discretion, judgment and risk-taking are essential. The first priority is to reform institutional procedures so that timely assessments and judgments of this sort can be made and that borrowing and investment at an appropriate scale can follow. Only in this way is it possible to assess whether the Public Sector Borrowing Requirement should be at its current level or a multiple of this.

Exported services

Internationally-traded services are important for at least two reasons – balance of payments and employment. For a country such as Britain, facing a potential balance-of-payments constraint, the role of services is important to counter the visibles deficit and to complement investment income. In addition to this concern with net receipts, tradeable services create employment opportunities. The two questions are somewhat distinct; for instance, a negative trade balance on the travel account, indicating a net outflow of tourist spending, may still generate jobs, since services are needed for inward and outward passengers. The two questions may also imply different approaches to the statistics. For balance-of-payments purposes, the relevant deflator of the net balance may be import prices, but the direct employment implications will be judged better if export prices are used.

On employment, there is reason to believe that traded services are slightly less labour-intensive (per unit value of sales) than manufacturing. The implication is that a balanced expansion of trade which resulted in increased manufacturing imports and higher services exports would reduce employment very slightly. However the skill content of traded services is higher than manufacturing and so the second-round effects of higher incomes would probably increase employment. In any case, there would be gains through increased trade (Sapir, 1983).

The prospects for growth in services exports are a little uncertain. The British Invisible Exports Council (BIEC) suggested caution in its evidence to the Aldington Committee inquiry (House of Commons, 1986), arguing that it would be unwise to assume too readily that the invisible-services sector is capable of an expansion of earnings (and thus the creation of new jobs) sufficient to absorb the millions of unemployed. Part of the reason for this caution must be that world trade in services is growing no faster than manufacturing, except in the area of financial and other services, where growth is about half as fast again (Bank of England, 1985, Table F). One reason sometimes offered for slow growth in services trade is that some services – maintenance, design, advice or entertainment – can now be incorporated in physical goods. Yet this is unlikely to be the major explanation, since most of these services form part of the category that is growing fastest. The slowest-growing area is transport, where barriers to trade are considerable.

Trade restrictions apply to many services, not just transport. They include direct quantity controls (air transport, film, advertising), subsidies (construction, data processing, transport), government procurement (business services, construction, transport), technical and customs barriers (business services) and personal restrictions on travel (Sapir, 1983). It is possible that, in the long run, growth in services will result from trade liberalisation in these areas, but the British body investigating this – the Liberalisation of Trade in Services Committee (LOTIS) – has pointed to many difficult questions involved: 'any international initiative will not show significant results in the short or possible even in the medium term' (p. 7). In arguing for liberalisation, it stressed the importance of trade within the EEC.[9]

A good deal of attention has been focused on trade in

services with developing countries, and US representatives have been pressing hard for services to be incuded in GATT negotiations. But services only account for about a quarter of all North–South trade and it seems likely that the US is mainly concerned at the implications of services for merchandise trade.[10] A World Bank view has been that unilateral reduction in protectionism on the part of developing countries is not politically feasible and the 'only realistic objective . . . is intra-industrialised country liberalisation' (Sapir and Lutz, 1980, p. 65).

The prospects for autonomous growth in services depends to some extent on how independent it is of trade in general and manufacturing exports in particular. BIEC reacted strongly to the tone of the Aldington report (House of Commons, 1986) which appeared to characterise services-trade as totally dependent on manufacturing. It is certainly true that some services such as tourism are largely independent (BIEC, 1985); nevertheless some writers have suggested that a new complementarity may be arising in the 'other services' category between goods and services (Petit, 1986): 'Exports and imports of these heterogeneous items such as financial, business and cultural services have increased relatively rapidly in all countries and this gives credence to the hypothesis that the general growth in this trade is linked to the continuous expansion of trade in goods' (p. 100). The argument here is a little opaque. It is probably true that trade in business services such as communications, licensing, R&D and prospecting follow to some extent multinational global investments and are loosely connected with goods-production and trade-flows, though transfer pricing may also play a role. The opposite causal pattern, whereby goods-exports follow a service contract, may also apply to some services such as construction and air transport. However these points do not detract form the large degree of autonomy in the other-services category. This autonomy, which also extends to tourism and travel, should not be taken to mean that prospects for growth are necessarily good; that, separate, question is investigated below.

Prospects for traded services

Exported services account for about 30 per cent of all British exports. Britain's share of traded services has fallen faster than that for manufacturing in recent decades. However import penetration in services has remained low, for whatever reason, in contrast to manufacturing. The trade ratio for services (value of exports to imports) trended upwards until the late 1970s, largely because of the increasing receipts from travel. Since then the ratio has fallen, despite a steep off-setting rise for a few years on the financial and other services account.[11]

Table 5.9 shows UK export receipts and trade balances for service categories – travel, transport, financial and other services – deflated in each case by estimated export prices.

It is difficult to provide a background theory for interpreting these figures. Sapir (1983) argues somewhat tentatively that comparative advantage can explain some of the variation between countries with abundance of physical capital, conferring advantages in transportation services, and a high skill-rating being important elsewhere. But it is clear that historical, geographical and language influences are also important. A cross-section study of forty-four developed and developing countries showed that net travel receipts per head tend to fall with GNP and GNP per head; put differently, residents of richer countries spend more abroad than poorer ones. By contrast, the net exports of financial and other services rises with GNP (Sapir and Lutz, 1980).

Sea transport has been in long-term decline, falling on average by 9 per cent a year in real terms between 1974 and 1984. Britain has still one of the largest fleets, so significant earnings still accrue, but the loss of share, mainly to Asiatic and Soviet-bloc countries, is expected to continue. The decline is a Europe-wide phenomenon and other countries' fleets have shown larger percentage falls. The best hope for diversification probably lies in joint ventures with other countries and in knowledge- and management-intensive roles such as chartering, registering, short-sea ferries and offshore supply. Oil-related transport can be expected to show a negative balance as oil receipts drop.

Table 5.9 Internationally-traded services: UK export volume index (A) and trade balance at 1980 prices (B)

Category		1973	1974	1975	1976	1977	1978	1979	1980	1981	1982	1983
Sea transport	A	138	152	133	127	125	110	105	100	84	77	68
	B	47.6	398.1	518.3	473.1	690.8	338.9	74.6	141.0	−175.6	−185.4	−565.2
Civil aviation	A	51	53	59	65	67	79	92	100	98	91	93
	B	147.0	227.5	233.0	293.0	246.5	330.2	290.8	395.0	296.3	32.7	95.1
Travel	A	65	76	86	109	124	115	112	100	89	87	94
	B	418.7	908.7	1122.7	1913.2	2330	1762.3	1153.3	223.9	−294.4	−326.2	−201.1
Financial services	A	79	84	103	108	103	110	107	100	113	119	130
	B	1337.5	1422.1	1743.8	1828.4	1743.8	1862.3	1811.5	1693.0	1913.1	2014.7	2200.9
Other services[a]	A	75	78	78	84	89	97	100	100	99	97	99
	B	2041.9	1960.4	1482.1	1729.2	1882.1	2500.1	2629.1	2601.0	2620.5	2386.3	2506.6

[a] Including consultancy, inter-firm transactions, R&D, and overseas students.

Source: 1984 Pink Book.

Civil aviation, despite its strong growth in receipts, has shown only a small positive balance, which has declined in recent years due to a fall in domestic-airlines' share of passenger traffic into and out of Britain. The travel balance tends to fluctuate considerably, partly in response to exchange-rate changes; it does not indicate any favourable long-term trend, though, as mentioned earlier, there is probably no simple correspondence between travel employment and the travel balance.

The only consistent source of growth is financial and other services, as may be seen from Table 5.9. However, financial services are difficult to measure properly. Debits may be under-recorded, and credits, too, may be under-stated as the estimates shown do not include net interest receipts, some of which may reflect services provided. The difficulty of measuring financial services in real terms is reflected in the widely-varying official estimates of growth between 1974 and 1984. The Central Statistical Office records strong growth for this period, while the Bank of England (1985) suggests a growth figure close to zero. The discrepancy is due to choice of deflator, with the Bank using the retail price deflator throughout and the CSO using international currency deflators for many items. Apart from these measurement problems, there is also a conceptual difficulty, in that some of the recent expansion in financial services simply reflects the switch to securities and away from bank lending as a result of the lowering of the credit ratings of commercial banks and their exposure to Third World debt. Variable interest rates have also led to a proliferation of credit instruments and some of these costs must be considered as *'faux frais'* (Marx, 1972).

Other services comprises a heterogeneous group, described in the footnote to Table 5.9. Growth here has been strong, but perhaps not remarkable. These services are clearly important since they account for a third of all service receipts and a tenth of all export earnings. The real balance has been flat since the late 1970s, probably reflecting the high UK exchange rate. The total of two sub-categories – consultancy (mainly construction) and company services provided abroad by UK firms – accounts for a similar value of exports as the receipts of financial services – about £3bn in 1984. As with manufacturing, faster volume growth in these areas could be achieved with a lower exchange rate. An International Monetary Fund model of trade in services shows that travel and other services are 'strongly influenced by relative prices and exchange rates with price elasticity of -2.3 for foreign travel and -2.7 for other services (Bond, 1979).

Four-fifths of the British earnings from consultancy come from engineering activities. Examples are urban transport systems, railways, airports, communication systems, waterworks, roads, bridges, electrical power-systems and process plant. Export subsidies and tied aid are used by nearly all exporting countries to obtain contracts, and competition is fierce. These exports have a double significance in that they result in follow-on trade in goods, estimated to be as high as three-to-one in value terms. Studies in the US have identified direct merchandise trade in excess of the services trade that gave rise to it (US International Trade Commission, 1982).

To conclude, the growth rate of financial and other services, while not outstanding, is faster than travel and transport. Furthermore, for Britain the differential between growth in this category of services and growth in traded non-oil goods is such that within ten years the former category could rise from less than a fifth of the latter to a quarter. This, however, may be an under-estimate. One part of these services – traded information – is projected to see some very fast growth. According to Sapir (1983): 'not only are we witnessing the start of a formidable expansion in communications and information services trade, but also in the process many other services are becoming tradeable' (p. 86). A recent British report of tradeable information (ITAP, 1983) defined the sector as comprising financial and business information, printing and publishing, on-line technical information, consultancies, entertainment and education. It estimated that the sector employed a million people, corresponding to 5 per cent of GDP. It seems likely that British firms will take a high share of new growth in these services, given advantages of language, historical involvement, skill structure and industrial contacts. However extra trade in these activities will have to be generated. Many of the factors that will encourage or inhibit growth in these exports are the same as those that will affect the growth of domestic information services, referred to earlier. It is worth noting that many of the activities concerned can be provided through a computer terminal which can be located anywhere; this has implications for jobs in the British regions.

6 Small wonder?

Chapter 4 has argued that the most hopeful path for stimulating employment is one leading to the development and take-up of new products. This could be helped by the planning of consumer expenditure and by public procurement. Many would add another ingredient – the fostering of a dynamic small-firms sector. Such firms, it is often argued, promote jobs at a rapid rate and have a better track-record on innovation. These claims and other similar ones are investigated in this chapter.

What is a small firm? The definitions used by the 1971 Committee of Inquiry on Small Firms (Bolton Committee) centred on the criteria of small market-share and owner-management.[1] The data on such firms is poor, often excluding the smallest categories. It is mainly establishment-based rather than enterprise-based and is very patchy outside manufacturing. Given these problems, it is not surprising that there are competing views on the role and performance of this type of firm.

This chapter consists of three parts. The first deals with the general questions of employment generation of small and new firms in the economy, including innovation performance. The second part addresses in greater detail the questions of employment generation of small and new firms. Finally, part three discusses the potential of various support schemes.

The role and performance of small firms

The increase in the share of larger firms in the economy,

particularly over the past thirty years or so, is often seen as a policy-induced change or one brought about by firms taking advantage of various scale economies. In fact, as Prais (1976) has elegantly shown, concentration will always increase where growth rates of firms tend to differ, unless measures are taken to prevent this. Some firms increase in size; some firms decrease in size; both lead to greater dispersion. The firms that have grown will account for a larger share of output and employment. Concentration is, therefore, a 'natural' process, though this explanation is not adequate to account for all the observed changes in recent times; governments have also encouraged concentration.[2]

It is by no means clear that it is always sensible to discuss the relative performance of large and small firms. These types of firm may simply occupy different terrain in the economy, each of them performing an important function but having different strengths and weaknesses. The task of assessing relative efficiency according to some common criterion is very difficult. Profitability cannot be considered a suitable comparative indicator unless the same degree of competitive pressure is assumed to operate for both groups of firms. Measures such as total factor-productivity are suspect for the same reason and rely on restrictive assumptions. For what it is worth, the Bolton Committee report utilised the latter measure and concluded that small firms were neither more nor less efficient than large ones.

It is not possible to draw policy conclusions on the basis of microeconomic considerations alone. The existence of a fringe of small firms, even inefficient ones, might well maintain competitive pressure on putative oligopolistic or monopolistic market structures. On the other hand, the predominance of very large firms in the economy may have beneficial effects, either in terms of commitment to training, technological diffusion, ease with which reforms may be legislated or in terms of the greater stability of investment and forward planning that is thought to characterise such a market structure.

Table 6.1 presents a picture of the evolution of small manufacturing firms in relation to the total, between 1963 and 1982. The proportion of net output and employment accounted

Table 6.1 Small[a] enterprise data, manufacturing industries, UK, 1963–82

	No. of small enterprises (thousands)	As % of all enterprises	Employment in small enterprises as % of total	Net output (by value) of small enterprises as % of total
1963	65.7	94.1	21.3	18.02
1968	66.1	94.9	20.8	18.1
1970	70.9	95.2	21.3	18.5
1971	71.4	95.3	21.0	17.9
1972	69.0	95.4	21.5	18.4
1973	74.1	95.7	20.7	17.1
1974	81.1	96.0	21.5[c]	17.7[c]
1975	83.4	96.3	21.9[c]	18.0[c]
1976	86.3	96.5	22.6[c]	18.2[c]
1977	86.7	96.6	22.5[c]	18.7[c]
1978	87.2	96.7	22.8[c]	19.3[c]
1980[b]	87.3	96.8	24.3[c]	21.5[c]
1982[b]	82.9	97.1	26.7	22.6

a 'Small' is defined as an enterprise employing less than 200 persons.
b Manufacturing plus mineral extraction. The latter category is negligible.
c Data based on establishment not enterprise figures.

Sources : *Interim Report of the Committee to Review the Functioning of Financial Institutions*, Cmnd 7503, HMSO, 1971, Tables 2.1, 2.2 and 2.3; *Reports of the Censuses of Production*, 1974–5, 1976, 1977, 1978, 1980 and 1982 published HMSO, 1978–81. Except for 1980 and 1982, all data is taken from Curran and Stanworth (1981).

for by small firms has been approximately constant but has shown a recent rise. However, it is likely that this rise largely reflects trends in labour-saving and the cyclical effects of the recession. Many medium-sized firms will have become 'small' as their employment has declined.

The data in Table 6.1 refer to manufacturing only. However, the Bolton Committee estimated that, on their definitions, manufacturing accounted for only a third of small-firm total employment. Put differently, small firms employ only one in five in manufacturing, but employ half or more in miscellaneous services, hotel and catering trades, and retail trades.

An alternative data source which can be used to measure the activity of small firms in all sectors is the VAT register of firms, introduced in the early 1970s. This has the advantage of including businesses in all sectors with a turnover in 1982 of £15,000 per annum, though exemptions are common in some sectors. Among its disadvantages is the fact that not all registered businesses trade. The sectoral breakdown of registration is shown in Table 6.2. From this it can be seen that 50 per cent of companies who registered were engaged in distribution or catering.[3]

Innovation and the small firm

In many small firms the scope for innovation is unlikely to be great, especially in sectors such as distribution. Even in manufacturing it seems likely that small firms will be less focused on innovation and less likely to do research and development. Williamson (1975) has argued that R&D is less likely to prove economically rewarding for small firms since the risk involved is difficult to insure against and transactions costs such as contracts will be relatively more costly.

Empirical observation needs caution because the independent occurrence of technological development in certain sectors could encourage the profusion of new or small firms. This would represent a reverse causation to that usually imagined, which goes from industrial structure to innovative performance. Prais (1976) has argued that the ten industries showing the fastest rise in the number of small establishments between 1958 and 1968 included 'scientific instruments, electronic apparatus, plastics fabrications and printing'. He concluded that 'technological developments thus remain of importance in promoting small firms' (pp. 15, 18). If this is correct there is a complex structure involved in the relationship of size-to-innovation, a structure which is obscured by simply investigating the relative degree of innovativeness of large and small firms.

Figures are given in Table 6.3 showing the percentage of significant innovations (as defined by technologists) introduced by small firms in manufacturing. The percentage has stayed relatively constant over thirty-five years at about 14 per cent of the total, somewhat lower than the corresponding percentages for employment and output (Townsend et al., 1981).

The results of the latter study do not suggest that small

Table 6.2 Businesses registered 1974–82, percentage of total by sector

	Retailing	Construction	Other services	Catering	Production	Wholesale
Sole proprietorship or partnerships	18	17.1	14.5	7.6	10.2	9.2
Companies	30.2	11.7	9.2	14.5	7.1	5.5

Source: *British Business*, 12 August 1983.

Small wonder?

Table 6.3 Percentage of innovations in each firm-size category for each five-year period in manufacturing industry

No. of employees	1945–9 (%)	1950–4 (%)	1955–9 (%)	1960–4 (%)	1965–9 (%)	1970–4 (%)	1975–80 (%)	Total (%)	% of total manufacturing net output in 1980
1–199	16.0	12.0	11.0	11.0	13.0	15.0 (11.0)	17.0 (12.0)	14.0 (12.0)	21.5
200–499	9.0	6.0	8.0	6.0	7.0	9.0 (7.0)	7.0 (6.0)	7.0 (7.0)	6.9
500–999	3.0	2.0	7.0	5.0	5.0	4.0 (4.0)	3.0 (3.0)	4.0 (4.0)	6.8
1,000–9,999	36.0	36.0	25.0	27.0	23.0	17.0 (19.0)	14.0 (13.0)	23.0 (23.0)	30.3
10,000 and over	36.0	44.0	50.0	51.0	52.0	55.1 (59.0)	59.0 (66.0)	52.0 (54.0)	34.5
Total	100.0	100.0	100.0	100.0	100.0	100.0	100.0	100.0	100.0
No. of innovations	94	191	274	405	467	401	461	2293	

Note: numbers in brackets for the periods 1970–4 and 1975–80 are the weighted percentage contributions, assuming the same sectoral mix as in the period 1945–69.
Source: Townsend et al. (1981), Table 5; *Report on the Census of Production*, 1980.

firms (up to 200 employees) have become relatively more important sources of innovation in the 1970s than in the 1950s and 1960s. They remain relatively unimportant in mechanical engineering and instruments; they make very little contribution in transport equipment, chemicals and – at least in Britain – in most parts of the electronics industry (p. 108). However, the study notes that while the average size of innovating firm in the sample has increased steadily since 1945, that of innovating units (including large-firm subsidiaries) has been decreasing since the mid-1950s.

The above sketch of innovation by size-category is based on an analysis of major innovations, and it may tend to understate the role of small firms in incremental innovative activity. Cannon (1982) considers that this is where the independent role of small firms is greatest. Certainly, small firms are more likely to succeed in the minor role than in major innovations since the proportion of R&D expenditure accounted for by small firms tends to be far less than their contribution to output or employment (Rothwell and Zegveld, 1982).

In the development of innovative products it may well be that the minor role is the more importnat one, i.e. the adaptation of existing research to new-product development. Certainly a major expression of consumer and public demand for high-technology products could not be adequately met by the existing large domestic firms and it would be important to encourage the rapid growth of new ones. Rothwell and Zegveld (1985) identify opportunities in scientific instruments, electronics, specialist machinery, computer-aided design, and conclude that 'innovation-oriented public purchasing, especially at the local level could provide niche-strategy small and medium sized firms with many new opportunities' (p. 218).

Employment generation in new and small firms

The growth of small firms cannot be satisfactory gauged by noting the proportion of employment or output accounted for by firms in any chosen size-category over time. Such an analysis does not provide information on the likelihood of growth, contraction or liquidation of small firms in relation to larger ones. An alternative dynamic analysis of a cohort of firms over time is needed and a number of such studies have been carried out, both for the US and the UK. These studies track the performance of a set of particular firms over time. This type of analysis, however, is fraught with statistical perils, and has led to popular myths which overstate the importance of small firms in job generation. Two qualifications in particular should be borne in mind.

1   The analyses are usually based on establishment rather than enterprise data. The fact that one can observe a negative relationship between establishment size and employment growth over some size-ranges has led some commentators to conclude that small firms are more important as job creators. However, Macey (1982) has shown that it is not possible on the basis of establishment studies to conclude that small firms grow more rapidly than large firms. The reasons for this are set out in Panel 6.1.

Panel 6.1
Problems with growth-comparisons based on establishment data

1   Large firms are more likely to be multi-establishment; a higher proportion of this growth relative to small firms will therefore be in new establishments. This will cause an under-estimation of relative growth rates of large firms when establishment employment-growth data (proxying firm data) is related to size.
2   Growth of large firms via acquisitions will not be recorded by establishment data. Of course, there are arguments for and against including acquisitions when engaging in growth comparisons.
3   It is known from Prais (1976) that large establishments grow more slowly than large firms, the implication being that firms keep plant sizes small.

2 The notion of a net job gain is a very elusive one. Displacement effects elsewhere in the economy resulting from new entry or expansion are extremely difficult to trace. A comparison between the net jobs generated by small and large firms will be vitiated if the displacement effects are not properly measured and if the probability of displacement occurring outside the relevant size group differ between existing large and new small firms.

Different writers express contrasting views on the employment potential of small firms.

1 Birch (1979) is probably the best-known study, if only because his conclusion that US firms employing less than twenty workers contributed 66 per cent of new net jobs created between 1969 and 1976, while firms younger than four years accounted for 80 per cent. In a critique of Birch's findings, researchers at the Brookings Institute disputed that small firms had any advantage in employment growth (Armington and Odle, 1982). In any event, there is a problem in expressing percentages in this way, since the net totals are obtained by subtracting much larger gross gains and losses. If the net gain were zero, Birch's statistics would perforce be infinity! If the net gain were negative, as in UK and US manufacturing industry in this period, the statistics would be meaningless.

2 Gallagher and Stewart (1984) carried out a study similar to Birch's in the UK for all industries – service and manufacturing. They concluded that firms under twenty employees (covering 13 per cent of employment) provided 31 per cent of all gross new employment between 1971 and 1981. But this conclusion must be qualified, if not discounted completely, by their use of a commercial database where credit rating and marketing determined the choice of firms within the sample. The database is thus biased towards more successful, and therefore growing, firms.[4]

3 Fothergill and Gudgin (1979) confined themselves to a study of manufacturing in the East Midlands region of the UK, 1968–75. They found that larger plants have been responsible for a net loss of jobs, while very small plants

(less than twenty-five employees) have experienced a small rise in employment. New (post-1947) independent firms, large and small, accounted for one in six of all gross job gains. New firms also provided the only dynamic element of small-firm job generation. The fact that high growth in small-firms employment is confined to new, i.e. post-1947, businesses leads the authors to conclude that 'for many firms, their period of buoyant growth may be tied to the life of their founder' (p. 14). This view is certainly consistent with the profiles of typical small-firm manager-owners evident from the literature (Belbin, 1980; Bannock, 1981; Curran and Stanworth, 1981). According to a study by Scase and Goffee (1983), attitudes to employing staff and its effect on the independence of the manager-owner placed a severe limit on the growth of small firms. A desire for independence may also limit a firm's access to external capital. The Unlisted Stock Market, which allows cash to be raised with only a small percentage of public shares, is intended to lessen this problem.

4 The Department of Trade and Industry has published a job-generation study of manufacturing for the period 1972–5 (Macey, 1982). Table 6.4, collated from a number of Macey's tables, shows the components of employment change between 1972 and 1975 and the extent to which each component is attributable to small firms. Some

Table 6.4 Employment in 1972 and components of change by size 1972–5 (manufacturing)

	Total (000s)	Of which, in firms employing 11–200
Employment in 1972	6,488	1,852.5
Closures	−248.3	−173.5
Contractions	−667.4	−185.5
Expansion	+552.8	239.4
Openings	90.0	62.8
Net change in employment excluding openings, 1972–5	−411.4	−120.6

Source: Macey (1982)

caution must be exercised in interpreting the figures since small firms are by their nature more likely to close than contract, relative to large firms. The greater volatility of small firms in terms of both upward and downward movements is evident from the data. Reading down the table, the data show the extent of the net change in employment in total and for small firms attributable to each component of employment change – expansion, contraction or closure. The net changes exclude openings so as to focus on firms already existing at the start of the period. The figures show substantial net job losses, reflecting the balance of large gross changes. The figures also show that 'small' establishments (11–200 employees) made a sizeable contribution (over one-quarter) to net job-loss over 1972–5. The results for this period do not appear to be very stable over time, however. A later analysis by the Department of Trade and Industry (unpublished) showed that there was an inverse relationship between size and employment growth for the 1975–8 period, but not for 1972–5 (Mawson, 1984). The relationship can be shown by expressing the net job gain as a ratio of employment in the initial size-band. Table 6.5 shows the results obtained in a number of recent studies, including Macey (1982) and the later updating by the DTI. Macey's conclusion, based on the second-to-last row of the table, is that net-employment performance declines with size until the 51–200 band is reached, but then net-employment performance in establishments larger than this improves. Some confirmation of this may be gleaned from the other studies reported in the table, though the pattern is rather varied. The conclusion is important because, as mentioned earlier, net-employment performance would be expected to decline with size for purely statistical reasons. The conclusion that can be drawn is that, over the time studied, for manufacturing industry 'size was not a major determinant of net employment performance' (Macey, 1982, p. 54). Nor is there any support for the view that over a much longer period, small-firms' net growth in jobs increases markedly. This view is confirmed by a unique twenty-year data series for Scotland reported in Macey (p. 35). However, the DTI

Table 6.5 Net employment change by size of establishment: various studies[a]

	\<10	10–20	20–25	25–50	50–100	100–200	200–500	500+
East Midlands, 1968–75		+12.6		−3.2		14.9		−14.8
Cleveland, 1965–76	+56.0		+16.3		−28.3	−20.9		−26.2
Scotland, 1969–74	n.a.	−1.0		−11.0	−12.0	−15.0	−12.0	
UK, 1972–5	n.a.	+1.3		−6.4	−7.6		−6.8	−6.1
UK, 1975–8	n.a.	+7.5		+3.1	−1.4		−4.7	−7.3

Employment size band[b]

[a] Establishments in existence at beginning of period only.
[b] Figures are expressed as a percentage of initial employment in size band.

Sources: 1 Fothergill and Gudgin, 1979; 2 Storey, 1980; 3 Scottish Economic Planning Department, 1980; 4 Macey, 1982; 5 Internal Department of Trade and Industry paper (unpublished). Taken from Mawson (1984).

study for the period 1975–8 finds that the pattern has changed, possibly because of the structural changes in the economy which have seen large closures in the past decade. It is not clear, however, how long-lasting this feature will be or how dependent it is on policy choices.

New small firms and new job generation

It has already been noted that new firms are the most dynamic element of small firms. But how many jobs can be expected from this source? Table 6.6. shows the average employment per plant accounted for by new firms after they have been in business for a period of time.

Average employment of new firms tends to be low, even after a number of years. However, if new firms survive they may make a substantial contribution to jobs over the very longrun. In Fothergill and Gudgin's study, post-1947 firms accounted for less than 9 per cent of employment twenty years later, though by 1979 this had risen to 23 per cent. Recent studies, however, do not give much credence to the view that many existing small firms will grow even to medium size (Lloyd and Mason, 1985).

Table 6.6 appears to indicate some differences in job generation between different types of firms. Storey's results indicate that manufacturing provides a higher average-job level than other activities, though the higher content of subsidiaries in the manufacturing sample may partly account for this difference. In Macey's study of manufacturing firms, two thirds of the new jobs created (almost all in small establishments) were in branch plants as opposed to new independent plants. When attention is focused on independent firms, the average job content is much lower – probably less than twenty after the first five years. This result does not appear to differ greatly from that observed for high-technology firms. The low numbers of jobs created by new firms, even in a period of some growth, cautions against relying on new openings as a source of job growth. As Gudgin *et al.* (1979) point out, individual employment would only be expanded by about 0.5 per cent over ten years by doubling the rate of

Small wonder?

Table 6.6 Average employment in new plants

Study	Firm sample	When checked	Average employment	Comment
Macey (1982)	Firms existing in 1972 that survived to 1975	1975	60 (branch plants) 26 (new firms)	Manufacturing only. The average is artificially raised by the exclusion of establishments with under 10 employees.
Oakey (1983)	Firms founded within 5 years of survey date		16 (Scotland) 24 (South-East) 57 (Bay Area, California, USA	Independent firms employing less than 200 workers. High-technology manufacturing firms only. The high California average is largely attributable to 3 firms that grew rapidly.
Fothergill and Gudgin (1979)	Opening in 1947–56 Opening in 1956–68 Opening in 1968–75	1956 1968 1975	12 14 15	Leicestershire: manufacturing, independent firms only.
Storey (1982)	Firms new to Cleveland between 1971 and 1977	1977	56.7 (manufacturing) 24.8 (total) 7.3 (independent, single plant) 27.5 (parent) 11.4 (branch) 43.2 (subsidiary)	The manufacturing subsidiaries in the sample employed an average of 126.
Robson Rhodes Dept of Trade and Industry (1983a)	Anticipated average employment by borrowers under Loan Guarantee Scheme.		4 (services) 9 (manufacturing)	New business only. Likely to be over-optimistic.
Segal Quince and Partners	Firms in Cambridge surviving to 1984		29 (six to ten years old) 16 (up to six years old)	High-technology firms only; non-independent firms (*Source*: Table 6 of Storey and Johnson (1985)

company formation, even assuming no displacement effects elsewhere in the economy.

The argument made in many of the British job-generation studies is that closures and contractions destroy many more jobs than can be matched by new-firm openings, at least in the medium term. It is also argued that a reliance on new firms as a source of jobs is regionally and socially divisive. This is because new-business formation shows regional disparities, being heavily concentrated in the South-East (Ganguly, 1982). Storey (1983) argues that the less-prosperous regions are disadvantaged because entrepreneurs emerge from employment in occupations related to their business; for the old, declining industries that characterise many regions, this option is not possible. Fothergill and Gudgin (1979) also report that all but the smallest plants in their sample of small firms (less than twenty-five employees) fared worse in the slow growing areas. All of this points to the need for measures to encourage diversification of existing firms in threatened sectors and regions.

Displacement effects

When new jobs are created, some may simply displace others, so that the gain is questionable. Few studies have tackled this question, but Gudgin *et al.* (1979) attempted a crude assessment of likely displacement effects for a sample of forty-seven independent new firms in the East Midlands. The approach was to ask the firms where they sold their products. Forty-one per cent served markets within the East Midlands and only 19 per cent of firms were exporters, suggesting that the displacement effects might be high. Results from Cleveland (Storey, 1983) indicate that 'approximately 80 per cent of the output of new firms in the service sector is sold within the administrative country of which the firm is located . . . without an exogenous increase in demand, new entrants will merely displace existing firms' (p. 461). However, this seems a rather crude method of assessing displacement effects. A better approach might be to identify which firms or sectors are meeting or creating new needs, whether in the form of goods or services. A survey of new small manufacturing-firms in

Manchester and Merseyside by Lloyd (1980) is informative here. He concluded that 'a clear and important feature of all the firms in the quota sample was that very few offered new products or new processes' (p. 16). This was confirmed in a Nottingham study which showed that only four out of a hundred firms made significantly new products or used new techniques.[5]

Some small firms are of course in the high-technology sector. This is important, not only because displacement effects may be lower here but also because of the induced demand generated in skilled labour-intensive industries such as software and components. But Storey and Johnson (1985) report that new high-tech manufacturing firms directly created only about 1,000 jobs in each of the two regions studied – East Anglia and Northern England.

A useful categorisation of firms in relation to displacement effects is contained in the Bolton Report (1971). This considered three roles for small firms – as satellites, specialists and marketeers. The satellites (6 per cent) performed subcontracting work for larger firms and were heavily dependent on one large customer; the specialists (16 per cent) performed activities that large firms did not find profitable to perform; and the marketeers (78 per cent) operated in direct competition with larger firms. The percentages in brackets refer to manufacturing and the report suggested that an even higher proportion of marketeers may be found outside manufacturing (p. 32). The breakdown between these categories does not seem to have been investigated since Bolton, though Storey (1982) argues that the proportion of marketeers has probably declined. The lack of hard information on this question is unfortunate because the three functions seem quite distinct. The specialist firms are exploiting a gap in the market and job-displacement effects are likely to be minimal if this type of small firm were encouraged.

Atkins *et al.* (1983) argue that job generation in marketeer and satellite small firms is likely to lead to redundancies in established companies since many survive only by virtue of working long hours with implied low labour-costs. This is the obverse side to the comment in *British Business* that 'even if there were total displacement of existing UK output . . . the winning of business by new small firms must imply some gains in efficiency/customer satisfaction' (16 July 1983, p. 465).

Franchising

One of the problems with small business which checks their growth is that customers find it difficult and costly to monitor quality and choose between competing suppliers. This makes it easier for inefficiency and poor quality to thrive, in many areas of consumer services in particular. The resulting impediment to growing market-demand could be overcome by the creation of a brand image which identified companies in quality or price terms. Franchising is the main route by which this could be achieved, and there has been quite rapid increase in this recently. Franchising has also other advantages. The support of the parent business implies economies of scale as well as financial and management advice. It is estimated that only 15 per cent of franchised businesses fail within five years of start-up – about a third of the failure rate for new businesses in general. Nevertheless, franchising turnover in Britain is only about 2 per cent of that in the US, where it accounts for about a third of all retail turnover.

Policy measures relating to small firms

One of the points to emerge from the previous discussion is that a focus on very small firms is unlikely to contribute much in jobs over the medium term and the numbers involved are certainly dwarfed by the scale of frequent large closures. Nor is there much evidence that this will improve in the longer term. Lloyd and Mason (1985), on the basis of a sample of 460 firms in Manchester and Merseyside, have considered the possibility 'that out of the normal population of new starters . . . the seeds of a new ICI or GEC may emerge'. They conclude from their sample, however, that only one or two firms had the potential to grow to even medium size. This is the context in which the balance of support between small-firms aid and other measures needs to be examined. Some aid measures are discussed below; the level of such aid was estimated at £½ billion in 1982.[6]

Enterprise Allowance Scheme (EAS)

This pays marginally more than single-person unemployment for an unemployed person who sets up in business. About 60,000 people, mostly men, are involved each year. The scheme is largely concentrated in a new service sectors such as distribution and construction and it could be regarded as a way of exerting downward wage-pressure in these industries. The chance of displacing an existing employed person is estimated by the Department of Employment to be 50 per cent. Over 40 per cent of those joining the scheme have no educational qualifications and one-third applied because they couldn't find paid employment.[7] These considerations effectively make the scheme one of support for the self-employed, though one in two take on one extra worker in some capacity.

Loan Guarantee Scheme (LGS)

This is also heavily oriented towards the smaller businesses. Sixteen thousand firms obtained a loan (mean value £33,000) between 1981 and 1985. Initially, one-third of those who took the loans failed (Robson Rhodes, 1983a). Later, as banks became more experienced in vetting proposals and as economic activity recovered from the trough, the failure rate fell to one in four or five. The government tightened the loan terms in 1984 and demand subsequently fell to under £30m a year. The scheme was given new encouragement in the 1986 budget which halved the 5 per cent premium on interest rates charged by the government to cover defaults.

The average existing business under the LGS employed about ten people and half were entirely new. A surprising proportion were in manufacturing (45 per cent). One-fifth claimed to be in high technology, though 'many of these were in computer bureaux, computer selling companies, or systems design companies' (Robson Rhodes, 1983b, p. 11). The poor judgment of some banks and the poor use of accounting methods by applicants has led some to argue for greater involvement of advisers such as the Department of Trade and Industry's regional network. But it is unlikely that a higher level of monitoring could be justified given the small size of these loans. Larger-scale cooperative ventures, arranged through an initial vetting procedure, might be a way forward.

Business Expansion Scheme (BES)

This involved about 500 companies in 1983–4. The mean investment was about £2 million, though this includes some very big loans; the typical investment was only £150,000. Individual investors are given tax relief up to the highest rate, on condition that the investment is committed for at least five years. The 1986 budget partially restricted the more blatant abuses; the value of land and building cannot be more than half the funds raised above £50,000 a year. The average business has tended to employ about thirty, and one-half of the funds have been placed in start-up or very young firms. One-third of investment has been in manufacturing.

The estimated impact on employment of these three schemes is shown in Table 6.7.

Table 6.7

	EAS	LGS	BES
Number of businesses per year (historical average)	54,000	5,000	500
Employment increase per surviving business	1.65	8	14
Failure rate	40%	30%	15%
Employment[a]	50,000	30,000	5,000
Cost per year (£m)[a]	111[b]	15[b]	50[c]

a These figures take no account of displacement or additionality.
b These figures would be lower if unemployment benefit and income tax were taken into account.
c Cost of foregone tax revenue.

Sources: *Department of Employment Gazette*, August 1984; Robson Rhodes (1983b); Small Business Research Trust.

Venture capital

The BES is open to many criticisms: it assists useless speculation; it does not create many jobs; the investors are by law distanced from the company in which the investment occurs. One-half of BES funds have been invested in the South-East or East Anglia. Although a third of BES funds went into manufacturing, the predominant use appears to have been to finance working capital. It also appears that BES funds are less involved in technology-based rapid-growth companies than are other funds (CFI, 1986).

Other important sources of funds apart from stockmarkets, are venture capital funds and local enterprise boards. Venture capital is where institutions fund, advise and oversee projects which exploit market opportunities in long-run projects, the aim being an eventual capital gain rather than a regular income stream.[8] In recent years the amount of venture capital raised has been over £200 million a year, including funds raised on the unlisted stock market. The mean amount invested is about £0.5 million. One of the advantages of venture-capital finance is that it can offer a 'hands-on' approach where the investor continually offers marketing, technological, management and financial advice to the presumably less-experienced client companies. Often the investing institution is in a position to hear of rival product developments, including international ones, and marketing and technological changes. The cross-fertilisation of projects within the investor's portfolio, perhaps through licensing or joint ventures, is also common.

Corporate venturing is a form of venture capital where the investor – a large firm with surplus cash or management resources – takes a stake in a smaller project. Sometimes the aim is to diversify through new-product development which the client company licenses. Alternatively, as with the British Steel Corporation, the aim may be to find jobs for displaced workers. This approach to small-firm promotion avoids many of the usual problems since the client firm is able to use the larger firms distribution and marketing network. It might be worthwhile to encourage further this activity, especially in depressed areas; indeed, some argue that firms should be obliged to create an equivalent number of new jobs before redundancies can be declared.

The importance of corporate venturing lies in its power to contribute to accelerated restructuring and expansion, possibly in collaboration with small-firm units. It does so firstly by giving support and stability to those small firms which possess special skills but which do not have the resources to exploit them fully. There are many cases where the absence of large-firm support has resulted in the failure of small innovative projects in Britain, or their exploitation elsewhre, mainly by US firms.[9] Encouragement of small new-firms, even in the high-tech sector, is an inadequate policy; links with larger firms and access to their resources are also important.

Corporate venturing can help with new-product activity. A Dutch study, reported in Rothwell and Zegveld (1985) shows that corporate spin-offs frequently take place from firms which have new ideas which do not fit in well with their strategy or management structure. Spin-offs from parent companies can save a developed idea which otherwise would remain unexploited. Other liaisons between small and large firms can also engender new-product development. A number of large firms such as Elf-Acquitaine in France offer subsidised R&D advice to smaller innovative firms. This has obvious advantages for industrial activity; it also benefits the larger firms by providing a listening post for new ideas.

The examples above of joint large–small company cooperation indicate that a strategy of prompting new industrial activity needs to be more sophisticated than throwing money at small firms. In particular, the practice of corporate venturing needs to be encouraged. It appears that at present only eight large British companies are involved in this, some only peripherally.[10]

Local bodies have been playing an increasing role in new business expansion, though the amount of funds they manage is relatively small as yet. The local enterprise agencies are largely advisory bodies. Local enterprise boards, on the other hand, of which the Greater London (GLEB) and the West Midlands Board (WMEB) are the largest, administer and manage investments of about £20 million.

The scale of the problems faced by these bodies is enormous. In the West Midlands County, for instance, one-third of its manufacturing employment was lost between 1979 and 1985 (a quarter of a million jobs). This context provides a sobering backdrop to the achievements of WMEB, which has £9m invested in twenty-seven companies, supporting 2,500 jobs. Although there have been a number of failures, the cost per job is estimated at under £500 if the investment write-offs are considered the only cost. Another scheme, which gives interest relief to firms, is the estimated to have a cost-per-new-additional-job of about £8,000. The Board is also involved in technology transfer (from universities) and training in high-quality skills. Of the 7,000 trainees, 82 per cent are said to have found relevant jobs, a far higher proportion than the lower-skill Youth Training Scheme. The activities of the WMEB and the associated increases in employment are set out in Panel 6.2.

The boards also fund cooperatives. One of the advantages of these over traditional small firms is that they are more likely to be able to count on wider experience. The average applicant for small-firm funds, by contrast, is only 50 per cent likely to have had experience in each of the areas of marketing, production, finance and purchasing (Robson Rhodes, 1983b). However, cooperatives are problematic as job creators as the experience of professional partnerships makes clear; there may be a tendency to maximise revenue per worker rather than going for rapid expansion of the numbers employed.

The role of local enterprise boards is important in view of the regional bias in new-firm formation (Storey, 1982; Whittington, 1984). Whittington has offered statistical evidence which suggests that new-firm formation is closely associated with high home-ownership and a small proportion of manual workers. As a result:

> Government reliance upon policies to stimulate new firms will . . . be discriminatory. Regions with low levels of entrepreneurship will not receive the same support through these policies as the more fortunate regions of the South. Moreover those regions with low entrepreneurship are also regions of economic decline where the displacement of existing businesses by the formation of new ones may be expected to be greater. (p. 255)

Small wonder?

Panel 6.2

West Midlands Economic Development Committee – summary of jobs associated with employment schemes

		Number of jobs
Direct employment in Economic Development Unit and West Midlands Enterprise Board Limited		100
WMEB Ltd		
Current portfolio	2,635	
Realised portfolio companies	46	
		2,681
Interest relief scheme		
Existing jobs preserved	5,191	
New jobs	499	
		5,690
Land and premises		
Industrial units	1,700	
New enterprise workshops	188	
Purchase, leaseback, etc.	280	
		2,168
Warwick University Science Park		168
Worker cooperatives		393
Business advice and training for ethnic minorities: 100 trainees, 71 jobs		71
Urban Programme voluntary schemes		
Direct	74	
Indirect	1,363	
		1,437
Training		
Urban Programme	1,056	
Main Programme	7,000	
	8,056 with 82% placement success rate	6,605
Total jobs associated with EDC schemes		19,313

Source: Mawson (1986)

Conclusion

Financial incentives or support for firms is offered for many reasons, only one of which is to create employment in the medium term. However, in so far as that is the aim, the focus should be on areas where:

1 there is a focus on new product or service development.
2 the market for the product can accurately be assessed – local authorities with significant purchasing power can assist here;
3 the financing body can stay in close touch with the assisted firm, monitoring its progress;
4 the screening and monitoring costs are justified in terms of the scale of the finance;
5 the regional dimension is taken into account

These conditions are most likely to apply to local enterprise boards and corporate venturing, both of which should be encouraged. One way of doing this would be for central government to offer incentives to pension funds to hold funds in these bodies. Surplus funds in pension funds could also be released in the form of investments in employment, creating boards or venture institutions. Redundancy payments could also be used to set up corporate ventures under experienced management. The role of secondment of experienced managers is also important. At present some enterprise agency staff are secondees, but more could be done to encourage this at a wider level.

7 Special measures

It is often argued that much unemployment is irrational because the money used for unemployment pay could be used either to subsidise existing insecure jobs or to finance new-job creation. The first approach is generally less favoured, partly because it might allow failed industries to carry on without adjustment.[1] There is, none the less, a rationale for subsidising jobs to prevent redundancies. Decision-making on employment by individual firms does not take into account all the costs involved, only those that fall on the firm. However, the cost of unemployment has to be borne by society; even in narrow economic terms this can be quite high. For instance, a social audit by local councils of the closure of the Rowntree-Mackintosh plant in Edinburgh showed that on plausible probabilities of re-employment, the 1,000 or so redundancies would cost central government £15m.[2] For the country as a whole, the cost of unemployment in 1985 was estimated to be £20 billion.[3]

Employment subsidies could often be a cheaper option. Clearly these could not be permanent and must contain some stimulus to adjustment, otherwise the burden of subsidy would rise without limit. There is also a problem in identifying those to whom the subsidy should go; there is an incentive for all firms to engage in special pleading. Furthermore, subsidies to existing jobs may not be the best way to spend public money, assuming that that is limited. Training or new job creation may be superior choices, especially where adaptation under the subsidy would be slow.

Special measures

What principles might be used to judge when and where job subsidies should be offered? Subsidies may have an effect on output, or on employment only (through a substitution effect). Output subsidies are similar to protectionist measures and might infringe trade regulations, since they simply pass the burden of adjusting to over-capacity to producers elsewhere.[4] Employment subsidies encourage greater labour intensity and have to be in a process where substitution is relatively easy. An important criterion is that any switch to increased labour intensity or the slowdown in planned capital intensity must not impair the ability to compete. In many markets, competitive performance hinges largely on 'non-price' aspects such as incremental product improvement. It would be foolish to engage in labour subsidies where quality, brand image and reliability would suffer from any delay in increasing capital intensity or from any attempt to substitute unskilled for skilled labour. This would apply with even greater force if a subsidy were to delay the acquisition of new skills associated with advanced techniques, as for instance in financial services. Subsidies are only justifiable in areas of the economy that do not compete in terms of differentiated products or services, i.e. in areas where non-price aspects are less important. Examples here are those industries that produce homogeneous tradeable products such as coal or bulk chemicals or some non-traded services. Subsidies could also be justified in industries such as crafts or tourism which might benefit rather than suffer from a higher labour-intensity.

It is sometimes thought that while tradeable sectors have to be lean and competitive, a lot more labour could be absorbed in the non-traded, largely services, sector.[5] However there are evident dangers in this approach, given the many levels at which the economy is integrated. Who would want to discourage cashless shopping, with its attendant spin-offs in terms of new services? Automated stock-handling is often part of a wider programme of automating customer services. Office information, too, has increased not only worker satisfaction but also the quality of the service, and is capable of enabling new leaps in the way in which society is organised; the computerisation of the Inland Revenue, for instance, will allow a far greater flexibility in the design of macroeconomic and fiscal policy. It is not impossible to identify particular activities where labour subsidies could result in job preservation without a loss of quality or competitiveness, but the implementation of such a policy would require detailed case-by-case investigation.

One case where such detailed investigation has been carried out is the coal industry. It is perhaps ironic that this industry, producing a largely homogeneous product, should have been singled out as a target for labour saving by the government in 1984, since there would appear to be no complicating non-price aspects to take into account.[6] Davies and Metcalf (1984) have examined the case for shutting down high-cost pits with a loss of 40,000 jobs. They pointed out that it was quite possible for pit closures to have been financially desirable for the Coal Board but economically undesirable for the community as a whole. The study valued coal at its world market price. The alternative to employment was costed by assuming that it took ten years for all displaced jobs to be re-created. Where workers and their families moved to other areas, the extra costs in providing housing, health and education were costed. The overall conclusion was that on average the pits involved should be kept open for five years; there would be some immediate closures and some would stay open for as long as ten years. Of course the exact calculations depend to some extent on guesswork and the prospects for coal have changed at least twice since the report was written, but it demonstrates how subsidising jobs can at times be rational.

Some have argued that differential labour subsidies should be aimed at identifiable groups of unemployed workers. Since it is known that unemployment is particularly high among the lower paid, it might be thought advisable to offer subsidies here, especially where training is not thought to be a feasible or desirable option. This thinking stimulated proposals to reduce employers' national insurance contributions on low-paid workers. Some account was taken of this proposal in the 1985 budget; this involved a change in employers' contributions – a fall at the lower end, financed by a continuously rising scale in place of the previous maximum limit. The reform was seen as leading to lower labour costs and thus higher employment in low-wage industries and, given inelastic supply of high-wage earners, was expected to lead to a squeeze on their wages and only small employment losses. Some commentators put the likely increases in employment at about 100,000, but it is difficult to discern whether any significant boost occurred; the elasticity of demand for labour is usually much exaggerated. In any event it is not desirable in many industries to encourage labour intensity, especially of a low-skill sort; any future modification of the national insurance charge should be industry-specific.

The remainder of this chapter looks at specific contexts in which special employment measures might be used. The following sections examine:

1. the regional question and the need for regional subsidies;
2. the promotion of labour-intensive services;
3. special job-creation schemes;
4. infrastructure projects.

The regional question

Job subsidies may be particularly appropriate in depressed regions since alternative employment prospects are low (Department of Trade and Industry, 1986). Failure to offer subsidies could result in inappropriately large migration of the more able and dynamic workers, accelerating the decline and adding to the eventual cost. Unless it is inevitable that depressed regions be more or less abandoned, it seems sensible to maintain employment while helping the area to adjust to a new structure of production. This is not to say that migration should be discouraged, but if migration is to be actively aided by measures such as greater access to housing, it should go hand in hand with extra aid to deprived regions if they are to remain well populated. It is particularly difficult for regions to make necessary adjustments if incomes are falling.

Unemployment is higher in some regions than others; the four 'southern' regions have unemployment levels between 9 per cent and 13 per cent, whereas the figures for the West Midlands, Wales, Scotland and the northern English regions range from 15 per cent to 19 per cent. The latter regions account for 47 per cent of employees, but they have 60 per cent of the unemployed and 70 per cent of those unemployed for more than three years.

Economic activity in Britain is very regional-specific in terms of occupational structure. Maps published by the Office of Population Census Surveys show that concentration of manufacturing employment occurs in quite different parts of the country than concentration of services employment (OPCS, 1984). It is important to know whether the regions that have suffered particularly heavy falls in manufacturing employment in recent years have compensated for this by a rise in employment in other activities. Table 7.1 records growth rates of employment by broad sector, 1977–85, for Britain and the regions.

The table shows the difficulty that many regions have had in filling the hole created by the losses in manufacturing. Employment in British manufacturing fell on average by 3.6 per cent a year between 1977 and 1985. The figures in brackets in the table show regions that have suffered faster falls – Scotland, Wales, West Midlands, Yorkshire and Humberside, the North and North West. Northern Ireland, not included in the table, has also been hard hit. The North is the only region where every sector has grown more slowly than average, but for many regions hard hit by manufacturing losses, the impact was also felt strongly in other sectors. In four of the hard-hit English regions, public and community services and construction have all fared worse than average, compounding the effect of government cuts in regional aid. The main compensating employment in these English regions has been in banking and business services, which has grown faster than the British average. In Scotland and Wales the only offsetting influences are public services and, in the case Scotland, oil.

It is mildly encouraging that there has been any increase in employment above average in the hard-hit regions. On the basis of input–output linkages, it would be expected that every unit fall in the manufacturing wage-bill would lead to a fall of over 0.04 in banking, etc., and about 0.15 in distribution, catering and transport (Driver, 1987). This is before any account is taken of income-multiplier effects, i.e. only the knock-on effect on intermediate supply to manufacturing is

Special measures

Table 7.1 Employees in employment by industry and region, end-point exponential growth rates 1977–85

Industry (SIC – standard industrial classification – code)	Great Britain	South East	East Anglia	South West	East Midlands	Scotland	Wales	Midlands Midlands	Yorkshire and Humberside	North West	North
Manufacturing (2–4)	−3.63	−2.40	−1.83	−2.30	−2.52	(−4.54)	(−5.15)	(−4.46)	(−4.35)	(−4.91)	(−5.18)
Distribution, hotels, catering (6) and transport, communication (7)	0.59	0.73	2.61	0.69	0.74	(0.53)	(0.34)	0.79	(0.33)	(0.16)	(−0.82)
Banking, finance, insurance business services (8)	3.21	(2.94)	3.60	3.40	4.46	2.60	2.91	4.14	3.74	3.42	2.84
Public and other services (9)	0.50	0.56	1.32	0.96	(0.22)	0.89	1.02	(−0.29)	(−0.13)	0.68	(−0.16)
Construction (5)	−3.0	(−1.50)	−2.40	−1.10	−2.14	(−3.84)	(−3.88)	(−3.68)	(−3.48)	(−3.85)	(−8.53)
Energy and water supply (1)	−2.09	−1.20	0	−1.79	(−3.55)	+1.93	−3.60	−1.96	(−3.13)	−1.59	(−4.74)

Source: Department of Employment

included. It appears, however, that the depressed English regions have not only shown a rise in financial jobs here, but have done better than average. There is no great comfort to draw from this, however; the relatively fast growth in these areas has been going on for some time and it did not accelerate in response to the dramatic recession of the early 1980s. Full-time job losses are also being balanced by part-time job gains and this imbalance is apparently worse in the North.[7] Furthermore, other indicators present a worrying picture. The percentage net gain in rated commercial office-space – a proxy for skilled-service employment – grew only half as fast in the depressed regions between 1982 and 1985 as in the remainder.

The positive employment growth of some services in the depressed regions also needs to be seen in context. Table 7.2 attempts to do this by expressing employment gains and losses as a proportion of total initial employment in each region in 1977. From this it can be seen that the effect of banking, etc., has been to add 1 or 2 per cent to employment in regions where the loss of manufacturing generally meant falls of over 10 per cent. Similar orders of magnitude are observed for transport, distribution and tourism, except for East Anglia, which is already a favoured region.

The system of regional aid in Britain was recast in 1983, with a new emphasis on achieving a low cost-per-job created. This was viewed with mixed feelings by some. Certainly the old system was somewhat bizarre, being biased in favour of a few capital-intensive industries. Between the mid-1960s and 1970s, 30 per cent of regional assistance went to chemicals and metal manufacture – industries which lost 14,000 jobs. By contrast, only 15 per cent went to engineering and vehicles, which created 100,000 jobs (Tyler, Moore and Rhodes, 1983).[8] The new system offers lower grants per job and is more selectively aimed at employment growth. However it is set in a context of a halving of total regional aid. The result is that industries which have high income-elasticities, such as many services, are disadvantaged. The system works to attract some footloose manufacturing industry towards the regions, but this involves a high displacement effect and it is not likely to make a great difference to regional unemployment, given that the total injection of regional funds is smaller. No

Table 7.2 Proportion of total initial (1977) employment gained (+) or lost (−) by 1985 in each industry for each region

Industry (SIC code)	Great Britain	South East	East Anglia	South West	East Midlands	Scotland	Wales	West Midlands	Yorkshire and Humberside	North West	North
Manufacturing (2–4)	−0.083	−0.046	−0.044	−0.049	−0.074	−0.093	−0.107	−0.138	−0.062	−0.123	−0.118
Distribution, hotels, catering (6) and transport, communication (7)	0.012	0.017	0.061	0.016	0.013	0.011	0.006	0.013	0.004	0.003	−0.015
Banking, finance, insurance, business services (8)	0.020	0.028	0.020	0.020	0.018	0.013	0.011	0.018	0.009	0.017	0.010
Public and other services (9)	0.011	0.014	0.030	0.023	0.004	0.020	0.025	−0.005	−0.001	0.014	−0.003
Construction (5)	−0.012	−0.005	−0.011	−0.005	−0.007	−0.020	−0.016	−0.012	−0.007	−0.013	−0.036
Energy and water supply (1)	−0.005	−0.002	0.000	−0.003	−0.016	0.005	−0.016	−0.004	−0.008	−0.003	−0.019

Source: Department of Employment.

assessment of the new system of regional aid has yet been made, and the observations above are prompted by a detailed study of five small areas of regional deprivation (NEDC, 85(74)). These areas, described below, have all contained their unemployment increase at or below the national average, but starting from a higher base. Despite the battery of instruments used, there has been little sign of any major turnaround.

1 Corby. The population is 53,000. Half the workforce were put out of work in 1980 or shortly after, mainly as a direct or indirect result of plant closures by British Steel. Unemployment is 21 per cent.
2 Sunderland. The population of 300,000 was heavily dependent on declining industries – shipbuilding, heavy engineering and coal mining. Unemployment is currently 22 per cent.
3 Wolverhampton. The population of 125,000 is typical of the West Midlands area; manufacturing employment is heavily concentrated in metals and engineering. Unemployment is running at 18.6 per cent.
4 Irvine. The town and its hinterland has a population of 57,000. Various closures – ICI, Dunlop, Massey Ferguson – have contributed to an unemployment rate of 24.5 per cent.
5 North-East Clwyd. This is a low population-density area, again heavily dependent on heavy industry. Shotton is said to have been the largest steel closure in Europe and there have been heavy plant closures also by Courtaulds. The unemployment is about 18 per cent.

In each of the above cases a large number of policy measures were used to contain unemployment.[9] A study of the jobs created show that most of them are in manufacturing and are drawn from other parts of Britain, along with some inward investment. There is no indication of any large rise in service employment, which would be needed to make a major dent in unemployment; this is constrained by low incomes. Nor is there much evidence that entirely new firms are contributing much in employment terms. In Corby, for instance, start-ups accounted for about 500 jobs in five years, compared to 7,000 in total, most from firms migrating from other parts of Britain.

The implication of these findings is that the cuts in regional aid should be restored and used to enhance the purchasing power of local buyers. This could be achieved by a regional labour subsidy to particular industries, especially those with high local content. Alternatively, money could be channelled through local enterprise boards where sufficient expertise exists. Deprived regions also need early involvement in tradeable services, where the service provision can be done at a distance. Apart from mail order, these generally involve the information sector; the ESRC (Economic and Social Research Council) is studying possibilities in this area and it is research which should receive priority support.

It is important to note that, while service employment can be stimulated by income transfers to the regions, the provision of service employment, unless it is traded outside the region or substitutes for products that are so traded, will not be a source of increased prosperity. That is why it is also important to stimulate manufacturing activity in the regions. This is, of course, the historical approach. However Storey (1983) has argued that the branch plants of large firms in the 1960s and 1970s 'did little to diversify the technical, management or skill base which is a precondition for self-sustaining economic growth' (p. 40). This is confirmed by Thwaites and Gillespie (1983), who found in a study of the Northern region that:

> the North has an under-representation of employment creating technological change and an over representation of job displacing technological change . . . Northern establishments either failed to carry out R&D on-site or employed fewer workers in these tasks than did equivalent plants associated with the non-assisted areas . . . [this constrains] participation in those information flows relevant to technological change. (p. 13)

The authors propose the encouragement of regional technology centres. Storey (1983) advocates management buyouts as a solution – these have increased in recent years but there is a marked regional bias towards the better-off areas; Oakey (1984) favours local authority equity-stakes in emerging firms.

Encouraging labour-intensive services

It may seem surprising that a boost to service employment should be considered at all, since it is often ssumed that the British economy in recent years has been kept afloat on a rising tide of jobs in this area. This is largely a myth. Between 1978 and 1983, service employment rose by 5 per cent, as against a drop of 23 per cent in manufacturing. Service employment has also risen less fast than in most other advanced capitalist countries. An even starker picture can be presented by looking at the longer-term picture and counting each part-time worker as half a full-time one. In Table 7.3 the high-tech, high-productivity services - communications and banking - are grouped along with manufacturing to show a contrast with lower-productivity services and construction - activities that might have been expected to absorb the unemployed into jobs. Nearly 2 million jobs disappeared in the former sector between 1973 and 1983, only one in seven of which was compensated by an equivalent job in these other services. Part of the reason is that even low-productivity industries are substituting capital

Table 7.3 Output growth and change in employment 1973–83 by sector[a]

	Output growth (%)	Change in employment 1973–83 (full-time equivalents, thousands)	Employment in 1983 (full-time equivalents, millions)
'High-productivity growth' sector[b]	3.6	−1,847.2	8.09
'Low-productivity growth' sector[c]	−1.59	+275.8	8.24

a Agriculture, utilities and public administration are not included. High and low productivity are defined as above and below 1 per cent growth per annum respectively.
b Manufacturing, post and telecommunications, banking and other financial services.
c Hotels and catering, distribution, transport, construction, other services.

Sources: CSO, Department of Employment

for labour, and of course part-time working has increased. In distribution, for instance, full-time equivalent employment fell by 16 per cent between 1979 and 1984, while retail sales-volume increased by 11 per cent and the net capital stock at constant prices rose by a quarter. In hotels and catering, too, capital labour substitution has increased, with the introduction of computer booking, electronic tills, self-service machines, etc. These developments again raise the question of whether the same degree of substitution would take place if decisions were based on an accounting (shadow price) system which took into account the alternative use of displaced labour. There is a good discussion of this issue in Britton (1986), but he confines his attention to the use of shadow prices in the public sector, 'assuming for present purposes that there is no means of applying shadow prices outside the public sector' (p. 137). It seems imperative, however, that if shadow prices are to be used they must apply also to the private sector; many have expressed concern that public-sector employment will become a dustbin for the unemployed, and morale will accordingly suffer.[10] It would of course be necessary to adopt a case-by-case (and hence bureaucratic) approach to shadow prices, given the large number of considerations outlined earlier: it is in the nature of externalities that they involve information flows too complex for the price system. Any attempt to introduce non-selective labour subsidies or subsidies directed at a general increase, say, in unskilled labour are likely to work against desired structural changes taking place where they are most needed.

There are many ways, other than through labour subsidies, of encouraging the expansion of labour-intensive services. Two of these are considered below.

1 Poor quality and reliability can depress demand. The incentive for firms to produce a quality output is not so great in many service activities because the ease of entry and exit, in turn reflecting low economies of scale, means average life is short. This applies with special force to geographical areas where customer mobility is also high, such as the inner city. In catering and car repairs, for instance, the failure rate of businesses in terms of the

proportion of turnover ceasing to trade is nearly 40 per cent higher than for production industries. This instability militates against quality and makes it difficult to arrange a good system of quality grading. It also discourages the industry from taking the question of skill-training seriously. The result is that a high proportion of people carry out their own repairs; one-third of house and car repairs are done outside the market. In cases such as these, consideration should be given to compulsory licensing and quality grading.

2 Demand can also be depressed because service firms have decided not to develop brand images, backing this with large-scale investment and advertising. Consumer advertising in services is 20 per cent of that for all goods and services, yet it accounts for 40 per cent of expenditure.[11] The answer here may be not so much a rise in advertising as an increase in franchising, as discussed in Chapter 6.

New job-creation schemes

The theoretical backdrop to most job-creation schemes is the rather conservative theme that a general demand expansion would increase inflationary pressures (mainly through the labour market), whereas a properly-targeted expansion would not. In particular, it is argued that the long-term unemployed exert no significant upward pressure on inflation (Layard, 1985; Layard and Metcalf, 1985; Buxton, 1986). The argument may prove politically persuasive, though the evidence offered is rather dubious. Not only are there grounds for doubting the orthodox systems of equations linking inflation and unemployment (Beckerman, 1985), but the introduction of separate variables for long- and short-term unemployment raises problems of interpretation. Briefly, since the ratio of long-term to short-term unemployment depends partly on the change in unemployment, there are good grounds for believing that the specifications used are inadequate.

Nevertheless, whatever one's view of the econometric arguments, it can be accepted that job creation measures should be directed at cases where it is most difficult to revive employment by other means. Special measures will be with us for some time. Expenditure on these measures at 1985 prices rose from £20m in 1975 to £640m in 1979 and reached £1,600m in 1983 (Davies and Metcalf, 1985). The numbers on the schemes have remained fairly flat since then. By January 1986 there were 670,000 people on these schemes, although government spending plans allow for over a million people by 1988.[12] Most of those affected are on the Community Programme, youth training, or taking early retirement. The Community Programme is of interest here in that it is a direct job-creation scheme. It had 130,000 places in 1985, with a net PSBR cost-per-place of around £2,000 and is projected to double in numbers in future years, though even then it will only cover a quarter of those who have been out of work for over a year. Recruitment is restricted to those in receipt of benefit and who have a history of long unemployment. The projects usually involve environmental improvement, energy conservation or building work. Since workers get the going rate of pay for the job, and average pay is limited to £68 a week, most jobs are manual and part-time. Over half go back into unemployment after their year on the Programme.

Some have argued for alternative schemes to the Community Programme. Proposals for a three-year build-up to a million extra places to be filled by the long-term unemployed – in effect a job guarantee for them – have been made by Layard and Metcalf (1985) and endorsed by the all-party House of Commons Select Committee on employment (House of Commons, 1986).[13] A more modest version of these ideas, with a net cost of £1bn rather than £3.3bn, has been proposed by the CBI (1985). This focuses on urban development and early retirement.

The proposed Select Committee Scheme (House of Commons, 1986) goes beyond the Community Programme in a number of respects. It enhances the quality of jobs by proposing that people on the scheme should be integrated into regular employment, much of it full-time. Employment would be split between three areas: privately-managed construction and rehabilitation; health and social services; and other employment, mainly in distribution and catering. The construction projects would be prioritised centrally and offered for tender so as to minimise the deadweight of subsidy to projects that would go ahead anyway. The scheme would also avoid one of the drawbacks of the Community Programme, where skilled workers and managers can only be used sparingly due to the strict limitation on the average wage; the maximum average pay under the new scheme is 50 per cent higher. In social services and health an extra 100,000 places are suggested, with workers providing extra manual help in hospitals or helping with those discharged. Given the high turnover rates of regular staff, many of these jobs could become permanent. Finally, the extra jobs in private services are to be encouraged by a subsidy of £40 a week for each extra worker, provided that non-subsidised employment does not fall.[14] This seems a weak part of the scheme, given that many of the sectors likely to be affected are already increasing employment; a more stringent requirement that employment should be above trend might be more appropriate. The choice of sectors is also important and the criteria for applying subsidies should be as discussed earlier. The scheme was costed in the House of Commons report at £3.3bn net, at full operation, or a net PSBR cost per job of £4,000–£5,000. Under pressure from the CBI and government, the Committee later revised the proposals and scaled them down to provide a job guarantee for the half million or so who have been unemployed for more than three years.

Infrastructure projects

The physical infrastructure includes six major items – roads, water, housing, schools, hospitals and central government property. Job creation in these areas deserves special mention; its importance is borne out by the weight of attention given to the state of the infrastructure by other observers. At the time of writing it was being monitored or had recently been investigated by NEDO, the Policy Studies Institute, the House Builders' Federation, the Economic and Social Research Council, the Institute of Civil Engineers, the CBI, the TUC, the Audit Commission, the House of Commons Environment Committee and many government departments.

The basic problem is not in doubt. Public capital expenditure has dropped like a stone, falling continuously in real terms by 60 per cent between 1973 and 1982. Only recently has it shown a moderate increase, but projections for the future are flat or falling, with heavy projected cuts in housing and education.

Capital expenditure can be distinguished, at least to some extent, from repair and maintenance. A backlog of the latter has built up in many areas: 'The examples encountered include many which arise from delays in maintenance which so sharply increase necessary expenditure in subsequent periods that no rational discounting process can justify them' (NEDC, 1985, p. 5). The various reports make sombre reading. There is a £2bn backlog of repairs to hospital buildings and over £20bn in public housing. The housing problem is not confined to the public sector. In 1981 nearly a million houses in England were judged by the House Condition Survey to need repairs of at least £7,000. The addition of many low-income buyers in recent years will have added to that problem. Expenditure on local-authority road maintenance is around a half or a third of that needed if more costly repairs are not to be needed later. The condition of many schools built in the 1960s is giving cause for concern; many buildings are not properly designed for modern curricula and fail to provide a proper educational environment; the school inspectors report for 1984 (Department of Education and Science, 1985) stated that school buildings were below an acceptable standard and were adversely affecting the quality of pupil work.

None of this amounts to an argument for increasing capital expenditure to the level of the 1960s. Much of the desired infrastructure, especially in the case of roads, is in place. It is far more important to maintain the existing stock rather than add to it. Nevertheless, capital expenditure and maintenance are to some extent substitutable options, and this raises difficult policy choices. Three points stand out.

1 Public money is limited, even for 'good' projects, given the attitudes of the financial community – in Britain, public investment is included in the Public Sector Borrowing Requirement.

2 Structural change and productivity are vital to long-run growth prospects.
3 Employment creation is a priority.

Items 2 and 3 are to some extent in conflict. The reason is not so much that the infrastructure is an activity that is traded internationally – though consultancy and contracting abroad are important – but rather lies in the trade-off between the current jobs created by maintenance work and the future opportunities opened up by some capital-intensive projects. These latter projects have a high cost-per-direct-job. The PSBR cost of a job-year created by housing investment averages out at between £23,500 for the Treasury model in 1985 and a somewhat lower figure of £16,000 obtained by Davies and Metcalf (1985). These figures are much higher than the cost-per-job of repair and maintenance which is probably lower than £10,000, the difference being partly due to the import content of new construction. However the option of new construction also frequently has something to recommend it and may even be necessary in areas such as communications and integrated transport systems. New capital-intensive projects were what characterised the major infrastructure developments in US inner cities, rather than a focus on direct employment in construction. This too is the approach in some British schemes such as the London docklands, where one-third of the total investment is in roads and transport.

It is not universally true that there is a trade-off between the labour intensity of construction projects and the degree of structural change facilitated. One area where the conflict between the two may be non-existent is in housing, which is one of the barriers to mobility between regions. A greater emphasis on refurbishment of the existing stock in areas of high labour-demand is a good candidate for a free lunch.

In cases where there are conflicts between the need for capital-intensive projects and employment creation, the constraints on public finance necessitate the involvement of private capital. However state investment will be needed in infrastructure projects where private capital is unwilling to shoulder all the risk; an example here may be the mooted rapid-transit scheme for the West Midlands, where the rate of return is positive but the pay-back period is long.

One attempt to mix public and private finance for infrastructure development in the inner cities was the Financial Institutions Group (FIG) set up after the 1981 riots, and which, through the Urban Development Grant, stimulated some investment from the institutions. interestingly, the TUC has called for the FIG to be revived and set up on a tripartite basis (NEDC 85(77)). This would seem necessary if potentially successful projects such as London docklands are not to exacerbate distributional problems or promote a geographically-concentrated underclass in the cities; it would also allow a much closer coordination of public-spending plans and private investment.

Conclusion

This chapter has considered four categories of special measures: regional measures; encouragement of labour-intensive services; direct job creation; and infrastructure schemes. These measures bring short-term social gains but they also absorb a great deal of resources. It is important that they be located in the context of a longer-term strategy in each case. Regional measures will be most successful if they are directed to activities with 'import substitution' or export-enhancing characteristics. Labour-intensive services need to reflect future demand patterns in so far as these can be assessed – the discussion in Chapter 4 deals with this. The same applies to direct job-creation schemes. Finally, in regard to infrastructure projects, it may often make sense not to choose the lowest-cost option, especially where the project in question is a key element in enabling further growth.

8 Making the jobs go round

Previous chapters have examined the scope for increasing employment by means of demand-side or supply-side initiatives. In this chapter attention is focused on a different theme – worksharing. A recent OECD report argued that 'a combination of cautious demand and active supply policies *accompanied by appropriate work-sharing arrangements* might be an optimal policy strategy to bring the economy back to full employment' (OECD, 1982, p. 10).[1]

The notion of sharing out existing work in order to contain unemployment has an obvious intuitive appeal. According to the British Social Attitudes Survey, six out of ten people support government schemes for worksharing.[2] There are a variety of views as to how this should be achieved. Some trade union leaders would like to see a reduction in the amount of overtime being worked. Others see merit in other forms of worksharing such as longer holidays, early retirement, or raising the school-leaving age. More usually, however, the main policy instrument for job sharing is seen in terms of a cut in average weekly hours of work for those in employment.

The following sections look in some detail at proposals to reduce the average work-week. Later in the chapter the question of early retirement is examined; this is especially important in view of the arguments in White (1986) that it is an easier reform to implement in a low-wage economy like Britain than cutting weekly hours. The difficulty in the latter approach lies in the need to maintain growth in weekly wages, which limits the extent of possible reduction in weekly hours.

It is a difficulty which could be offset without having to reduce the trend of wages if lower non-labour costs could be achieved by better work organisation and greater utilisation of capital. Greater efficiency might also, in a suitable macroeconomic climate, lead to higher output. An argument along these lines is made towards the end of the chapter, focusing on the need to open up a large number of thirty-hour-per-week jobs and to 'uncouple' the period of commercial operation from the personal work-week.

Attitudes to the standard work-week

In a society that places a premium on choice, it is surprising that few of us can choose the length of time we work. Of course, where overtime is a normal practice, workers can often vary their hours upwards. However only those workers willing and able to negotiate part-time contracts can work below the standard work-week. There are many reasons for this fixity of hours, especially in regard to the organisation of the flow of work. However, it is certainly possible that some of these reasons have more to do with managerial conservatism than with other forms of inflexibility. It has been pointed out that rigid working hours were introduced in Victorian times only because it was the only way to measure the work people did (Clutterbuck, 1983).

It seems sensible to investigate whether a freer choice of hours could lead to worksharing without causing too much organisational distribution. It is also worth investigating whether a general reduction in working hours, as suggested for instance by the EEC Commission, could have the effect of reducing unemployment substantially.

The worksharing approach is certainly not without its problems. Those who work longest often have the lowest incomes or, especially if they are male manual workers, are at the point in life where family responsibilities are heaviest. It would be difficult to achieve a reduction in hours worked for this group if it involved a *pro rata* loss in pay. At the other end of the scale, it is clear that society incurs a cost in accepting a lower work-week for highly qualified people that have invested a lot in education and skills. If shorter hours lead to a bigger workforce in such areas, the costs of training and administration will increase, at least to some extent.

In the face of such complex issues, it is perhaps not surprising that policies on hours of work have not crystallised into a clear political pattern. In Britain, it is true that there is a certian opposition between the government and the employers' organisations on the one hand and the TUC on the other, with the latter calling for a thirty-five hour week. The same conflict was glimpsed in the lengthy metal-workers' strike in West Germany in 1983 and in the response of European employers' organisations to the attitude of the EEC Commission. But it seems that these disputes revolve more around the implications of hours-reductions for costs and pay rather than being directly concerned with the basic question of hours. Many industrialists welcome the trend to part-time work and home-working for the flexibility and lower costs that it brings. Many are also prepared to move towards agreeing annual-hours contracts, where workers can negotiate to work an agreed number of hours during the year in a flexible way.

The political complexity of the hours-of-work debate is heightened by the fact that it impinges on social questions which are outside of the traditional ambit of union–management conflict. With higher participation of women in paid work, there is often the desire to share childcare and housework between partners. Evidently this is only possible where hours of formal work are either short or flexible and this gives an added reason for worksharing schemes.

Despite the many arguments for job sharing, there is a strong feeling – and one that crosses political lines – that it constitutes a retreat from genuine job creation. Unlike measures such as public spending or reforms achieving greater efficiency, worksharing in itself does not increase the amount of employment measured in total hours and does not increase the national output as conventionally measured.

It is impossible to discuss this view sensibly without considering the extent to which work is to be regarded as preferable to alternative uses of time. In the next sections we will ask whether worksharing is in fact a retreat from employment generation, as well as addressing the question of whether a reduction in formal hours worked is a good thing in itself.

The economists' view

However supportive the general public may be of worksharing, the same approval is unlikely to come from any representative group of economists. The *Financial Times* journalist Sam Brittan has trenchantly attacked the notion as a 'flawed, dangerous nostrum . . . there cannot be too many workers so long as there are unsatisfied human needs and desires' (Brittan, 1984). Some economists view the proposals as disguised wage claims while others argue that the problem is one of expanding demand for labour rather than reducing its supply. Richard Layard has even attacked the case for early retirement, arguing that a reduction in the excess supply of labour would generate greater wage pressure: 'we cannot cut unemployment by cutting the labour force'.[3] Behind all this lie the arguments that the economy will either return naturally to a state of full employment or can be made to do so by judicious demand-led expansion and measures to improve the inflation–unemployment tradeoff. These arguments imply that the present unemployment is a transitional problem of structural adjustment to new technology and world trading patterns. They take no account of the possibility of 'jobless growth', where productivity continues to match or outstrip output growth and where, in consequence, employment growth is low, even though output may be growing strongly.

There is an element of unsupported optimism in these views. It is interesting to contrast the cautiousness of technological forecasting experts with the certainty of those who forecast the economic reactions to such changes. Some economists and technologists have, however, taken the question seriously enough to consider whether the certainty of the orthodox economists is justified in this matter.

The former director of the London-based Technical Change Centre, Bruce Williams, has argued against the likelihood of 'jobless growth', but he admits that 'we cannot know for certain whether there will be such a revival of employment and growth after this current depression as there was after the depressions of the 1880s and 1930s' (Williams, 1984, pp. 7, 8). On the other hand, Nobel prize-winner Wassily Leontief, reporting on a study of the Austrian economy, argues that new investment and growth will make only a limited contribution to alleviating technological unemployment (Leontief, 1982). A Study by the Sussex-based Institute of Manpower Studies reached fairly pessimistic conclusions on the employment potential of the labour-intensive financial services sector, though the study was admittedly limited to the period 1983–7 (Rajan, 1984). The Department of Employment, in reviewing the existing literature in this field, were surprisingly cautious: 'it is possible that the overall effects on employment of new technology may be positive once account is taken of the wider effects neglected in those studies which predict large employment losses' (*Employment Gazette*, May 1984, p. 215). The OECD, too, is uncertain as to the implications of new technology for employment, and a recent report declared itself agnostic as to whether the latest technological revolution 'will or will not destroy more jobs than it will create new ones' (OECD, 1982, p. 51).

It seems clear from this brief survey of forecasts that there is little sense in pursuing an approach which takes as certain the early re-emergence of opportunities for large expansion in employment. The policies suggested by the analysis in earlier chapters would certainly give a significant boost to employment, but the scale of the problem is such that it will endure for some time. Society may have to choose between reduced working hours or a continued polarisation between those in and out of work.

The benefits of shorter hours

Any policy initiative to cure unemployment is likely to involve costs, but sometimes there can be substantial offsetting benefits of a non-monetary kind. Is this the case with proposals to reduce hours of work? Put differently, is a reduction in hours of work a good thing in itself, quite apart from employment implications? To discuss this question at all may smack of a *dirigiste* approach, but few people at present have the option of choosing their hours of work and some may prefer greater leisure. There is little evidence of any sudden shift in leisure–income preferences, but a more flexible system of working hours would allow those who wanted to to work less and some may choose this. The maxim that time is money contains only a partial truth: time is also just time; it is needed for reflection, development of interests, deepening social relationships, appreciation of nature and the arts and for pure entertainment. It is arguable that the present level of hours in work is far too high to permit the enjoyment that current levels of material prosperity offer. Table 8.1 shows that weekly hours of work have changed over the last couple of decades for various workers. It is clear from these figures that there has been a certain reduction in hours since 1960, especially for manual workers, but the pace of reduction seems to have slowed in the 1970s.

Table 8.1 Average weekly hours worked 1960–81 (full-time workers only)

	Men		Women	
	Manual	Non-manual	Manual	Non-manual
1960	49.7	41.9	42.7	39.9
1965	48.2	39.8	40.9	37.8
1970	46.9	38.5	40.1	36.9
1975	45.5	38.7	39.4	36.6
1980	45.4	38.7	39.6	36.7
1985	44.5	38.6	39.5	35.6

Source: Armstrong (1984), Table 13 and New Earnings Survey (1985).

Much of the creative potential of people is repressed by long hours spent in formal routine work. This may be less true as the work process becomes more complex and requires greater skills, but, as this happens, the education and perceptive skills of workers also grow so that opportunities for creative leisure expand. Confirmation that few people regard work as a vehicle for self-expression or development comes from a survey carried out by the British organisation, Work and Society. Across a range of countries, the average percentage of respondents who gave self-development as their prime reason for working was less than 20 per cent. The UK came bottom of the countries surveyed at around 10 per cent (*Employment Gazette*, February 1984, p. 54).

It can be argued that the greater leisure time would not be spent constructively. This issue was investigated in a French survey in 1978 which attempted to discover the effects of reducing the work-week to thirty hours. The figures in Table 8.2 are extracted from that survey.

It may seem from the answers in Table 8.2 that shorter hours in formal work would simply mean more time spent working in the home. To a certain extent this is indeed the case, but it seems clear that such informal activities are not always regarded as work, as the figures in Table 8.3 reveal.

Table 8.2 Effects of reducing the work-week to thirty hours

	Percentages who would engage in particular activities[a]	
	Men	Women
Devote more time to family	57	50
Engage in home activities to substitute for bought articles	35	42

a Multiple answers were allowed. Other high-score answers were retraining (32 per cent), reading and theatre (32 per cent), local administration (25 per cent), social life (22 per cent).

Source: Cuvillier (1984).

Table 8.3 Attitudes to housework

Activity	Percentage of those who would consider particular activity as:	
	Work	Pleasure
Cooking or child-care	40	60
Shopping for food	70	30
Other housework	80	20

Source: *Planning for Social Change Survey*, Henley Centre, 1983.

To sum up this section, it is at least arguable that the home environment offers many workers a greater source of creative personal development than does the work environment. Many do not even seem to regard home-based activities as work, but rather as enjoyment. It also seems that people have well-formed views as to the sort of activities they would engage in, were they to be less constrained by formal work-times.

Why have we got a forty-hour week?

Any study of the feasibility of reducing working time must start from an understanding of the forces that make for any particular number of hours at any given time.

The length of the standard work-week is determined partly by employers and partly by the wishes of the workforce. The government also has a role, in that it can influence the behaviour of either, partly by varying income tax or overhead labour-costs such as national insurance contributions.

There have been many attempts in different countries to ascertain the wishes of individuals in regard to reducing hours of work. Unfortunately, the fact that these studies are invariably based on interview surveys makes the answers somewhat questionable. Interviewees may have difficulties in conceptualising the changes of pay and hours that are involved in hypothetical situations. This is particularly true when people are asked to contemplate a tradeoff between *future* income and leisure time.

One striking finding from a comprehensive US study in 1978 was that people were willing on average to trade more than half of a 10 per cent rise in future income for more leisure (OECD, 1982). This would have represented a dramatic rise in the leisure–income tradeoff, but in fact hours of work in the US have hardly declined since the late 1970s, despite a substantial rise in income per head. Of course, it may be the case that this outcome has been imposed by employers, but it also seems likely that the attraction of money over time tends to increase as a gradual evolution of needs emerges, leading to new norms of consumption and spending. It should be said, however, that the same US survey found that a quarter of those questioned were willing to trade 2 per cent or more of their *current* income for various forms of reduction of formal work hours.

Back on this side of the Atlantic, the evidence in favour of a desire for more leisure time is rather more striking. A survey by the European Commission found that when people were offered the stark choice between more pay or fewer hours, 40 per cent chose the former and more than half opted for a cut in hours (OECD, 1982). In some of the poorer countries (though not Britain) the order of preference was reversed, while shorter hours were preferred by a factor of more than two in Denmark and the Netherlands.

An attempt to infer changes in the leisure–income tradeoff, without resorting to survey methods, has been made by Armstrong and Williams in works referred to earlier. The problem here is that in attempting to infer choice from actual data on growth of hours and incomes, the question is begged as to whether the length of the working week is freely negotiated, even where collective bargaining is the norm.

Average annual hours of work for males in the UK since 1870 are graphed in Fig. 8.1. The corresponding data for

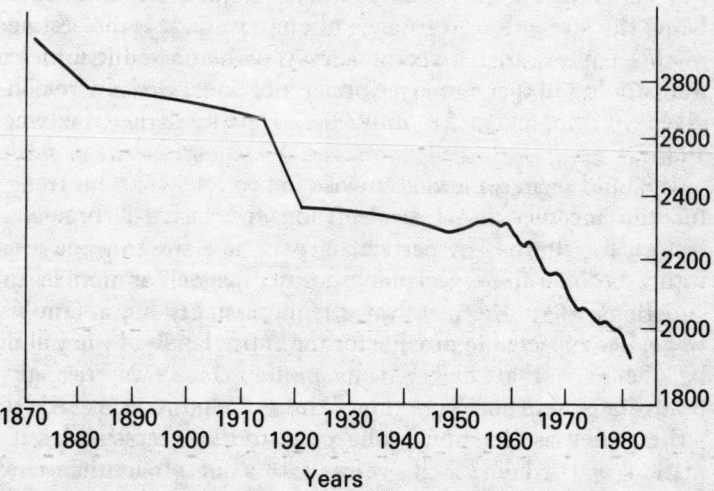

Figure 8.1 Male annual hours of work, UK. *Source*: Armstrong (1984), *Technical Change and Reduction in Life Hours of Work*, London, The Technical Change Centre.

females cannot so easily be interpreted due to the vast changes over time in participation rates and extent of part-time work. It is clear from this graph that the evolution of hours is dominated by a long-run downward trend, with two major deviations, the first associated with the introduction fo the eight-hour day immediately after the First World War and the second, upward, in the period of dismantling of war-time constraints in the late 1940s and early 1950s. The downward trend may appear to conflict with the relative constancy of average hours shown in Table 8.1, but this contrast is explained by the rise in the proportion of non-manual workers in the total, these having lower average hours. The underlying trend follows closely the trend in hourly productivity over the entire period, the implication being that there is a fairly constant proportion of productivity gains which are taken in the form of reduced hours.

Williams seems to interpret this data as evidence for a constant leisure–income tradeoff over time, though it is not clear that the data can be interpreted in this way if hours are determined by employers. Armstrong, who constructed the data set, has referred to subjective desires of workers as only one factor in the determination of hours of work, the other being the strength of resistance of employers. it is interesting in this context that a recent survey of hours reductions in industry found that employee preference was a *minority* reason given by employers for implementing the change (White, 1982).

It would seem somewhat unwise to project a constant trend for the income–leisure tradeoff on the basis of previous historical patterns. In particular, part-time working may in future become more acceptable to men as well as women in situations where the male wage is increasingly not a 'family' wage, i.e. expected to provide for the entire family. It may also be the case that higher consumption levels increasingly necessitate more non-work time. This is the position argued by writers such as Gershuny, who point to the increasing 'automation' of the home as it evolves into a site of simultaneous production and consumption, displacing previously purchased services such as laundry and entertainment.[4] In this view, people are increasingly prepared to produce for their own satisfaction by means of informal work in the home.

Commentators such as Gershuny point to the possibility of fundamental social changes in perceptions of work and leisure. It is difficult to square this view with that of Williams, however, who sees a certain constancy in income–leisure preferences. Indeed, Armstrong has calculated that, if the trend-change in hours between 1961 and the mid-1970s was extrapolated to the end of the century, the average working week would still be over thirty-seven hours. But if underlying social causes do make for a desire for shorter hours it is going to require a deviation from trend perhaps as significant as either of the two historical divergences apparent in the graph in Figure 8.1.

It is obviously difficult to assess the likely strength of future demand for reduced work hours. However, a quantitative analysis can reveal whether the most recent trends in hours suggest a strengthening of the historical downward movement. The results of one such analysis are described below for average male hours of work.

Determinants of work time

This section describes the results of a model where the average annual hours of work are seen as reflecting the influences of productivity, unemployment and non-wage labour costs. Productivity increases not only allow for the financing of reduced hours but also create labour slack since output volume does not always rise to compensate fully and redundancies do not always immediately remove the slack. Unemployment reflects cyclical influences on the demand for average hours; with high or rising unemployment, labour slack internal to firms should be high due to labour hoarding and this should depress overtime and average hours. Finally, non-wage labour costs such as national insurance contributions would be expected to have a positive relationship with hours in that these have to be paid, regardless of the length of the workweek. The functional form for the regression analysis is discussed in Panel 8.1 and the results are shown in Table 8.4.

A detailed discussion of the regression results may be found

> **Panel 8.1**
>
> One approach to modelling variables that are trended is to allow the trend in the conditioning variable (productivity, P) to explain the trend in the dependent variable (hours, H). The functional form used in the analysis was:
>
> $$H_t = B_0 + B_1 P_t + B_2 P_{t-1} + B_3(H_{t-1} - P_{t-1}) + B_4 t + e_t \ldots [1]$$
>
> where t is a time trend which may be superfluous and e_t is an error term, and where H and P are in log form.
>
> With a dynamic equilibrium such that $\Delta \log H = g_H$ and $\Delta \log P = g_p$ it may be shown that the long-term effect of P on H is given by:
>
> $$H_t = \exp[(g_H - B_0 - B_1 g_P)/B_3] \cdot P_t^{(1 - B_2/B_3)}$$
>
> Equation [1] was modified by the addition of terms in unemployment (U), non-wage labour costs (F), and a dummy variable for the years of unusually large falls in average hours in the early 1960s (D_1). The time trend was persistently insignificant. Ordinarily least squares (OLS) and two-stage least squares (TSLS) were used. In the latter case, the productivity and unemployment variables were treated as endogenous, with capacity utilisation and shift productivity dummies as extra instruments. The results shown in Table 8.4 show that specifications in the last three columns are all broadly acceptable.

in Driver (1986c). Here the discussion will focus on whether recent hours of work indicate any major deviation from the predictions of previous structural relationships. The first point to note is that there appears to be no recent structural break in the relationship. A test for the stability of the parameters failed to locate such a break. Furthermore the annual-hours figure for 1984 is only about 2 per cent below that predicted by the long-run relationship between hours and productivity, despite the existence of mass unemployment. Even this modest deviation may have been erased in the most recent period as productivity has continued to rise sharply.

Two conclusions can be drawn from these results. Firstly, there is no evidence at present that any putative demand for lower hours has influenced management to behave differently than in the past. Secondly, since no unusual fall in hours has

Table 8.4

Dependent variable	$\Delta \log H$ OLS estimation 1956–84		1960–84 TSLS estimation	
	(1)	(2)	(3)	(4)
Constant	3.845 (2.35)	3.508 (2.62)	7.537 (5.70)	7.538 (4.70)
$\Delta \log P$	−0.193 (−1.72)	−0.11 (−1.18)	−0.322 (−3.85)	−0.349 (−2.44)
$\log P_{t-1}$	−0.67 (−2.63)	−0.611 (−2.89)	−1.487 (−5.97)	−1.50 (−4.54)
$\Delta \log U$	−0.020 (−2.26)	−0.022 (−3.09)	−0.030 (−5.22)	−0.036 (−4.13)
$\log U_t$	−0.003 (−0.35)	−0.007 (0.87)	−0.020 (−3.26)	−0.178 (−2.29)
$\Delta \log F$			−0.027 (−3.11)	−0.151 (−0.63)
$\log F_t$			0.073 (4.22)	0.068 (2.40)
$(\log H_t - 1 - \log P_{t-1})$	−0.551 (−2.49)	−0.498 (−2.75)	−1.127 (−5.85)	−1.133 (−4.67)
D1		−0.015 (−3.55)	−0.011 (−3.79)	−0.015 (−3.55)
DW	1.34	1.50	2.05	2.49
S/ME	1.12	0.92	0.67	0.63
R^2	0.39	0.61	0.81	−
AR	$F(2,21)=4.58$	$F(2,20)=1.03$	$F(3,17)=0.32$	$F(1,15)=1.57$
ARCH	$F(2,21)=0.73$	$F(2,20)=0.52$	$F(2,18)=0.03$	$F(3,13)=0.42$
Normality	$X^2(2)=1.25$	$X^2(2)=0.61$	$X^2(2)=9.52$	$X^2(2)=0.25$

DW = Durbin Watson; S/ME = ratio of standard error to mean of dependent variable; AR and ARCH are tests for residual autocorrelation and autoregressive conditional heteroscedasticity.

taken place, there may be a role for public policy to anticipate future changes in hours and accelerate the pace of change. The prospects for achieving this without adverse effects on efficiency or production costs are enhanced at present by the unusually fluid state of the industrial structure (Atkinson and Meager, 1985).

The employer's view

The major resistence to cutting work hours comes from the employers' organisations. Although some companies, such as ICI, Metal Box, Imperial Tobacco, the National Health Service and many others, have been willing to negotiate significant reductions in hours in exchange for more flexible working practices, the general view among employers is that the proposal, if implemented, would add to costs and increase production difficulties. It appears also that among the various methods of worksharing, a reduction in the length of the working week is the least favoured by management (Armstrong, 1984).

Management attitudes in this respect are entirely understandable. Even if a shorter working week were compensated to a large extent either by offsetting wage reductions or by higher levels of efficiency, there would still be likely to be some increase in costs per unit of output. Individual managers have their eye on their own company's fortunes. They cannot be expected readily to appreciate that the macroeconomic consequences of such a move might be increased employment which in turn might allow for an eventual reduction in the corporate tax burden.

Before any sensible judgment on the issue can be made, it is essential to understand the difficulties involved from the employers' point of view. Basically, there are two objections that carry weight. Firstly, reducing hours leads to increased costs since workers will not agree to compensating wage reductions. If, somehow, costs are contained through efficiency agreements, the resulting higher productivity would remove the incentive to increase employment. The implication here is that unrealistic expectations are being set up in regard to employment-generation which industry cannot meet. Increased employment would, in any case, increase costs for companies, given the large overhead component of wage costs, consisting of hiring and potential redundancy costs, training costs, fringe benefits and national insurance contributions.

Secondly, the employers argue that labour is not a homogeneous entity and that labour time cannot be redistributed at will. There are a wide variety of modes of work within industry – time-work, piece-work, continuous and discontinuous shift-work, overhead, supervisory and operative labour. Each category has different conditions relating to time and pay. An example of the difficulties that can be caused by the coexistence of different forms of labour is the case that arose when many engineering firms cut their basic working week from forty to thirty-nine hours. Supervisory staff, who had formerly been paid overtime beyond their standard week of thirty-seven hours, had in some cases to be guaranteed the previous cash pay that had been paid as overtime.

Differences between industries also highlight particular problems that can arise in translating shorter hours into increased employment. In areas of industry with skill shortages, a reduction in hours would be difficult or costly. In cases where capital utilisation is already high, extra employment would necessitate increased outlay on plant. Alternatively, fewer hours per person might be accommodated by increased shift-working, but this might not always be acceptable to the workforce.

Many of the objections cited above are undoubtedly valid, but they are not necessarily insuperable, and it should also be remembered that a shorter working week would offer the advantage of greater flexibility to many employers. They would also reap the benefits of productivity agreements, which might not otherwise be achieved. A study by the independent group Incomes Data Services, referring to productivity agreements in the early 1980s, reported that 'a number of industrial relations managers have expressed the view to us that without the change in climate (consequent on reduced hours) the implementation would have been much more costly' (Incomes Data Services, 1982, p. 6).

Fewer hours for the same pay?

The question of linking hours reductions with corresponding adjustments to pay levels or overtime premiums is one of the thorniest issues in the whole debate on hours. The unions' case is for a standard thirty-five hour week with no reductions in pay; a demand that the employers, not surprisingly, regard as inflationary. It is, however, quite conceivable that such a reduction in hours could be achieved without inflationary consequences if it was arranged as part of a package whereby future potential productivity gains were taken largely in the form of increased leisure.

A cut in the standard working week to thirty-five hours is approximately a 10 per cent reduction for manual workers. If productivity were to show a compound growth of 2½ per cent a year over the next six years, this would raise real output per hour by 16 per cent, which could be split into a 6 per cent rise in real incomes and a 10 per cent rise in leisure time, giving a thirty-five hour week. Assuming that overtime did not rise to compensate for the drop in standard hours, this would ensure that employment was more than 10 per cent higher than it otherwise would be, at least in those areas of the economy where the present standard work-week is of the order of forty hours.

It is of course possible that the projected tradeoff between income and leisure is too optimistic. It is possible that shorter hours might be negotiated in return for even higher productivity levels than would otherwise have been the case. It is also likely that not all the reduction in standard hours would be reflected in a drop in actual hours. Particular difficulties arise for a cut in working time below thirty-seven and a half hours, as negotiations must then begin with both manual and non-manual workers, this being the typical work-week for the latter category.

Despite these *caveats*, however, there is evidence that cut in hours is attractive to workers and that some at least are prepared to finance the cut by flexibility over pay. An example of this flexibility is the building industry agreement which cut the standard week to thirty-nine hours but maintained the threshold for overtime pay at forty hours. There is also evidence that the 1981 pay agreements of firms that reduced hours were lower than they otherwise would have been (White, 1982).

The role of government

The previous sections have reviewed the conflicting pressures from workers and employers in regard to hours. It is clear why progress towards a shorter work-week has been painfully slow. The union side is simultaneously negotiating on hours and pay and is representing a heterogeneous workforce with varying interests. it does not want to commit itself to long-term agreements on pay, but would happily negotiate a phased reduction in hours. The employers' concern is to contain cost-increases occasioned by cuts in hours. Firms are conscious of overhead fixed-costs of extra employment and seek to offset higher costs by increased hourly productivity which minimises the need to increase the workforce. Government has a role in mediating these conflicts. Unhappily, the role of the British government has not been constructive in this matter; it has dragged its feet on all forms of worksharing and has set itself firmly against any further shortening of the working week.

Elsewhere in Europe the situation has been quite different. In Belgium, for instance, legislation and financial aid have helped employers create more jobs through changes in working-time arrangements. In 1983 the government approved a bill to restrict both hours of work and salary levels for new public-sector recruits to 80 per cent of the normal rate in the first year of appointment. In Austria a phased movement has been agreed towrads a five-week legal minimum holiday entitlement. Early retirement schemes have been encouraged by state assistance in several countries. In Norway, employees aged sixty-four or over could choose to work half normal hours and receive half their pension until full retirement at sixty-seven. Similar provisions of a temporary nature were made in France and Germany. In the Netherlands, where unemployment rose very rapidly in the early 1980s, many large companies, including the multinational Phillips, moved to a thirty-eight-hour week at the beginning of 1985. In the public sector the government has imposed a thirty-two-hour week on reduced wages against the wishes of some public-sector unions who preferred a slower pace of change.

The British government has pursued no such schemes with

any enthusiasm. The much trumpeted job-splitting scheme which had been promoted as a major initiative to create hundreds of thousands of part-time jobs scarcely succeeded in generating 2000 new posts. Clearly there is a lack of commitment to worksharing at the highest level of government. Indeed employment ministers have vigorously opposed shorter hours on the grounds that it would weaken European competitiveness against the USA and Japan (*Employment Gazette*, June 1984, p. 251). Clearly, this view represents a pessimistic attitude towards the prospect of agreeing a combined programme of worksharing and income sharing.

The reluctance of the British government to take seriously the question of worksharing is all the more disturbing because of the high hours worked by manual workers in the UK relative to other European countries. Unemployment is highest among manual workers so it is here that worksharing could have its greatest value in terms of job creation, yet, as shown in Table 8.4, not only are the hours for UK manual workers among the highest in Europe but the rate of reduction in recent years has been slowest.

Table 8.4 Manual workers' average weekly hours in EEC

	1972	1982	% reduction
Belgium	41.7	35.6	14.6
France	45.0	39.5	12.2
Italy	41.9	38.1	9.1
Luxembourg	43.9	38.9	11.4
Netherlands	43.9	40.6	7.5
UK	43.0	41.5	4.0
W. Germany	43.2	40.8	5.6

Source: *European Economy*, Nov. 1983, quoted in *Labour Research*, Feb. 1984. 1982 UK estimate from Labour Research Department.

Economic consequences of reducing hours

The possible consequences of reducing work hours can be presented as follows.

1. First, there is a potential decline in production which can be offset either by:
   - increased overtime;
   - increased work intensity, higher productivity through reorganisation, less absenteeism, higher morale, etc.;
   - recruitment of additional workers.
2. Secondly, there is a potential rise in costs per unit of output incurred, either because:
   - wages per unit of output rise, or;
   - because of the need to increase employment or investment.

These various possibilities are outlined in the flow diagram in Figure 8.2. This is a complicated diagram, but the main point is that the effect on employment (shown on the bottom right) is largely conditioned by the extent to which companies choose to make up for the shorter hours in ways which do not increase employment (shown in the middle left of the diagram). The response of wage earnings to the cut in hours is also important in that any change in the wage costs per unit of output will affect not only the absolute level of employment but, to a certain extent, the choice between labour-intensive and capital-intensive methods of production.

It is clear that the employment response to reduced workhours could well vary by industry and possibly by company. Consider, for instance, the different extents to which changes in shift-working could offset reduced hours. The employment response could also be expected to depend on the manner in which the hours reduction was achieved – whether, for instance, it involved twelve minutes off each working day, or the working of an additional shift.

Case studies of four different industries in West Germany (chemicals, electrical and engineering, vehicles and retailing) show marked differences across industries and across forms of working-time reduction as regards the potential for offsetting the reductions in hours by productivity gains (Lapping, 1983). This diversity was confirmed in the findings of the UK industrial study of engineering, pharmaceuticals, printing and construction carried out by the Policy Studies Institute for the Department of Employment (White, 1982).

Making the jobs go round

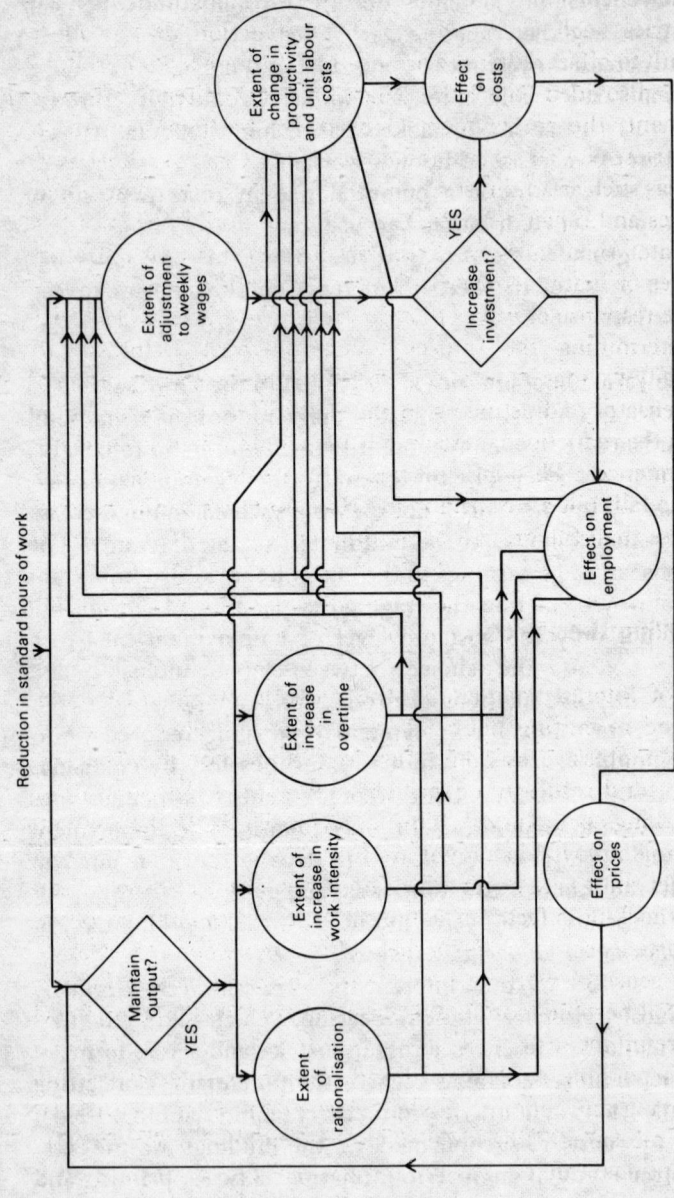

Figure 8.2 Flow diagram showing possible consequences of reducing work hours.

One conclusion that stems from these studies is that service industries such as retailing and construction find it most difficult to offset reduced working-time through higher productivity. Provided therefore that the cost effects are not dominant, the employment gains might be highest in these industries. Not all service industries are of this type, however. In areas such as administration, supervisory work, commercial services and repair services, the scope for work intensification is greater than in more direct production work, whether in services or manufacturing.

The response of wages to hours-reductions is clearly crucial in determining the impact for employment. Unless the company savings ratio is too high (it may be so at present), compensatory adjustments to the path of weekly earnings to match the reductions in hours would heighten the employment consequences. This does not mean that weekly earnings would have to fall, but in return for shorter hours they would have to rise less than the growth of productivity.

Modelling the effects

It is of interest to quantify the possible employment gain involved in cutting hours. A back-of-the-envelope approach yields impressive answers. Just two hours off the working week would result in a 5 per cent increase in the workforce, other things being equal. This is not negligible in the context of an unemployment rate of around 14 per cent.

Other things are never equal, however. Wage costs will rise, with knock-on effects for competitiveness. Productivity deals will partially compensate for the reductions in hours. Overtime, in the sense of working more than the new standard hours, may well become more prevalent and may have to be paid for at a premium.

It is possible to deal with these complex interactions by employing an economic model to assess the effect of various policy measures – this is called simulating the model. Various assumptions can be fed in on the behaviour or response patterns of some economic variables and this information can be used to work out the implications for other key variables such as output, inflation, employment and the balance of payments. The answers obtained will, of course, only be as good as the assumptions, but at least a consistent set of responses to various different assumptions can be generated.

In 1980 the Treasury published a set of simulations on the effects of a two-hour cut in the standard working week (Allen, 1980). The results showed that significant gains in employment could be achieved if the reduction in hours did not lead to increased hourly wages. However, where weekly wage levels were maintained on the same path as before the cut in hours, the simulated response of the economy was more problematic. The model predicted that in this case, after four years inflation would be over 10 per cent higher than it otherwise would be and that the employment gain would be small or maybe even negative. These perverse reactions to a cut in hours stem from the rise in employers' costs per unit and from the corresponding loss in competitiveness that would follow a cut in hours unmatched by compensating wage adjustments.

The results of the Treasury simulations were not dissimilar in some respects to a more up-to-date set of simulations run by the author on a condensed version of the model at the end of 1984. These results are tabulated in Table 8.5 and refer to a cut of two hours off the standard week in the private sector.

Table 8.5 Effects of a two-hour reduction in standard weekly hours. Figures represent % deviation from the expected path, except for the balance of payments, where the deviation is expressed in £ million.

Earnings assumption		Private employment (%)	Inflation (%)	Output (%)	Balance of payments (£ million)
No change	1985	1.2	0.7	0	−372
	1989	1.0	2.5	−0.1	−1,180
Hours reduction fully matched by fall in earnings	1985	1.2	−0.3	0.1	−230
	1989	1.8	−1.9	0.6	−210

The results show that a two-hour cut in the working week could increase employment by about 1 per cent or a quarter of a million, assuming no hike in average earnings. An employment increase of 2 per cent could be expected if the growth in average earnings were to be adjusted downwards to match the cut in hours.

It should be said, however, that a full adjustment of wages is most unlikely, if for no other reason than the existence of overhead labour-costs – training, administration, etc. It is also the case that very few agreements have been negotiated which involve a *pro rata* reduction in earnings for a cut in hours.

The extent to which wages would adjust is a fairly open question. The 1981 survey by the Policy Studies Institute (PSI) found that one in seven managers thought that the 1981 wage settlement of firms that had reduced hours was lower than it otherwise would have been. However a follow-up survey a year later found little evidence of a continuing tradeoff between hours and wage levels. This finding must be interpreted carefully. To the extent that the hours-reductions were accompanied by heightened work-intensity or new flexible working-practices, there would be little presumption that a reduction in earnings would also be requried. The union side cannot be expected to pay twice over for the hours reduction – once in the form of new working practices and again in the form of reduced earnings-growth.

Returning to the figures in Table 8.5, in the case where there is no earnings adjustment, there is an implicit cost to the economy in that the rate of inflation is some 2.5 per cent higher than it would otherwise have been.[5] This is, however, substantially less than the corresponding figure in the earlier Treasury simulation, perhaps because inflationary expectations are now lower. As well as the inflationary consequences, there is a repercussion also on the balance of payments, which deteriorates in the simulation by about £1 billion. While these developments may be an acceptable price to pay for reduced unemployment, they indicate that the provision of new jobs by cuts in hours is not a costless exercise.

Unlike the Treasury paper, the results in Table 8.5 do not contain figures for the case of a rise in average earnings. This could happen if overtime payments increased substantially as standard hours were cut. There is some evidence that overtime would rise somewhat to offset a cut in hours unless the government discouraged such a move by tax measures or legislation, but the effect is probably nowhere near the level assumed in the Treasury study – 40 per cent of potential output fall being made up by increased overtime working, paid for at the full premium. In the study by the Policy Studies Institute, less than 1 per cent of the total sample expected a worse performance due to a rise in overtime costs to effect efficiency, though 10 per cent expected that there would be increased overtime working. It is possible that many firms were able, as in the construction industry, to ensure that overtime costs did not rise.

The productivity assumptions underlying the simulation results of Table 8.5 are rather conservative. It has been assumed that 70 per cent of any potential loss in output was made up by rises in hourly productivity rates. The available evidence in this regard is rather mixed.

The PSI studies showed that hourly productivity rose strongly to offset the reduction in hours, but this response may have been specific to the particular time of the study – the early 1980s. This was a period of rapid productivity growth. In the absence of a study on a control group of firms that did not reduce hours, it is not clear how much the productivity increase of firms is attributable to agreements on shorter hours. In so far as some of the productivity agreements were of the form of a reduction in tea breaks or other time allowances, there is no guarantee that they will last. Figure 8.3 shows the movement of an index of work intensity over a number of years. This measures the extent to which industry operatives are literally working during their time at work. It is interesting that the index tends to fluctuate over a constant value in the long run, indicating that concessions on time allowances tend to be ceded and won back again successively by the workforce. It is clear that the period of the early 1980s was one when the intensity of work rose strongly, but it would be wrong to take this as a measure of permanent productivity gain due to the hours reductions that occurred. In this sense the simulations reported above may give an unduly conservative picture of the employment potential of reduced hours, in that if the productivity response was less, greater employment might result in the short run. This view is supported by the results of a number of policy simulations carried out on the disaggregated model of the Institute for Employment Research at

Making the jobs go round

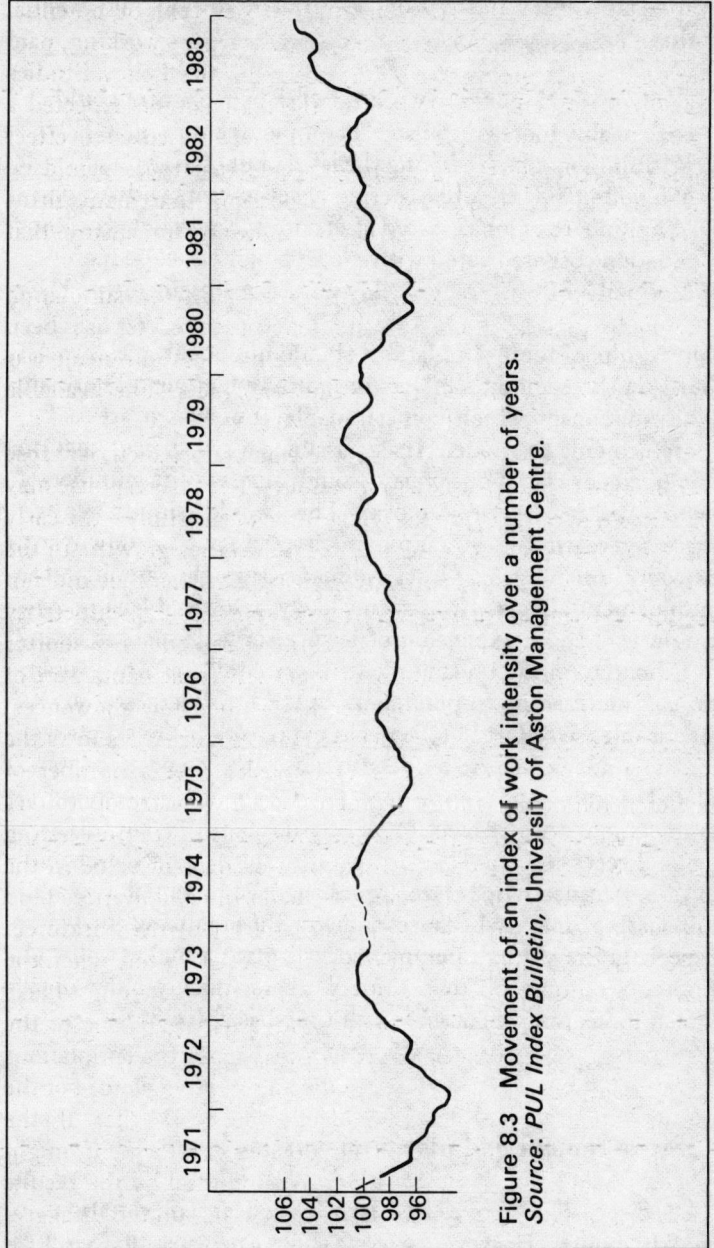

Figure 8.3 Movement of an index of work intensity over a number of years.
Source: PUL Index Bulletin, University of Aston Management Centre.

Warwick (Whitley and Wilson, 1986). The authors' conclusion is that:

> a policy of reducing the working week by 5 per cent could conceivably increase the level of employment in the UK by ¾–1 million jobs (reducing the level of unemployment by 450,000–650,000) after a period of seven years with around ½ million extra jobs created after three years. However, the inflation cost associated with such a policy could be high, especially if the average weekly wage is maintained. (p. 15)

The results of these simulations should not be taken as the last word on the economic effects of hours reductions. There are other influences which come into play but which are rather more difficult to model. It is possible, for instance, that an increased level of hourly pay would increase the number of people willing to seek work. This would simultaneously increase registered unemployment and put a downward pressure on wages. Other influences might amplify the employment effects. If, as seems likely, increased leisure time would lead to an expansion of leisure services such as eating out, holidays and entertainment, there could be a disproportionate increase in employment, as these services are largely labour-intensive. Drèze (1985) has expressed 'polite skepticism' on the ability of these models to assess the changes contemplated, arguing that too little is known about the elasticity of employment with respect to weekly hours in the context of a general recession (p. 41). However, despite this scepticism of exact quantification, Drèze argues that the potential exists for job-sharing, mainly because 'some of those looking for work, especially the young unemployed will place a higher value on finding a regular job than some workers (mainly older ones) attach to keeping their son a full-time basis' (p. 26).

Early retirement and part-time working

The discussion above has largely concerned variation in weekly hours. However worksharing can operate in other ways. A scheme to encourage older workers to relinquish their jobs has been in operation in Britain since 1977 – the Job Release Scheme. This allows workers near retirement to retire early on a weekly allowance on condition that the job is replaced from the unemployed register. A few thousand jobs have been created each year, but the effect is marginal because eligibility is confined to those very close to retirement. Metcalf (1985a) has proposed a cost-effective reform of the system, extending the eligible age-group and increasing the allowance so as to reduce the unemployment register by about 150,000.

The TUC has also suggested cost-effective schemes for early retirement. Recognising that a reduction in retirement age for men from sixty-five to sixty would cost over £2bn, it has proposed various ways of phasing in such a change, including:

1 a partial scheme to allow those over sixty-one to work a four-day week with compensation;
2 a lower retirement age for industries that are hazardous or involve stress or physical fatigue.

It seems clear that there is further scope for early retirement in Britain. The participation rate among sixty-to-sixty-four-year-old men is still 10 to 15 percentage points higher than in France or Germany, despite a greater discouraged worker effect from higher unemployment in Britain (White, 1986).

An increase in part-time working also seems promising. Drèze (1985) is pessimistic on the prospects for creating employment by marginal reductions in basic hours for all workers, mainly because many firms are still hoarding labour and will not respond to shorter hours by new hirings, except in expanding industries (where shorter hours would cause other problems) or where there is flexibility in shift systems to allow greater capital utilisation.[6] Increased part-time work might overcome this difficulty, but the problem is that hours worked part-time are largely concentrated at or near the half-time mark. There is a potential supply of part-time workers near the thirty-hour mark but it does not seem to be matched by corresponding demand.

The alternative approach favoured by Drèze is to open up a

significant number of thirty-hour-per-week jobs; this would cause new hirings, though it would be costly in terms of reorganisation of work practices.[7] It is timely to consider this issue now as many recent studies have confirmed that the reorganisation of work-practices is at a fluid stage, with companies responding to new technology and weak trade-union bargaining strength by implementing measures to obtain greater flexibility. These steps include greater 'functional' flexibility with multi-skilling and, more often, 'numerical' flexibility – overtime working, shift working and employment of casual, part-time or temporary staff. If these changes merely occur haphazardly or in response to temporary bargaining advantages, a big opportunity will have been missed to introduce comprehensive reforms that would have lasting benefit all round. In the current fluid climate there is a strong case for state intervention to ensure that patterns of work organisation develop along lines which minimise work time and job insecurity and which maximise the opportunities for functional flexibility. The need for such intervention stems not only from the greater stability and social cohesion that would result, but from the discontinuous, discrete nature of present changes which imply reforms not only at firm level but throughout society. Drèze (1985) puts this point rather well. If the trend reduction in working hours is expected to continue, there will, at some stage, have to be an 'uncoupling' of the average work-week from the period of business activity. This is, of course, already done in some cases with shift working or continuous operation, but a radical departure for the whole economy may be necessary – one suggestion is for a four-day work-week and a six-day business period. This would require 'a new coordination between production activities, services, leisure activities, schools, etc.' (p. 47). Many may doubt whether this is feasible even in the medium term. Some tentative evidence that such a change would be acceptable is contained in a survey carried out by the European Commission in member countries (Commission of the European Communities, 1985b). About a third of workers in all countries would agree to work one Saturday in four or do evening work if annual working hours were reduced by 2 per cent. The exact question and replies are reproduced in Table 8.6.

Table 8.6 New working arrangements

Question

Supposing you were offered the *following working time arrangements*: You work for example one Saturday a month, or else you work five times a month up to 22h in the evening, and as a counterpart, your working time per year is reduced by 5% (that could be 2 hours less work per week in the average or else it could be two weeks more vacation a year). What is your personal opinion on such arrangement?

Are you
1. Very much in favour.
2. Rather in favour.
3. Rather against.
4. Very much against.
5. Indifferent.

(Answers in %)

	1	2	3	4	5	No answer	TOTAL
Belgium	15	19	29	18	12	7	100
Denmark	11	19	14	20	16	20	100
W. Germany	8	28	17	9	24	14	100
Greece	26	20	12	18	15	9	100
France	14	33	23	13	13	4	100
Ireland	25	28	11	12	13	11	100
Italy	14	25	20	18	11	12	100
Luxemburg	10	26	20	19	16	9	100
Netherlands	12	20	19	29	12	8	100
UK	13	21	18	13	25	10	100
All	12	26	20	14	18	10	100

Source: Commission of the European Communities, 1985b.

Concluding comments

The present unemployment catastrope is, in part, a problem of the distribution of work and to this extent worksharing can help. There is a potential added bonus to companies who adopt worksharing in that it leads to more flexible and efficient working practices, though this will paradoxically minimise new employment opportunities in the short run. If the only gain were higher efficiency, the emergence of new employment opportunities might be too slow. There is some evidence that companies can accurately determine the threshold to which working time can be reduced without creating new jobs and that employers refuse to accept a reduction in working time that goes beyond this.[8] If this is the case, it points to the need to consider ways in which employers can be persuaded or directed towards translating hours reductions into jobs. The role, not only of government but also of the trade unions, is clearly crucial in this regard. The scope for encouraging job creation at the thirty-hour mark is clearly in evidence.

9 Summing up

The scale of job creation needed to restore reasonably full employment is disturbingly large. The figure of a million jobs a year for five years (Glyn, 1986) probably overstates the number, but only marginally. Metcalf (1985b) has accurately assessed the numbers who might actively seek work in an improved climate of job opportunity. He has modified the unemployment statistics up and down, adding to the count some of those on low-paid special measures, some of those excluded by new methods of counting and those discouraged workers who will seek work only when prospects improve. Allowing for an extra half million or so rise in the labour force between 1985 and 1989, he obtained a figure of 2.1 million net new jobs required just to reduce unemployment to 2 million by 1989.

This figure has been confirmed by the Employment Institute (1986). It suggests that in addition to a progamme of job measures to reduce long-term unemployment by 750,000, an extra 1.4 million jobs, mainly full-time, would have to be found. Metcalf's total probably presents a more accurate picture, however, as it is not clear whether existing low-paid community-type work is either practicable or desirable, even for a majority of those who have been out of work for long periods.

It is possible to extend Metcalf's figures in an ambitious direction to estimate the implications of reducing unemployment to an acceptable half million or effectively to full employment. This would require a further 2 million jobs, reducing the registered count by another 1½ million. At a minimum, therefore, a fully successful employment-creation strategy would need to involve 4 million new jobs, mostly full-time – a higher rate of job growth than that achieved between 1932–7 when employment rose by 2.4 million or 1945–8 when civilian employment increased by nearly 3 million.

Knowing the scale of the problem is salutary, though the exact figures matter rather less. There is no economic method or model at present that could work out the precise effects of policies calculated to achieve change of the order necessary to restore full employment. The existing economic models all treat as fixed a number of social and economic relationships that would change, and in any case, the models differ greatly when used in unorthodox policy simulations. It is not possible, therefore, to show that full employment can be restored; only to indicate the direction of paths that most plausibly point in that direction.

The answer some propose is to cajole, subsidise or push the long-term unemployed into work, thus increasing competition for jobs and lowering wage pressure while simultaneously 'solving' a social problem. This approach is at least strategic, but the strategy is deeply flawed. The problem of unemployment is largely a problem of growth, not one of labour market malfunctioning. It will not help structural adjustment or long-term growth to put money and effort into prioritising low-paid unskilled jobs. In the short term, job-creation expedients are necessary, but these should be set so far as is possible in a training context and there should be a clear objective to achieving a transition to a high-skill structure. Shorter hours of work should also be seen not only in the context of 'work-sharing' or 'income-sharing' but as a means of creating the flexibility of lifestyle that is important if new consumer patterns are to evolve readily.

Chapters 4 to 6 have dealt with the problem of growth in new products and services in a regime of heightened uncertainty. This is an international problem and requires international cooperation. However individual countries also need to act. The promotion of a constellation of new activities (balanced between public and private) will have to be accelerated by encouraging specific consumer and public patterns of expenditure. This planning framework for consumption will give a boost to investment far beyond that achievable by marginal investment incentives that have been tried in the past.

The choice of activity for support will depend on several considerations. These include a political process that weighs in the balance indications of market preferences and redistributive considerations. It will also be important to determine whether the outcome of individual market preferences is such as to allow sustainable growth. This will depend on the extent to which important sectors can be expanded through backward linkages (as happened in the interwar years) and on the extent to which the balance-of-payments problem can be minimised. The point of planning consumption is not only to lessen uncertainty over the pattern of domestic output; it will also ensure that expansion is not dissipated in an unsustainable surge of imports. This policy will operate without having to resort to overt import controls which would be irresponsible in the present climate of world trade, when a slide to protectionism is a real possibility.

The creation of stable demand-patterns needs to be part of a wider strategy which ensures that production units in the economy are innovative and flexible. A heavy responsibility falls on management, both in the private and public spheres. The present imbalance of cautious expansionary investment and relatively high labour-saving investment is a reflection of the poverty of management strategy and culture. In particular it is highly serious that large firms have failed to pioneer new growth points in the form of corporate venturing or sponsored spin-offs. Policies are needed to persuade firms to prioritise these activities.

Chapter 4 has shown that mature industries tend to be characterised by relatively low investment in relation to profitability. This is disturbing. Problems arising from market distortion are probably minimised as long as surplus profits generated by firms with market power are used for new developments or acquisitions. However, there must be serious concern when surplus profits are not so used or when a country is – as Britain is – top heavy with mature industries, leading to excessive transfers abroad. Policies for consideration here include price controls on mature industries or a combination of dividend control and encouragement of internal diversification ventures.

In newer industries the major constraints seem to be risk and management resources. These constraints must be broken to encourage the exploitation of the stock of potential developments that firms have identified as non-central to their current strategy. There is a choice of policies here, including government measures to encourage spin-offs, whether by public or private bodies, and reforms of management decision-making to focus it less on the benefit of the particular firm and more on the contribution to the economy. The latter course involves a greater acceptance of risk by the corporate sector; subsidy or legislation can be used to push firms in this direction. One option might be to allow employees the option of developing projects that top management has shelved for more than a specified period. This step would have to be balanced by other measures to increase R&D, perhaps by making it obligatory on companies to disclose expenditure on research. Risk can also be minimised for pioneering firms by penalising short-term holdings of equity or by encouraging long-term holdings, particularly by institutional investors.

The problem of management affects the public sector as well. Here the challenge is to raise the quality and heterogeneity of the service provided. Any limitation on the public's desire to expand these services is also a limitation on jobs. The attitude to public services is in part a function of the extent of innovative and responsive management in these areas. Reforms here are not costless, but funds must be released for 'research and development' of social and community services. As Rothschild (1980) has remarked 'consumption and production are out of joint' in the sense that demand has grown strongly for collective or environmental services, while the delivery systems for these services have not kept pace with innovative trends in industry. Little improvement is likely without an injection of funds in these fields; demoralisation, defensive postures and short-term thinking are the more likely effects of a spending squeeze.

The previous point highlights a general difficulty with the reforms indicated by the analysis in this book; they require an injection of public funds with no guarantee of a quick payback.

This will involve a rise in the government deficit and in borrowing as a ratio of national income. It is not entirely clear why this is resisted so strongly in financial circles. The notion that it will 'crowd out' private investment has no basis if the finance is used to encourage investment: 'if the policy looks after investment, there is no reason to be concerned with crowding out' (Blanchard, Dornbusch and Buiter, 1986, p. 24). One argument sometimes put in favour of containing public expenditure is that the ratio of debt to GDP is set to rise sharply in many Western countries and Japan in the next century due to pension commitments and demographic changes. However it is a bizarre logic that constrains present investment and thus future GDP so as to contain future debt ratios.

The conflict between the objective need for higher debt-ratios and the conservatism in financial circles points to the need for a permanent review body of interested parties, including city institutions. This group would be required to report on the level of debt that would be reasonable to incur in providing for accelerated social and industrial structural change. An unusual degree of structural change in the economy requires a higher temporary debt-ratio, both to facilitate acceptance and to take advantage of new opportunities. The review body should find some consensus method of assessing the degree of change and the increase in debt that it warrants. A natural assumption would be that long-term inflationary pressure would be lowered, not raised, by public borrowing to finance the transition of an economy through a turbulent period of structural adjustment.

Such an approach would mark an abrupt change from the first half of the 1980s in Britain, when conventional wisdom was the exact opposite. During much of this period, the fiscal stance was actually contractionary and the ratio of debt to GDP fell. During this period, also, the net capital stock in manufacturing fell continually and fixed investment in the economy as a whole was sluggish compared with the trend in profits. The extraordinary disregard for investment in education and training in this period has already been remarked on on Chapter 3. Structural change did accelerate in this period, but largely in the form of unbalanced loss of industrial capacity. Indeed, mobility of individuals between jobs actually fell, despite the shake-up in industry, showing that flexibility was reduced. All this is evidence of a failed restructuring and one which will leave behind a legacy of high unemployment and inflationary pressure.

Concern may be felt that the proposed review system for national debt would usurp the function of government, but an independent voice on sustainable debt and structural change is in the mould of existing consensus institutions that offer advice and judgment. The merit of the reform is that it broadens the forum in which such decisions are taken and ensures that the voice of the City is more in harmony with other interests. Such an institution would not, in any event, depoliticise the issue entirely; nor should it. There is still a need for political debate on the appropriate amount of debt to finance social consumption over and above investment in the social and physical infrastructure.

Industry, no less than the economy, will gain from faster growth. However in our industrial culture with decentralised decision-making and with heightened uncertainty, that potential gain is not a sufficient spur to long-term commitment of resources. On the three crucial fronts of training, R&D and fixed investment there has been a serious slippage in recent years relative to potential. These deficiencies can be put right by a steer from the centre to coordinate and support aspirant growth in the private and public domains. This will involve a sensitive commitment to planning, from product development through to consumption. Acceptance of change will have to be bought by higher debt ratios. The risks involved will have to be minimised, firstly, by involving as broad a range of interest groups as possible in the planning process and, secondly, by a determined commitment to disengage at an early stage from mistakes that are clearly evidenced. Doubters there will be; but these policies are probably the only route to full employment in a reasonable time span.

Notes

1 No future?

1 The OECD labour force did grow more rapidly in the 1970s than earlier, but job growth was greatest in the area where the labour force grew most rapidly – North America.
2 The voluntary unemployment argument sugests that people are choosing not to work for a wage that reflects their productivity. It is important to take this view seriously, if only because the very intractability of unemployment and the need for radical measures to cure it will cause it to be given greater prominence. The alleged rise in voluntary unemployment used to be attributed to an increased generosity in benefit payments to the unemployed. Nickell (1979) suggests that a small part of the rise in unemployment up to 1973 was the result of better compensation for loss in income, but that unemployment kept rising when compensation no longer improved. It has become harder in recent years to argue that unemployment has risen because of more generous welfare benefits, but the notion of unemployment as voluntary has not been given up. Rather, the apparent rise in it is said to result from a shift in the leisure–income tradeoff, with people preferring to be idle for any given level of welfare benefits. This is difficult to test empirically, but an indirect test is possible. Since any increased proclivity for leisure would be expected to affect the population as a whole, one would expect to see an effect too on overtime worked by those in jobs. The facts are that between 1980 and 1985 the overtime premium has remained constant in proportional terms while the extra hours worked by those on overtime has increased by nearly 10 per cent. This is hardly evidence of a shift towards greater leisure preference.
4 Interesting evidence for the perceived seriousness or 'salience' of unemployment for different groups in the US is provided by Akerlof and Yellen (1985). By looking at the ratio of remembered unemployment to actual duration they conclude that over two

decades there has been a decline in salience for younger and older people, but no change for those of prime age.
5. See, for instance, Lindbeck (1985) or various articles in the *Oxford Review of Economic Policy*, vol. 1, no. 1. The term 'classical unemployment' is Malinvaud's: 'classical unemployment is a suitable description for a situation in which excess supply of labour and excess demand for goods both prevail' (1982, p. 24).
6. Demand is endogenous so in the long run there is a 'natural' level of output.
7. There is considerable doubt expressed in the literature as to whether greater labour-market flexibility, where it has been in evidence, has made a significant different to unemployment. See, for instance, Bell and Freeman (1985), Gordon (1986), National Institute for Economic and Social Research (1984) and Shackleton (1985).
8. Some economists identify a rise in structural change, and associated labour-market mismatch, as a reason for a rise in the non-accelerating inflation rate of unemployment (NAIRU). The debate on structural change has largely concerned its effects on the NAIRU, to the exclusion of other important considerations.
9. OECD sources based on McGraw-Hill surveys. There is of course a strong contrast between the US and Europe. In the US, investment rose 60 per cent and employment 40 per cent between 1970 and 1985. In the big four European countries, by contrast, investment rose by only 20 per cent, with employment static.
10. See Cripps and Tarling (1973), Cornwall (1977), Wragg and Robertson (1978).
11. The discrepancy between Michl (1985) and Cornwall (1977) appears to arise from the latter's restriction of equal constant terms across time periods. Unfortunately, all of these estimates for individual time periods have omitted variables, in particular capital intensity. An attempt at a fully-specified equation, though somewhat short on diagnostics, may be found for pooled cycles in Michl (1985), Table 3.
12. This finding contrasts somewhat with the earlier work of Briggs, Robertson and Goodchild (1982). It is possible that measures of capital investment in services, if available in greater detail, could resolve these differences.
13. One test of this is to compare the years 1966–72 with 1976–82 in terms of the variance of the balance of national forecasts as described in Llewwllyn *et al.* (1985), p. 107. There is a sizeable increase, both for the real GDP and for the inflation data between the periods.
14. See, for instance, the argument in Blanchard *et al.* (1985).
15. The causal pattern here may be complex. See Chan-Lee and Sutch (1985), Annex 2 for evidence of bicausality between investment and profitability. See Cowling (1985) for a discussion of the relevance of profitability for investment.
16. See Driver, Kilpatrick and Naisbitt (1986).
17. For data relating to the UK case, see Williams (1981).

18 See Tales 3 and 4 in Chan-Lee and Sutch (1985).
19 See the various graphs of marginal capital productivity in the four-volume study *Technological Trends and Employment* by researchers at the Science Policy Research Unit at Sussex University, published by Gower in 1985 and 1986.
20 Bruno and Sachs (1985), Tables 8.1 and 8.4.
21 See Sawyer (1986) for a more general critique of the equations underlying the natural rate hypothesis.
22 Among the models that have been developed are: Tobin (1975), Steindl (1979), Rowthorn (1981), Weitzman (1982). See also Kaldor (1985), with the comment by Tobin; and the symposium in the *Journal of Post-Keynesian Economics*, spring, 1985.
23 Some writers, e.g. Tanzi (1985), have observed an effect of government deficits on interest rates, but it is admitted that a large part of the increase in interest rates in the early 1980s were due to other factors. It should also be noted that the effect of interest rates on investment may also be less than traditional theory predicts (Eichner, 1986).
24 Table 13 in Geroski and Jacquemin (1985) shows large excess capacity in the European steel industry since 1960.
25 Referring to the need for a battery of controls in a demand expansion, the economic journalist Sam Brittan wrote: 'in the unlikely event of such measures succeeding, key concepts such as jobs and output will lose much of the meaning they have in a society based on free choice. So, ultimately, questions of value in the philosophical as well as in the economic sense' are involved' (*Financial Times*, 13 February 1986).

2 Workshop and the world

1 See Table 1, *Economic Progress Report*, No. 178, HM Treasury, June 1985.
2 See Table E, 'Services in the UK Economy', *Bank of England Quarterly Bulletin*, September 1985, p. 408.
3 In the six big EEC countries the implicit price index for all services value added has been more than 10 per cent higher than for manufacturing since 1970. (See *The Role of Service Activities in the Community Economy, the United States and Japan*, European Commission, document 849510, November 1984).
4 The inclusion of intermediate or 'producer' services such as wholesaling or business services complicates the situation somewhat. Taking account of these services tends to accentuate the apparent rise in the volume of service-sector output as a proportion of GDP. This is because many of these activities – car-fleet management, for instance – have been classified historically under other sectors such as manufacturing; it is only as the division of labour proceeds that they are identified separately as services in the

national accounts. This is thought to inflate the growth rate of services artificially by about 10 per cent (Ranga Chand, 1983).
5. Because of the positive intercept, the share falls slightly with GDP.
6. An exception to this is the data in Fig. 2.1.
7. For instance, it is possible to envisage performances involving semi-amateur or voluntary use of free time as formal work-time is reduced.
8. Sources used in this section are NEDO reports, the *Financial Times* series 'Can Europe catch up' (1985), *FT* survey, 17 December 1985, the *Economist*, 24 November 1984, M. Sharp (1983), as well as trade union sources and discussions with industrialists.
9. The argument on fragmented markets is often conflated with the distinct one of 'national champions'. For a good account of the arguments on this issue in relation to telecommunications, see G. Dang Nguyen, 'Telecommunications: a challenge to the old order' in M. Sharp (1985).
10. See OECD Science and Technology Indicators, June 1984 and October 1985.
11. See in this regard the House of Lords (1985), Select Committee on Overseas Trade, Report, vol. 1, paragraph 108.
12. New technology involves changing roles for workers as well as for technical managers. A good discussion of the potential problems involved in different methods of introducing flexible manufacturing systems (FMS) may be found in a review of academic work at Sheffield University Social and Applied Psychology Unit, by Nick Garnett in the *Financial Times*, 17 March 1986.
13. It can also, of course, be achieved at the expense of jobs and output. Between 1976 and 1983, Britain moved from lowest to highest position in terms of unit value per ton of advanced machine tools, but simultaneously the share of exports of these products fell astonishingly, from 36 per cent to 5 per cent (Horn *et al.*, in Chapter 3 of Sharp, 1983).
14. This is confirmed in the four-volume study *Technological Trends and Employment* produced by the Science Policy Research Unit (1984, 1985). These studies contain sensitivity tests on employment projections and report optimistic and pessimistic scenarios for each industry. In most cases the medium-term dispersion between the estimates is not very great.
15. This conclusion is confirmed, using a somewhat different methodology, in the evidence of Cambridge Econometrics to the House of Lords Select Committee on Overseas Trade.
16. Furthermore, much intangible capital, such as sales teams, contacts, marketing goodwill, etc., has been lost along with the loss of export volume. It will take many years to rebuild this.
17. See the *Financial Times*, 3 December 1985.
18. Correct and far-sighted intervention may of course still encounter opposition, as the interesting case of Japanese entry into car production confirms. The original decision involved a contest

between MITI and the Bank of Japan (Gibbs, 1980, p. 51).
19 For a study suggesting that the allocation of industrial aid in 1975–6 was based on principles other than picking winners, see Davies *et al.* (1980).
20 See *Monthly Labour Review*, November 1985.

3 High road or low road?

1 This is not to say that the unemployed are unemployable; while they are less qualified and productive on average than the average worker, their potential productivity is not necessarily any less than similarly-qualified workers who are employed. Evidence for this is provided by White (1983).
2 Hughes and Hutchinson (1986) say: 'It is not at all clear that an improvement in skills at the present time will be a guarantee of employment . . . it is the very young and the older skilled males who are facing the most rapidly growing unemployment rates, whereas the position of the unskilled has hardly changed' (p. 325). There are a number of points to be made in regard to this assertion. Firstly, the category of unskilled is drawn very tightly and excludes, for example, those 'older skilled males' with redundant skills. Secondly, the fact that the employment system protects and favours those with a job over those without, inevitably pushes unemployment on to the young. This may affect the chance of an individual unemployed person benefiting from higher skills, but it says nothing – and the analysis can by its nature say nothing – about the effects of a general rise in the skill level. The only safe conclusion to draw is that investment in skills may be sub-optimal as the return to the individual may not reflect its societal value.
3 This rather surprising feature may be a reflection of the fact that the study imposes a set of final demand levels – that forecast by the US Bureau of Labour Statistics. Different diffusion rates will, of course, change the pattern and accordingly bring further changes in the occupational structure.
4 See the second report of the House of Commons Employment Committee, 1986.
5 Hart and Trinder say: 'We need tax incentives to reverse the increase in the supply of some three million female part-time workers which occurred between 1951 and 1981' (p. 40).
6 See, for instance, M. Cross and P. Mitchell, *Packaging Efficiency – The Training Contribution*, London, The Technical Change Centre.
7 Implemented by the author at NEDO, in conjunction with Gallup.

4 New jobs and old

1 See 'All change on the production line' by Peter Bruce, *Financial Times*, 2 October 1986.

2. The analysis is confirmed by independent research on the PIMS database (Robinson, 1986). This showed that businesses in declining markets have on average lower capital-intensity, R&D expenditure, marketing effort an product innovation, but do not exhibit a significantly different profitability. The top 20 per cent of declining businesses averaged over 50 per cent profitability (net income over investment).
3. Direct evidence on the effect of market uncertainty on investment is available in Britain from the CBI Industrial Trends Survey, but the question has only been asked since the end of 1979. It is probable, however, that the question is interpreted as downward uncertainty.
4. Blanchflower and Oswald (1986) have investigated whether firms with profit-sharing schemes have superior performance to those who do not. They conclude that there is no evidence to support this claim.
5. Reported in the *Financial Times*, 20 June 1986.

5 Ways and means

1. A survey of possible areas of new job growth may be found in NEDO Long-Term Perspectives Group (1985).
2. The lack of standardisation is also reflected in some other characteristics thought to be typical of services – there is no inventory and there are difficulties in measuring output. The above distinction, while useful may also tend to confuse, since many activities which were once non-standardised are increasingly becoming so and are also being automated (an example here is fast-food catering). The national accounts divide the economy into services and manufacturing in a way which cuts across these distinctions and which takes little account of new technology; services in these accounts include a set of heterogeneous activities with little rationale for their common grouping, since many are more akin to manufacturing in terms of occupational structure, labour process and labour relations.
3. Quoted in GLC (1982).
4. The survey, *Attitudes to Services*, was carried out for the author at NEDO in January 1986.
5. See Driver (1980) for a discussion of this question.
6. Business Monitor MD14, *Industrial Research and Development Expenditure and Employment*.
7. OECD Science and Technology Indicators; Resources Devoted to R&D. The figures are the latest available and relate to the late 1970s.
8. The educational material too is costly to produce. Duke (1984) has described the skill input for interactive video material: 'Manpower contributions are necessary from the fields of subject expertise, teaching and curricular development, instructional design and

evaluation, text editing and graphics, computer programming and systems engineering, film and television production, and project direction and management.' (p. 122)
9 LOTIS was a subcommittee of the Committee on Invisible Exports, later renamed the British Invisibles Export Council.
10 A detailed account of the implications of traded services for merchandise trade may be found in a report by the US International Trade Commission (1982).
11 It may, perhaps, be the case that a high exchange rate is correlated with confidence in financial institutions. In this case there would be a compensating relationship between the two components of 'other' and 'financial' services, with the former benefiting from a lower exchange rate. This would explain the divergence between the growth of 'other' services and 'financial' services since 1980, the former growing much more slowly.

6 Small wonder?

1 Roughly speaking, the criteria amounted to a limit of 200 employees for manufacturing or 25 in construction. Turnover criteria were used in other sections; at 1980 prices there limits were about £1m in wholesale, £½m in motor trades and £¼m in retailing and miscellaneous. All of catering was included.
2 It is often argued that concentration in manufacturing will tend to be undermined by new technology which makes small batch-production more efficient. Bollard (1983) has investigated the likely effects of technology on a number of industries in this regard. In most cases the likely effects are ambiguous. Numerical control makes smaller batch-production efficient, but also allows centralised control to be more flexible. In industries such as printing, fibre-optics allow decentralisation without physical handling of text; but if advances in communication replicate earlier advances in transportation, the effect may be to undermine local units.
3 These figures are not representative of the stock of small businesses; failures will be more prevalent in some sectors than in others. Over 20 per cent of long-established small firms are in manufacturing (Economists Advisory Unit, 1983).
4 A series of detailed criticisms of the Newcastle study may be found in Storey and Johnson (1985). These authors note that the conclusions of the study appear 'to depend heavily upon the contribution to new jobs made by births, the methods for estimating which are highly questionable' (p. 11).
5 See *The Economist*, 5 May 1984.
6 See *British Business*, 6 May 1983.
7 See *Department of Employment Gazette*, August 1984.
8 Although venture capital funds are intended to be closely involved with clients, 'only a handful promote a decent appraisal and

monitoring service' (*Financial Times*, 3 July 1984). Many venture capital groups are under-funded and under-staffed (*Financial Times*, 2 April 1986).

9 This is certainly true of the developments in CAD/CAM in Britain in the 1970s and early 1980s; see Peter Marsh, 'A dream they never sold', *Financial Times*, 9 June 1986.

10 *Financial Times*, 24 June 1986.

7 Special measures

1 Note that Lindley (1986) has calculated that net cost per job is lower for job-preservation schemes than job-creation schemes.

2 See the study by City of Edinburgh and Lothian Councils, April 1985. The study may overstate the costs somewhat since the negative displacement effects of relocation are not considered.

3 The estimate is by Dr F. Robinson, senior research assistant at the Centre for Urban and Regional Development Studies in the University of Newcastle-upon-Tyne. It was reported in the *Listener*, 28 March 1985. It is broadly in line with the author's own estimate.

4 As pointed out in Layard and Nickell (1980):

> the fact that one is doing down the rest of the world by subtle rather than obvious means is not necessarily something to be pleased about, but then if the economically stronger countries of the world had not pursued such contractionary policies in the recent past, papers such as this might well not have been worth writing.

This was written before the UK contraction of the early 1980s. There was in fact a marginal employment subsidy in Britain until 1979, when it was outlawed by the EEC; the Temporary Employment Scheme (TES) paid £20 a week for up to a year for each redundancy averted. As Metcalf (1984) notes: 'from a European perspective it is plausible that the net increase in employment associated with the TES . . . merely means that employment elsewhere in the EC is correspondingly lower' (p. 95). Note that Lindley (1986) argues that subsidies must be long-term if they are to have a significant substitution effect; this makes it all the more difficult to combine them with adjustment measures.

5 Anatole Kaletsky has argued that while 'overmanning' exists in UK manufacturing, relative to other countries, the opposite applies to services. See 'Where the jobs are', *Financial Times*, 24 April 1984.

6 Bob Rowthorn, in private correspondence with the author, has suggested a 'twin-track' approach in the case of coal, with some pits adopting the most modern machinery and others having higher labour-intensity. This would develop or help to maintain managerial and professional skills in the industry.

7   See a review of an article by Alan Townsend, written in the March 1986 issue of the 'Northern Economic Review' in the *Financial Times*, 24 March 1986.
8   See also Metcalf (1984), who shows that the correlation across industries between regional development grants in the 1970s and the elasticity of substitution is positive; the industries that have received the most capital subsidy per head are the ones which make the biggest substitution away from jobs.
9   All the areas have regional selective assistance, local authority schemes, derelict land grants and EEC funding. Four out of five benefited from enterprise agencies, the Urban Programme and regional development grants. Three were new towns; BSC (Industry) helped in three; two were enterprise zones; and one was aided by an enterprise board.
10 The TUC view is also that marginal subsidies should not only apply to the public sector (Callaghan, 1986).
11 See the *Advertising Statistics Yearbook*, 1984.
12 See *NIESR Review*, May 1986, p. 6.
13 The House of Commons report scaled down the numbers at the outset to three-quarters of a million.
14 The scheme thus involves a marginal subsidy which is thought superior to a general subsidy. For the theoretical arguments here see Layard and Nickell (1980).

8 Making the jobs go round

1   It may be noted that while the British political and economic establishment has generally been opposed to reduction in hours and worksharing, this is not true in Europe generally.
2   British Social Attitude Survey, 1983, Table 3.9.
3   R. Layard, letter to the *Financial Times*, 24 July 1986. This extreme position would not be shared by most economists. In any case, subsidised early retirement could be restricted to certain categories so as to avoid a skills shortage. The chairman of United Biscuits proposed such a scheme in a letter to the *Financial Times* (1 August 1986).
4   Jonathan Gershuny, *Social Innovation and the Division of Labour*, OUP, 1983. Gershuny implicitly argues that hours of work are chosen by individuals and his cross-section data show that as incomes rise people first of all work longer hours and then, at higher income levels, work shorter hours in order to have the time to enjoy the fruits of their efforts. While such a pattern may indeed exist in cross-section, reflecting the preference of different income groups, this does not imply that changes in hours through time will occur which fit in with people's changing preferences.
5   Average weekly earnings actually rise by a small amount at the start

of the simulation in response to higher prices, incurred as output per person employed falls.

6 This is why Drèze is also pessimistic in regard to the effectiveness of marginal employment subsidies – many workers are already receiving more than their marginal revenue product. The pessimism on hours is not shared by all; employer sources in Germany suggest that the German metal-workers' strike for shorter hours in 1984 resulted in the employment of an extra 80,000 workers.

7 According to a European Commission survey referred to later in the text, only 4 per cent of Europeans work at around the thirty-hour mark, but 18 per cent would be interested in doing so, nearly all of them at present in full-time jobs.

8 *Survey of Workers: Reduction of Working Time and Worksharing*, FGT, Belgium, 1980.

Bibliography

Abernathy, W. J. (1978), *The Productivity Dilemma: Roadblock to Innovation in the Automobile Industry*, London, Johns Hopkins.

ACARD (1986a), *Software: A Vital Key to UK Competitiveness*, London, HMSO.

ACARD (1986b), *Medical Equipment*, London, HMSO.

ACARD (1986c), *Exploitable Areas of Science*, London, HMSO.

Advisory Board for the Research Councils (1986), *An International Comparison of Government Funding of Academic and Academically Related Research*, Science Policy Studies no. 2, Sussex, Science Policy Research Unit.

Aglietta, M. (1979), *A Theory of Capitalist Regulation: The US Experience*, London, New Left Books.

Akerlof, G. A. and Yellen, J. L. (1985), 'Unemployment through the filter of memory', *Quarterly Journal of Economics*, no. 3, August, pp. 747–74.

Allen, R. (1980), *The Economic Effects of a Shorter Working Week*, Government Economic Service Working Paper, no. 33, London, HMSO.

Arestis, P. and Driver, C. (1980), 'Consumption out of different types of income in the UK', *Bulletin of Economic Research*, November, pp. 85–96.

Arestis, P. and Driver, C. (1987), 'The effect of income distribution on consumer imports', *Journal of Macroeconomics*, forthcoming.

Armington, C. and Odle, M. (1982), 'Small business: how many jobs?', *Brookings Review*, Winter, pp. 14–17.

Armstrong, P. (1984), *Technical Change and Reductions in Life Hours of Work*, London, The Technical Change Centre.

Artis, M. J. (1982), *Why Do Forecasts Differ*, Papers presented to the Panel of Academic Consultants, Bank of England, no. 17, February.

Bibliography

Atkins, T. *et al.* (1983), 'New firms and employment creation', *SSRC Newsletter*, 49, June.

Atkinson, J. (1984), *Flexibility, Uncertainty and Manpower Management*, Report no. 89, Sussex, Institute of Manpower Studies.

Atkinson, J. and Meager, N. (1985), *Changing Patterns of Work*, London, NEDO Books.

Bank of England (1985), 'Services in the UK economy', *Bank of England Quarterly Review*, September, pp. 404–14.

Bank of England (1986), 'Fixed investment, the capital stock and factor utilisation', *Bank of England Quarterly Bulletin*, June, pp. 236–41.

Bannock, G. (1981), *The Economics of Small Firms*, Oxford, Blackwell.

Barras, R. (1984), *Growth and Technical Change in the UK Service Sector*, London, Technical Change Centre.

Batchelor, R. A. (1982), 'Expectations, output and inflation; the European experience', *European Economic Review*, vol. 17, no. 1, pp. 1–25.

Baumol, W. J., *et al.* (1985), 'Unbalanced growth revisited: asymptotic stagnancy and new evidence', *American Economic Review*, vol. 75, no. 4, September, pp. 806–17.

Beckerman, W. (1985), 'How the battle against inflation was really won', *Lloyds Bank Review*, January, pp. 1–12.

Belbin, R. M. (1980), 'Launching new enterprises', *Department of Employment Gazette*, April, pp. 362–5.

Bell, L. A., and Freeman, R. B. (1985), *Does a Flexible Industry Wage Structure Increase Employment? The US Experience*, Working Paper No. 1604, National Bureau of Economic Research, Cambridge, Mass.

Ben Zion, U. and Mehra, Y. P. (1980), 'Risk and determinants of aggregate investment', *Applied Economics*, vol. 12, no. 2, June, pp. 209–22.

BIEC (1985), *Response of the British Invisible Exports Council to the Aldington Report* (House of Lords, 1985).

Biggadike, R. (1979), 'The risky business of diversification', *Harvard Business Review*, May, pp. 103–11.

Birch, O. L. (1979), *The New Job Generation Process*, Cambridge, Mass., Massachusetts' Institute of Technology.

Blanchard, O., Dornbusch, R., and Buiter, W. (1985), *Public Debt and Fiscal Responsibility*, paper no. 22, Centre for European Policy Studies, London.

Blanchflower, D. G. and Oswald, A. J. (1986), *Shares for Employees: A Test of their Effects*, mimeo, London School of Economics.

Bollard, A. (1983), 'Technology, economic change and small firms', *Lloyds Bank Review*, January.

Bolton Committee (1971), *Small Firms*, Cmnd 4811, London, HMSO.

Bond, M. (1979), 'The world trade model: invisibles', *International Monetary Fund Staff Papers*, vol. 26, no. 2, pp. 257–333.

Borooah, V. K. (1986), *Expenditure and Price Elasticities and Consumers' Expenditure*, paper given to Cambridge Econometrics Conference, June.

Borooah, V. K. and Sharpe, D. R. (1984), *Aggregate Consumption and the Distribution of Income in the UK*, Cambridge Growth Project, paper no. 558, Cambridge, Department of Applied Economics.

Brittan, S. (1984), article in the *Financial Times*, 8 October.

Britton, A. (1985), 'Unemployment and the structure of labour demand', *National Westminster Bank Quarterly Review*, pp. 32–40.

Britton, A. (1986), 'Employment policy in the public sector', in Hart (1986).

Bruno, M. and Sachs, J. (1985), *The Economics of Worldwide Stagflation*, Oxford, Blackwell.

Burgess, C. (1985), 'Skill implications of new technology, *Employment Gazette*, October, pp. 397–403.

Buxton, A. J. (1986), *Some aspects of the UK Phillips Curve*, NEDO Economic Working Paper no. 22, London, NEDO Books.

Callaghan, W. (1986), 'Comment on A. Britton (*op. cit.*)', in Hart (1986).

Cannon, T. (1982), *The Role of Small Businesses in Economic Recovery: Myth and Reality*, University of Stirling.

CBI (1985), *CBI News*, no. 22, November.

CFI (1986), *External Capital for Small Firms*, NEDC Committee on Finance for Industry, London, NEDO Books.

Chambers, R. (1982), 'Information technology and education', in Rank Zerox, *Brave New World*, London, NEDO Books.

Chan-Lee, J. H. and Sutch, H. (1985), 'Profits and Rates of Return in OECD Countries', OECD Economics and Statistics Department Working Paper no. 20, Paris, Organisation for Economic Cooperation and Development.

Clark, P. K. (1979), 'Investment in the 1970's: theory, performance and prediction', *Brookings Papers on Economic Activity*, I, pp. 73–113.

Clutterbuck, D. (1983), *New Ways of Working*, paper given to the National Conference of the Institute of Personnel Management, October.

Bibliography

Commission of the European Communities (1985a), *Annual Economic Report 1985–6*.

Commission of the European Communities (1985b), *European Economy*, no. 10, October, Supplement B.

Cornwall, J. (1977), *Modern Capitalism; its Growth and Transformation*, London, Martin Robertson.

Cowling, K. (1985), *An Industrial Strategy for Britain; the Nature and Role of Planning*, mimeo, Coventry, University of Warwick.

Cripps, T. F. and Tarling, R. J. (1973), *Growth in Advanced Capitalist Economies 1950–1970*, University of Cambridge, Department of Applied economics Occasional Paper no. 40.

Curran, I. and Stanworth, J. (1981), 'Bolton ten years on: a research inventory and critical review', *Proceedings of the 1981 Small Businesses Research Conference*.

Cuvillier, R. (1984), *The Reduction of Working Time*, Geneva, International Labour Office.

Daly et al. (1985), 'Productivity, machinery and skills in a sample of British and German manufacturing plants: results of a pilot enquiry', *National Institute Review*, no. 111, February, pp. 48–61.

Davies, G. (1985), *Government Can Affect Employment*, London, Employment Institute.

Davies, G. and Metcalf, D. (1984), *Pit Closures – Some Economics*, specially commissioned for Independent Television 'Weekend World', September.

Davies, G. and Metcalf, D. (1985), *Generating Jobs; the Cost Effectiveness of Tax Cuts, Public Expenditure and Special Employment Measures in Cutting Unemployment*, Simon & Coates, London.

Davies, G., Kilpatrick, A. and Mayes, D. (1986), *Fiscal Policy Simulation: A Comparative Model Exercise*, NEDO Economic Working Paper no. 23, London, NEDO Books.

Davies, H. et al. (1980), 'State aid and industrial characteristics', *Applied Economics*, December, vol. 12, no. 4, pp. 413–28.

Davis, N. (1986), 'Training for change', in Hart (1986).

Department of Education and Science (1985), *HMI Report on the Effects of Local Authority Expenditure Policies on Education Provision in England in 1984*, London, HMSO.

Department of Employment (1983), *Family Expenditure Survey*, London, HMSO.

Department of Trade and Industry (1985), *Reply to the Report of the House of Lords Select Committee on Overseas Trade*, London, HMSO.

Department of Trade and Industry (1986), *UK Regional Development Programme 1986–90*, unpublished.

Drèze, J. H. (1985) *Work Sharing: Why? How? How Not . . .* , Paper no. 27, London, Centre for European Policy Studies.

Driver, C. (1980), *Productive and Unproductive Labour: Uses and Limitations of the Concept*, Thames Papers in Political Economy, London, Thames Polytechnic.

Driver, C. (1981) 'Aglietta, "A Theory of Capitalist Regulation"', *Capital and Class*, Autumn, pp. 150–68.

Driver, C. (1984), 'Testing the Gershuny hypothesis', *Futures*, vol. 16, no. 5, October, pp. 508–12.

Driver, C. (1986a), 'Transformation of the CBI capacity utilisation series: theory and evidence', *Oxford Bulletin of Economics and Statistics*, November, vol. 48, no. 4, pp. 339–52.

Driver, C. (1986b), 'Spare capacity and the scope for fiscal expansion', *Fiscal Studies*, August, pp. 67–75.

Driver, C. (1986c), *What Determines Average Hours of Work*, NEDO economic working paper no. 19, London, NEDO Books.

Driver, C. (1987), 'The employment effects of expanding service industries' in T. S. Barker and P. Dunne (eds), *Manufacturing or Services?*, London, Croom Helm, forthcoming.

Driver, C., Kilpatrick, A. and Naisbitt, B. (1985), 'The employment effects of changes in the structure of UK trade', *Journal of Economic studies*, vol. 12, no. 5, pp. 19–38.

Driver, C., Kilpatrick, A. and Naisbitt, B. (1986), 'The employment effects of UK manufacturing trade expansion with the EEC and the newly industrialising countries', *European Economic Review*, vol. 12, no. 5, pp. 427–38.

Duke, J. (1984), *Interactive Video: Implications for Education and Training*, London, Council for Educational Technology.

Dunning, J. H. (1985), 'Multinational enterprises and industrial restructuring in the UK', Lloyds Bank Review, October, pp. 1–19.

Economists Advisory Unit (sponsored by Shell UK) (1983), *The Small Firm Survivers*.

Eichner, A. S. (1986), *The Megacorp and Oligopoly*, New York, M. E. Sharpe.

Eliasson, G. (1984) 'The microfoundations of industrial policy', in Jacquemin (1984).

Eliasson, G. and Fries, H. (eds) (1983), *Microeconometrics, Yearbook of the Industrial Institute for Economic and Social Research*, Stockholm.

Eliasson, G. *et al.* (eds) (1983), *Policy Making in a Disorderly World Economy*, Stockholm, Industrial Institute for Economic and Social Research.

Employment Institute (1985), 'We can cut unemployment', *Bulletin of the Employment Institute*, May.

English, M. (1984), 'The European Information Technology Industry', in A. Jacquemin (ed., 1984).

Ergas, H. (1984), 'Corporate strategies in transition', in Jacquemin (1984).

Faxen, K-O. (1983), 'Stability in economic growth under uncertainty', in Eliasson *et al.* (1983).

Fothergill, S. and Gudgin, G. (1979), *The Job Generation Process in Britain*, CES Research Series no. 32, London, Centre for Environmental Studies.

Freeman, G., Clark, J. and Soete, L. (1982), *Unemployment and Technical Innovations*, London, Frances Pinter.

Gallagher, C. C. and Stewart, H. (1984), *Jobs and the Business Life Cycle in the UK*, Research Report no. 2, Department of Industrial Management, University of Newcastle upon Tyne.

Ganguly, P. (1982), 'Regional distribution of births and deaths of firms in the UK', *British Business*, 24 September, pp. 108–9.

Geroski, P. and Jacquemin, A. (1985), 'Corporate competitiveness in Europe', *Economic Policy*, no. 1, November, pp. 169–204.

Gershuny, J. (1978), *After Industrial Society*, London, Macmillan.

Gershuny, J. (1982), 'Social innovation: change in the mode of provision of services', *Futures*, December, pp. 496–516.

Gershuny, J. (1983), *Social Innovation and the Division of Labour*, Oxford University Press.

Gershuny, J. (1985), 'New technology – what new jobs?', *Industrial Relations Journal*, vol. 1, no. 16, pp. 74–84.

Gershuny, J. and Miles, I. (1983), *The New Service Economy*, London, Francis Pinter.

Gibbs, R. (1980), *Industrial Policy in More Successful Economies*, London, NEDO Books.

GLC (1982), *Cabling in London*, Greater London Council Economic Policy Group.

GLC (1985), *The London Industrial Strategy*, Greater London Council.

Glyn, A. (1986), *A Million Jobs a Year*, London, Verso.

Gordon, R. (1986), Text of a speech given to the Centre for Economic Policy Research, 11 June.

Grant, R. M. (1986), *Capacity, Adjustment and Restructuring in the UK Cutlery Industry 1974–84*, NEDO Economic Working Paper no. 21, London, NEDO Books.

Gudgin, G. *et al.* (1979), *New Manufacturing Enterprises in Regional Employment Growth*, CES Research Series no. 39, London, Centre for Environmental Research.

Harcourt, G. C. (1972). *Some Cambridge Controversies in the Theory of Capital*, Cambridge University Press.

Hart, P. E. (ed.) (1986), *Unemployment and Labour Market Policies*, London, Gower.

Hart, P. E. and Trinder, C. (1986), 'Employment protection, national insurance, income tax and youth unemployment', in Hart (1986).

Harvey Jones, Sir J. (1986), 'Does Industry Matter?', The Richard Dimbleby Lecture in the *Listener*, 10 April, London, BBC Enterprises Ltd.

Henley Centre (1985), *Survey on Leisure Futures*, London.

Henley Centre (1985), *The Real Future of the UK Economy*, Conference Papers, 12 December, London.

Hopkins, Sir Bryan (1984), *Real Wages and Unemployment*, Bank of England Panel of Academic Consultants, Panel Paper no. 24, October.

Horn, E. J. *et al.* (1983), 'Advanced machine tools: production diffusion and trade' in Sharp (1985).

House of Commons (1986), *Special Employment Measures and the Long Term Unemployed*, First Report from the Employment Committee, London, HMSO.

House of Lords (1985), *Report of the Select Committee on Overseas Trade*, July, London, HMSO.

Hughes, P. R. and Hutchinson, G. (1986), 'The changing pattern of male unemployment in Great Britain, 1972–81', *Oxford Bulletin of Economics and Statistics*, vol. 84, no. 4, pp. 309–30.

Incomes Data Services (1982), *Report* no. 264, April.

ITAP (1982), *Cable Systems*, London, HMSO.

ITAP (1983), *Making a Business of Information*, London, HMSO.

Jacquemin, A. (ed.) (1984), *European Industry, Public Policy and Corporate Strategy*, Oxford University Press.

Jones, D. (1985a), *The Import Threat to the UK Car Industry*, Science Policy Research Unit, University of Sussex.

Jones, D. (1985b), Chapter 2 in C. Freeman (ed.), *Technological Trends and Employment*, London, Gower.

Kaldor, N. (1985), 'Keynesian economics after fifty years', in Worswick and Trevithnick (1985).

Kalecki, M. (1971), *Selected Essays in the Dynamics of the Capitalist Economy*, Cambridge University Press.

Karlsson, C. (1986), 'Creation of new businesses in large established organisations', in Burton and Aabel (eds), *Innovation and Entrepreneurship in Organisation*, Amsterdam, Elsevier.

Katsoulakis, Y. (1986), *The Employment Effect of Technical Change*, Brighton, Harvester.

Klau, F. (1984), 'Comments' in Layard, Nickell and Jackman (1984).

Kleinknecht, A. (1984), 'Prosperity, crisis and innovation patterns', *Cambridge Journal of Economics*, 8, pp. 251–70.

Knight, Sir A. (1980), 'UK industry in the 1980s', Annual Lecture to the Institute of Fiscal Studies, London.

Lapping, A. (ed.) (1983), *Working Time in Britain and West Germany*, London, Anglo-German Foundation.

Layard, R. (1985), 'Cutting unemployment using both blades of the scissors', *Catalyst*, no. 1, vol. 1, Spring, pp. 41–51.

Layard, R. and Metcalf, D. (1985), *A New Deal for the Long-Term Unemployed*, Centre for Labour Economics Working Paper no. 812, London School of Economics.

Layard, R. and Nickell, S. J. 1980, 'The case for subsidising extra jobs', *Economic Journal*, March, vol. 90, no. 357, pp. 51–73.

Layard, R. and Nickell, S. J. (1985a), 'The causes of British unemployment', *National Institute Economic Review*, no. 111, February, pp. 62–85.

Layard, R. and Nickell, S. J. (1985b), *Unemployment, Real Wages and Aggregate Demand in Europe, Japan and the US*, Centre for Labour Economics Discussion Paper no. 214, London School of Economics.

Layard, R., Nickell, S. J. and Jackman, P. (1984), *European Unemployment Is Keynesian and Classical but not Structural*, CEPS Economic Paper, no. 13, London.

Leontief, W. (1982), 'The distribution of work and income', *Scientific American*, September, vol. 247, no. 3, pp. 152–79.

Leontief, W. (1985) 'The choice of technology', *Scientific American*, June, vol. 252, no. 6, pp. 25–33.

Leontief, W. and Duchin, F. (1985), *The Future Impact of Automation on Workers*, Oxford University Press.

Bibliography

Lindbeck, A. (1985), 'What is wrong with the West European economies?', *The World Economy*, June, pp. 153–70.

Lindley, R. (1986), 'Labour demand: macroeconomic aspects of state intervention' in Hart (1986).

Llewellyn, J., Potter, S. and Samuelson, L. (1985), *Economic Forecasting and Policy: the International Dimension*, London, Routledge & Kegan Paul.

Lloyd, P. (1980), *New Manufacturing Enterprise in Greater Manchester and Merseyside*, North West Industry Research Unit, University of Manchester.

Lloyd, P. and Mason, C. (1985), 'Spatial variation in new firm formation in the United Kingdom; comparative evidence from Merseyside, Greater Manchester and South Hampshire', in Storey (1985).

LOTIS (1982), *Liberalisation of Trade in Services*, November, Liberalisation of Trade in Services Committee of the British Invisible Export Council, London.

McCracken, P. *et al.* (eds) (1977), *Towards Full Employment and Price Stability*, Paris, OECD.

MacDonald, J. (1985), 'R&D and directions of diversification', *Review of Economics and Statistics*, vol. 67, no. 4, November, pp. 583–90.

Macey, R. D. (1982), *Job Generation in British Manufacturing Industry; Employment Change by Size of Establishment and by Region*, Government Economic Service Working Paper no. 55, London, HMSO.

McKay, C. (1985), 'A note on high technology manufacturing industry in Scotland', *Scottish Economic Bulletin*, December, pp. 10, 11.

McMahon, C. W. (1984), *The Scope for Industrial Expansion*, Lecture given by the Deputy Governor of the Bank of England, Birmingham and West Midlands Institute of Bankers, 22 February.

Malerba, F. (1985), *Demand Structure and Technological Change; the Case of the European Semiconductor Industry*, paper given to EARIE Conference, Cambridge, September.

Malinvaud, E. (1977), *Profitability and Unemployment*, Cambridge University Press.

Malinvaud, E. (1982), 'Wages and Unemployment', *Economic Journal*, March, vol. 92, pp. 1–12.

Marshall, M., Christian, C. and Virgo, P. (1984), *No End of Jobs: A Return to Full Employment Through New Technology*, London, Conservative Political Centre.

Marx, K. (1972), *Theories of Surplus Value, Part 1*, London, Lawrence & Wishart.

Mawson, J. (ed) (1984), Policy Review Section, *Regional Studies*, vol. 18, no. 3, pp. 257–66.

Bibliography

Mawson, J. (1986), *Report of the Director of Economic Development to the Economic Development Committee*, County Council of West Midlands.

Mayes, D. (1985), *Encouraging Technical Change*, paper given to ESRC group on Industrial Economics, November, London, NEDO.

Metcalf, D. (1984), 'Employment and industrial assistance' in Jacquemin (1984).

Metcalf, D. (1985a), *Shrinking Work Time and Unemployment*, Centre for Labour Economics Working Paper no. 708, London School of Economics.

Metcalf, D. (1985b), *Employment in the Second Half of the 1980s*, Centre for Labour Economics Working Paper, no. 757, London School of Economics.

Michl, T. R. (1985), 'International comparisons of productivity growth; Verdoorn's Law revisited', *Journal of Post-Keynesian Economics*, Summer, pp. 474–92.

Morris, D. and Sinclair, P. (1985), 'The assessment: the unemployment problem in the 1980's', *Oxford Review of Economic Policy*, vol. 1, no. 2, pp. 1–19.

Moylan, S. and Davies, B. (1980), 'The disadvantages of the long-term unemployed', *Employment Gazette*, August, pp. 830–2.

MSC/NEDO (1985), *A Challenge to Complacency: Changing Attitudes to Training*, London, Coopers Lybrand Associates.

MSC (1986), *Improving Information on Skill Supply and Demand; A Consultative Document*, London, HMSO.

National Institute for Economic and Social Research (1984), 'Some aspects of labour markets in Britain and the US', *National Institute Economic Review*, no. 110, November, pp. 51–61.

NEDC (1984), *Competence and Competition: Training and Education in the Federal Republic of Germany, the United States and Japan*, London, NEDO Books.

NEDC (1985), *Investment in the Public Sector Built Infrastructure; Overall Findings and Conclusions*, London, NEDO Books.

NEDO (1983), *The Impact of Advanced Information Systems*, London, NEDO Books.

NEDO (1984a), *Crisis Facing UK Information Technology*, London, NEDO Books.

NEDO (1984b), *Flexible Manufacturing Systems*, London, NEDO Books.

NEDO Long-Term Perspectives Group (1985), *IT Futures*, London, NEDO Books.

NEDO Long-Term Perspectives Group (1986), *IT Futures Surveyed*, London, NEDO Books.

Newell, A. (1984), *Annual Indices of the Changes in the Structure of Employment by Industry and Region*, Working Paper no. 617, London School of Economics.

Nickell, S. J. (1979), 'The effects of unemployment and related benefits on the duration of unemployment', *Economic Journal*, vol. 89, pp. 34–49.

Nickell, S. J. (1985), 'The government's policy for jobs; An analysis', *Oxford Review of Economic Policy*, vol. 1, no. 2, pp. 98–115.

Northcott, J. et al. (1986), *Robots in British Engineering: Expectations and Experience*, London, Policy Studies Institute.

Oakey, R. P. (1983), *Research and Development Cycles, Investment Cycles and Regional Growth in British and American Small, High Technology Firms*, University of Newcastle upon Tyne.

Oakey, R. P. (1984), 'Innovation and Regional Growth in Small High Technology Firms; Evidence from Britain and the USA', *Regional Studies*, vol. 18, no. 3, June, pp. 237–52.

OECD (1980), *Technical Change and Economic Policy*, Paris, Organisation for Economic Cooperation and Development.

OECD (1982), *Labour Supply, Growth Constraints and Worksharing*, Paris, Organisation for Economic Cooperation and Development.

OECD (1985a), *Economic Outlook*, Paris, Organisation for Economic Cooperation and Development.

OECD (1985b), *Science and Technology Indicators; Resources Devoted to R&D*, Paris, Organisation for Economic Cooperation and Development.

OECD (1985c), *Measuring Health Care 1960–83*, Paris, Organisation for Economic Cooperation and Development.

OECD (1986), *New Information Technologies: A Challenge for Education*, Paris, Organisation for economic Cooperation and Development.

OPCS (1984), *Population Trends 37*, London, HMSO.

Panic, M. (ed.) (1978), *The UK and West German Manufacturing Industry 1954–72; A Comparison of Structure and Performance*, London, NEDO Books.

Pasinetti, L. (1981), *Structural Change and Economic Growth*, Cambridge University Press.

Pavitt, K. (1983), 'A Failure to Adjust', Economic and Social Research Council Workshop on the competitiveness and industrial regeneration of British industry, 18 and 19 November, London.

Perez, C. (1985), 'Structural change and assimilation of new technologies in the economic and social systems', *Futures*, October, vol. 15, no. 5, pp. 357–75.

Peston, M. (1985), 'Higher education: financial and economic aspects', *Royal Bank of Scotland Review*, December, pp. 3–17.

Petit, P. (1986), *Slow Growth and the Service Economy*, London, Frances Pinter.

Prais, S. J. (1976), *The Evolution of Giant Firms in Britain*, Cambridge University Press.

Prais, S. J. (1986), 'Comment', in Hart (1986).

Rajan, A. (1984), *New Technology and Employment in Insurance, Banking and Building Societies*, Institute of Manpower Studies, University of Sussex.

Rajan, A. and Pearson, R. (eds) (1986), *UK Occupation and Employment Trends to 1990*, London, Butterworths.

Ranga Chand, U.K. (1983), 'Why the dramatic increase in service sector employment?', *Canadian Business Review*, vol. 10, no. 3, Autumn, p. 25–8.

Reich, R. B. (1982), 'Why the US needs industrial policy', *Harvard Business Review*, Jan.–Feb., pp. 74–81.

Robertson, J. A. S., Briggs, J. M. and Goodchild, A. (1982), *Structure and Employment Prospects of the Service Industries*, Research paper no. 30, Department of Employment, London, HMSO.

Robinson, B. and Wade, K. (1985), *Economic Outlook Forecast Release*, vol. 9, no. 10, pp. 1–4.

Robinson, S. J. Q. (1986), 'Strategies for declining industrial markets', *Journal of Long-Range Planning*, vol. 19, no. 2, pp. 72–8.

Robson Rhodes (1983a), *Small Business Loan Guarantee Scheme; a study of Some Early Claims*, Department of Trade and Industry, London, HMSO.

Robson Rhodes (1983b), *Small Business Loan Guarantee Scheme; Commentary on a Telephone Survey*, Department of Trade and Industry.

Rothschild, E. (1980), 'Individual comment' in OECD, *Technical Change and Economic Policy*, Paris, Organisation for Economic Cooperation and Development, 1980.

Rothwell, R. and Zegveld, W. (1979), *Technical Change and Employment*, London, Frances Pinter.

Rothwell, R. and Zegveld, W. (1982), *Innovation and the Small and Medium Sized Firms*, London, Frances Pinter.

Rothwell, R. and Zegveld, W. (1985), *Reindustrialisation and Technology*, London, Longmans.

Rowthorn, B. (1981), *Demand, Real Wages and Economic Growth*, Thames Papers in Political Economy, London, Thames Polytechnic.

Rowthorn, B. (1984), *Some Aspects of Employment Changes in the USA*, mimeo.

Sapir, A. (1983), 'Trade in services: policy issues for the 1980s', *Columbia Journal of World Business*, vol. 17, no. 3, pp. 76–83.

Sapir, A. (1984), *North–South Issues in Trade Services*, paper prepared for the Trade Policy Research Centre London.

Sapir, A. and Lutz, E. (1980), *Trade in Non-factor Services: Past Trends and Current Issues*, World Bank Staff Working Paper no. 410.

Sawyer, M. (1986), *Conflict and Aggregate Demand in Post-Keynesian Economics: The Problem of Over-Determinancy*, University of York, mimeo.

Scase, R. and Goffee, R. (1983), 'The small businessman as an employer', *SSRC Newsletter*, June.

Scherer, F. (1984), *The World Productivity Growth Slump*, International Institute of Management discussion paper 84-25, Berlin.

Shackleton, J. R. (1985), 'Is the UK labour market inflexible?', *The Royal Bank of Scotland Review*, no. 147, September, pp. 27–41.

Sharp, M. (ed.) (1985), *Europe and the New Technologies*, London, Frances Pinter.

Shepherd, W. (1975), *The Treatment of Market Power*, Washington DC, Columbia University Press.

Soete, L. and Freeman, C. (1985), 'New technologies, investment and employment growth', in OECD, *Employment Growth and Structural Change*, Paris, Organisation for Economic Cooperation and Development, 1985.

Stanback, T. M. *et al.* (1981), *Services: The New Economy*, New Jersey, Rowman & Allanhead.

Steindl, J. (1979), 'Stagnation theory and stagnation policy', *Cambridge Journal of Economics*, vol. 3, no. 3, pp. 1–14.

Steindl, J. (1985), 'Structural problems in the crisis', *Banca Nazionale Del Lavoro Quarterly Review*, September, pp. 223–31.

Stoneman, P. (1985), 'Local versus Global Optimality as a Basis for Technology Policy', presented to a joint meeting of NEDO and IESG, London, 8 November.

Storey, D. J. (1982), *Entrepreneurship and the New Firm*, London, Croom Helm.

Storey, D. J. (1983), 'Regional policy in a recession', *National Westminster Quarterly Review*, November, pp. 39–47.

Storey, D. J. (1985), 'The implications for policy' in D. J. Storey (ed.)

(1985), *Small Firms in Regional Economic Development*, Cambridge University Press.

Storey, D. J. and Johnson, S. (1985), *Job Generation – An International Survey*, Research Working Paper no. 2, University of Newcastle-upon-Tyne.

Tanzi, V. (1985), 'Fiscal deficits and interest rates in the United States: an empirical analysis 1960–84', *International Monetary Fund Staff Papers*, vol. 32, no. 4, December, pp. 551–76.

Thwaites, A. and Gillespie, A. (1983), 'Technology, information and regional economic development', *SSRC Newsletter*, 49 June.

Tobin, J. (1975), 'Keynesian models of recession and depression', *American Economic Review*, vol. 65, no. 2, pp. 195–202.

Townsend, J. *et al.* (1981), 'Science and Technology Indicators for the UK', Science Policy Research Unit Occasional Paper, no. 16, University of Sussex.

Tunzelmann, G. N. von (1982), 'Structural change and leading sectors in British manufacturing 1907–68', in C. P. Kindleberger an G. Di Tella (eds), *Economics in the Long View*, vol. 3, London, Macmillan, pp. 1–49.

Tyler, Moore, J. and Rhodes, B. (1983), *The Impact of Regional Policy on Different Types of Industry and the Implications for Industrial Restructuring*, Department of Land Economy, University of Cambridge.

US International Trade Commission (1982), *The Relationship of Exports in Selected US Service Industries*, published by the US Government.

Vernon, R. (1966), 'International investment and international trade in the product cycle', *Quarterly Journal of Economics*, May, pp. 190–207.

Vernon, R. (1979), 'The product cycle hypothesis in a new international environment', *Oxford Bulletin of Economics and Statistics*, November, pp. 255–67.

Weitzman, M. (1982), 'Increasing returns and the foundations of unemployment theory', *The Economic Journal*, vol. 92, December, pp. 787–804.

Weitzman, M. (1985), 'The simple macroeconomics of profit sharing', *American Economic Review*, vol. 75, no. 5, December, pp. 937–53.

White, M. (1982), *Shorter Working Time through National Industry Agreements*, Department of Employment Research Paper no. 38, London, HMSO.

White, M. (1983), *Long Term Unemployment and Labour Markets*, London, Policy Studies Institute.

White, M. (1985), *Information Technology and the Changing Structure of Employment*, mimeo, London, Policy Studies Institute.

White, M. (1986), 'Working time and employment: a negotiable issue?', in Hart (1986).

Whitley, J. D. and Wilson, R. A. (1986), *The Impact on Employment of a Reduction in the Length of the Working Week: Results of Simulations Using a Macroeconomic Model of the UK Economy*, Institute for Employment Research, University of Warwick.

Whittington, R. C. (1984), 'Regional bias in new firm formation in the UK', *Regional Studies*, vol. 18, no. 3, pp. 253–6.

Williams, B. (1984), 'Regional bias in new firm formation in the UK', *Regional Studies*, vol. 18, no. 3, pp. 253–6.

Williams, N. P. (1981), *Influences on the Profitability of Twenty-two Industrial Sectors*, London, Bank of England Discussion Paper, no. 15.

Williamson, O. E. (1975), *Markets and Hierarchies*, New York, Collier Macmillan.

Worswick, D. and Trevithnick, J. (eds) (1985), *Keynes and the Modern World*, Cambridge University Press.

Wragg, R. and Robertson, J. (1978), *Post-war Trends in Employment*, Research Paper no. 3, June, Department of Employment, London, HMSO.

Index of names

Abernathy, W.J., 12, 72
Aglietta, M., 78, 86
Akerlof, G.A., 205n
Allen, R., 190
Arestis, P., 109
Armington, C., 135
Armstrong, P., 174, 177, 179,182
Atkins, T., 142
Atkinson, J., 65, 68, 181

Bannock, G., 136
Barras, R., 97, 99
Batchelor, R.A., 12, 78
Baumol, W.J., 34–5
Beckerman, W., 163
Belbin, R.M., 136
Bell, L.A., 206n
Ben Zion, U., 78
Biggadike, R., 74
Birch, O.L., 135
Blanchard, O., 203, 206n
Blanchflower, D.G., 210n
Bollard, A., 211n
Bond, M., 125
Borooah, V.K., 98, 109
Briggs, J.M., 206n
Brittan, S., 172, 207n
Britton, A., 83, 162
Bruce, P., 209n
Bruno, M., 3, 207n
Buiter, W., 203
Burgess, C., 63–64

Butler, M., 40
Buxton, A.J., 163

Callaghan, W., 213n
Cannon, T., 133
Chambers, R., 118
Chan-Lee, J.H., 16, 206–7n
Clark, P.K., 83
Clutterbuck, D., 170
Cornwall, J., 8–9, 206n
Cowling, K., 206n
Cripps, T.F., 206n
Cross, M., 209n
Curran, I., 129, 136
Cuvillier, R., 175

Daly, A., 43, 68
Davies, B., 56
Davies, G., 22–3, 25, 153, 163,167
Davies, H., 209n
Davis, N., 68, 70
Dornbusch, R., 203
Drèze, J.H., 194–6, 214n
Driver, C., 34–6, 46, 58, 86,109, 155, 180, 206n, 210n
Duchin, F., 66
Duke, J., 210n
Dunning, J.H., 51

Eichner, A.S., 83, 207n
Eliasson, G., 81, 91–2

Index of names

English, M., 40
Ergas, H., 74

Faxen, K.-O., 12
Fothergill, S., 135–6, 139–41
Freeman, C., 4, 75, 78, 81
Freeman, R.B., 206n
Fries, H., 81

Gallagher, C.C., 135
Ganguly, P., 141
Garnett, N., 208n
Geroski, P., 207n
Gershuny, J., 34–5, 100, 178–9, 213n
Gibbs, R., 209n
Gillespie, A., 160
Glyn, A., 199
Goffee, R., 136
Goodchild, A., 206n
Gordon, R., 206n
Grant, R.M., 75
Gudgin, G., 135–6, 139–41

Harcourt, G.C., 79
Hart, P.E., 69, 209n
Harvey-Jones, Sir J., 56
Hobsbawm, E., ix
Horn, E.J., 208n
Hughes, P.R., 209n
Hutchinson, G., 209n

Jackman, P., 5
Jacquemin, A., 207n
Johnson, S., 140, 142, 211n
Jones, D., 50–1

Kaldor, N., 207n
Kaletsky, A., 212n
Karlsson, C., 75
Katsoulakis, Y., 19, 73
Kilpatrick, A., 25, 46, 206n
Klau, F., 81
Kleinknecht, A., 18
Knight, Sir A., 40

Lapping, A., 187
Layard, R., 3–5, 13, 28, 57, 163–4, 172, 212–13n
Leontief, W., 66, 79, 173
Lindley, R., 212n
Llewellyn, J., 11, 20, 206n
Lloyd, P., 139, 142–3
Lutz, E., 121–2

MacDonald, J., 74
Macey, R.D., 134, 136–7, 139–40
McKay, C., 74
Malerba, F., 77
Malinvaud, E., 20, 26, 206n
Marsh, P., 212n
Marx, K., 124
Mason, C., 139, 143
Mawson, J., 137–8, 149
Mayes, D., 17, 25
Meager, N., 68, 181
Mehra, Y.P., 78
Metcalf, D., 70, 153, 163–4, 167, 195, 199, 212–13n
Michl, T.R., 8–9, 206n
Miles, I., 34
Mitchell, P., 209n
Moore, J., 157
Morris, D., 3
Moylan, S., 56

Naisbitt, P., 46, 206n
Newell, A., 5
Nguyen, G. Dang, 208n
Nickell, S.J., 3–5, 13, 28, 205n, 212–13n
Northcott, J., 44

Oakey, R.P., 140, 160
Odle, M., 135
Orr-Ewing, Lord, 105–6
Oswald, A.J., 210n

Panic, M., 47
Pasinetti, L., 81
Pavitt, K., 44, 47
Pearson, R., 66–7
Perez, C., 12, 78, 86
Peston, M., 119
Petit, P., 100, 121
Prais, S.J., 68, 128, 130, 134

Index of names

Rajan, A., 66–7, 173
Reich, R.B., 51
Rhodes, B., 157
Robertson, J.A.S., 206n
Robinson, B., 57–8
Robinson, F., 212n
Robinson, S.J.Q., 210n
Robson Rhodes, 144–5, 148
Rothschild, E., 202
Rothwell, R., 133, 147
Rowthorn, B., 63, 207n, 212n

Sachs, J., 3, 30, 207n
Sapir, A., 120–2, 125
Sawyer, M., 207n
Scase, R., 136
Scherer, F., 17
Shackleton, J.R., 206n
Sharp, M., 208n
Sharpe, D.R., 109
Shepherd, W., 51
Sinclair, P., 3
Soete, L., 4, 78, 81
Stanback, T.M., 81
Stanworth, J., 129, 136
Steindl, J., 80–1, 207n
Stewart, H., 135
Stoneman, P., 86
Storey, D.J., 140–2, 148, 160, 211n
Sutch, H., 16, 206–7n

Tanzi, V., 207n
Tarling, R.J., 206n
Thwaites, A., 160
Tobin, J., 207n
Townsend, A., 213n
Townsend, J., 130, 132
Trinder, C., 69, 209n
Tunzelmann, G.N. von, 72–3
Tyler, P., 157

Vernon, R., 77

Wade, K., 57–8
Weitzman, M., 83, 207n
White, M., 61, 71, 118, 169, 178, 184, 187, 195, 209n
Whitley, J.D., 194
Whittington, R.C., 148
Williams, B., 172–3, 177–8
Williams, N.P., 16, 206n
Williamson, O.E., 130
Wilson, R.A., 194
Wragg, R., 206n
Wyplosz, C., 30

Yellen, J.L., 205n

Zegveld, W., 133, 147

Index of subjects

Advisory Board for the Research Councils (ABRC), 44
Advisory Council for Advanced Research and Development (ACARD), 40–2, 78, 92, 108
Aldington Committee, 120–1
Ashworth Report, 41
automation, 63–6

Bolton Committee Report, 127–9, 142
borrowing, government, 203–4
British Invisible Exports Council (BIEC), 120–1, 211n
British Social Attitudes Survey, 169
British Telecom (BT), 105–6
Business Expansion Scheme (BES), 145–6

cable communications, 101–6
capacity utilisation, 19–20, 28–9, 57–8
capital stock, 57
catch-up theory, 15
Charter for Jobs, 25–6
classical theory, 2–3, 13, 24–7
coal industry, 153, 212n
Commons, House of, Select Committee on Employment, 55, 69, 164–5
communications, *see* information technology

Community Programme, 25–6, 70, 164–5
competition, 15–16; British manufacturing, 41–5; and new technology, 36–41
computers: and education, 117–19; services, 108; *see also* automation
Confederation of British Industry (CBI), 6, 29, 55, 92
construction industry, 25–6, 55, 165–8
Construction Programme, 25–6
consultancy services, 124–5
consumption, 80–1; planning, 92–3, 200–1; services, 33–4, 200–1
cost-cutting, 6–9
creation of jobs, *see* job creation

debt, government, 203–4
deindustrialisation, 32–6
demand: for services, 95–8, 109–11, 162–3; for training, 70; and unemployment, 2–3
displacement effects, 106, 141–3

Economic and Social Research Council (ESRC), 160
education, 38, 101, 203; computer-aided, 117–19, 210–11n; technical, 43
efficiency, investment for, 6–9
elasticities, services, 95–8

Index of subjects

employers, and hours of work, 182–3
employment: full, requirements for, 199–200; and manufacturing, 45–9; and output, 9, 20; policy (*q.v.*), 53–4; and services, 94–126; and skills, 59, 209n; and small firms, 133–43; special measures for, 151–68; subsidies, 59, 151–4, 212n; trade experiments, 46–9; and work-sharing (*q.v.*), 189–94; *see also* unemployment
Employment Institute, 28, 199
engineering, 42–3, 125
Enterprise Allowance Scheme (EAS), 144–5
ESPRIT programme, 41, 52
Europe: consumer services expenditure, 33–4; hours of work, 185–6, 196–7; macroeconomic debate, 21–4; R&D expenditure, 17; technology, competitiveness, 36–41
European Commission, 9, 11, 170, 196–7
expenditure: capital, 165–6; consumer, 32–6, 83–5, 87–91; control of, 83–4; health care, 113–15; public, 113–15, 165–7, 203–4; on R&D, 17–18; on services, 32–6; special measures, 163–4; switching, 87–91
exports, services, 119–26

financial/business services, 124–5, 211n
Financial Institutions Group (FIG), 167–8
flexibility, 196–7, 204
flexible manufacturing systems (FMS), 44–5, 208n
forecasting, 11, 92
France, 17, 28, 30, 39; telecommunications, 103–4, 107–8

franchising, 143
full employment, requirements for, 199–200

Germany, 6, 17–18, 38–99
government, *see* policy
growth: and employment, 8–9, 20, 200–4; 'engines' of, 95; and productivity, 19–20; in services, 9, 94–126; and small firms, 134–5

health care: expenditure on, 113–15; innovations in, 78, 101–2
Henley Centre, 80, 107
hours of work, 111, 169–98, 200; attitudes to standard workweek, 170–2; benefits of shorter hours, 173–6; determinants of, 179–81; and employment, 189–94; government role, 185–6; part-time work, 170, 195–7; and pay, 183–4; reasons for forty-hour week, 176–9; reduction in, 186–94; *see also* work-sharing
housework, 175

imports, 109, 121, 201
incomes: distribution of, 80, 108–9; and hours of work, 183–4; and leisure, 176–8
Incomes Data Services, 183
industries, 72; mature, 73–6; new, 76–8; policy for, 50–2, 89–92; and skills, 59–61
inflation, 2–3, 20–4
information technology (IT), 87; applications of, 101–5; job implications of, 105–8; UK, 41
Information Technology Advisory Panel (ITAP), 104–5
infrastructure, 100–8; job implications, 105–7; special projects, 165–8
innovation: health care, 78, 101–2; and new industries, 76–8; product and process, 18–19,

Index of subjects

innovation (*cont.*):
72–3; and services, 116–19; and small firms, 130–3
Institute of Manpower Studies, 173
interactive services, 100–5
investment: for efficiency, 6–9; 'gap', 81; and government debt, 203–4; mature industries, 74–6; and profitability, 81–2, 201–2

Japan: education, 38; expenditure, 17, 33; planning, 92; R&D, 17; technology, 37–9, 87
job creation: and full employment, 199–200; low skill, 55–7; new industries and products, 71–93; special schemes, 163–5
Job Release Scheme, 195

Keynesian theory, 2–3, 13; and employment prospects, 24–7; structural critique of, 27–30; wage gap, 22–4
knitting machinery, 42

labour market, and unemployment, 2–3, 13
leisure, 174–9, 194
Liberalisation of Trade in Services Committee (LOTIS), 120, 211n
linkages, industrial, 73
living standards, 80–1
Loan Guarantee Scheme (LGS), 144–5
local enterprise boards, 147–9
Lords, House of, reports, 32, 53

McCracken Report, 6
McGraw-Hill survey, 6
macroeconomics: and Europe, 21–4; and policy, 19–21
management, 43, 201–2
Manpower Services Commission (MSC), 59, 63–5, 68–9, 92

manufacturing, 31–54; deindustrialisation, 32–6; employment prospects, 45–9; industrial policy, 50–2; and new technology, 36–41; and services, 95, 97; and skills, 43–4; small firms, 128–9, 139, 211n; and trade, 46–9; UK, 41–5
markets: inadequacy of, 23, 50–1; labour, 2–3, 13; rationalisation of, 74–5; and uncertainty, 80–1; and unemployment, 23
mature industries, 73–6
mechanical engineering, 42–3
multinational enterprises, 51

National Economic Development Council (NEDC), 42
National Economic Development Organisation (NEDO), 65, 101–3
National Institute for Economic and Social Research (NIESR), 25–6, 43
natural rate of unemployment (NRU), 22–3
new industries, 76–8; *see also* small firms
newly industrialised countries (NICs), 15–16, 48–9

occupations, and skills, studies, 61–7
Organisation for Economic Cooperation and Development (OECD): consumer services expenditure, 33, 113; forecasting, 11; growth and employment, 8–9, 20; investment for efficiency, 6, 8; macroeconomic policy, 19–20; productivity and profit, 15–16; R&D expenditure, 17, 116–17

part-time work, 170, 195–7
pay, and hours of work, 176–8, 183–4; *see also* incomes

Index of subjects

planning, 89–93, 200–1; consumption, 92–3; and industrial policy, 89–92; public sector, 116

policy, government: borrowing, 203–4; employment, 53–4; fiscal, 20–1, 30; and hours of work, 185–6; industrial, 50–2, 89–92; macroeconomic context, 19–21; and planning, 89–92; and small firms, 143–9; and theories of unemployment, 13

Policy Studies Institute, 44, 191–2

Prestel, 103, 106–8

producer services, 32–3, 207–8n

production technology, 44–5

productivity: and employment, 9, 20; and profit, 15–16; of services, 97–9

profitability: decline in, 13–19; and investment, 81–2, 201–2; and market share, 51; and productivity, 15–16

protectionism, 121, 201

public services, 111–19; health care, 78, 101–2, 113–15; innovation in, 78, 101–2, 116–19; planning of, 116; and public sector debt, 116, 119; R&D expenditure, 116–17, 202

rate of change of unemployment, 23

redistribution, 108–11, 201; *see also* hours of work

reflationary approach, 23–4, 28–30

regions, UK, 154–60, 213n

research and development (R&D), expenditure on, 17–18, 41, 44, 202–4; in public services, 116–17; in small firms, 130–3

retirement, early, 169, 194–7, 213n

risk, *see* uncertainty

'salience' of unemployment, 205–6n

services, 9, 94–126; assessment of, 94–5, 210n; consumer expenditure on, 33–4, 200–1; demand for, 95–8, 109–11, 162–3; elasticities, 95–8; expenditure on, 32–6; and expenditure switching, 87–91; exported, 119–26; and infrastructure, 101–8; interactive, 100–5; labour-intensive, 161–3; and manufacturing, 95, 97; occupation groups, 67, 96; producer, 32–3, 207–8n; productivity of, 97–9; promotion of, 161–3; public (*q.v.*), 111–19; R&D, 116–17, 202; and redistribution, 108–11; and skills, 60, 67; and technology, 34–5

skills, 55–70; and employment, 59, 209n; high *vs* low, 56–70; and industrial structure, 59–61; and job creation, 55–7; and manufacturing, 43–4; and occupational structure, 61–7; and services, 60, 67; shortages, 59; and technology, 63–6; and training, 59, 68–70; trends, 61–7

small firms, 127–50; Bolton Committee on, 127–9, 142; and employment generation, 133–43; and innovation, 130–3; and policy, 143–9; role and performance of, 127–31, 211n

social services, *see* public services

special measures, 151–68, 212–13n; infrastructure projects, 165–8; job creation schemes, 163–5; labour-intensive services, 161–3; UK regions, 154–60

structural theory of unemployment, 3–19; cost-cutting, 6–9; critique of Keynesianism, 27–30; and profitability decline, 13–19; structural change, 4–7, 203–4; uncertainty, 9–12

subsidies, employment, 59, 151–4, 212n

237

Index of subjects

switching, consumer expenditure, 87–91

technology: communications, *see* information technology; European competitiveness, 36–41; output and employment, 74; production, 44–5; and services, 34–5; and skills, 63–6; uncertainty, 79–80
teletext, 78–9, 100–4
Temporary Employment Scheme (TES), 212n
theories of unemployment, 1–30; classical, 2–3, 13, 24–7; Keynesian, 2–3, 13, 24–7; structural, 3–19; structural critique of Keynesianism, 27–30
trade: and manufacturing (experiments), 46–9; services, 119–26
training, 43, 70, 81, 203–4; and skills, 59, 68–70
transport services, 122–4

uncertainty, 9–12, 78–87; market, 80–1; solutions for, 81–7, 202; technology, 79–80
unemployment, 1; effects of reduction in hours on, 189–94; and growth, 200; natural rate of (NRU), 22–3; rate of change of, 23; 'salience' of, 205–6n; special measures for, 151–68; theories of, 1–30; voluntary, 2, 205n
United Kingdom (UK): consumer services expenditure, 32–5; education, 38; employment and output, 9; employment policy, 53–4; fiscal policy, 20–1, 30; incomes, 80–1; industrial policy, 50–2; information technology, 41; innovation, 73, 78–9; investment, 6, 10; manufacturing, 41–5; R&D expenditure, 17, 41, 44; regional problems, 154–60, 213n; services exports, 120–5; small firms, 130–41; telecommunications, 103–8; uncertainty, 10–11
United States of America (USA): consumer services expenditure, 33–5; education, 38; hours of work, 176–7; innovation, 77; investment, 6; Keynesian policies, 28; occupations and skills, 61–3; R&D expenditure, 17; recovery, 20–1; small firms, 134–41; technology, 37–9

venture capital, 146–9, 211–12n
voluntary unemployment, 2, 205n
voucher system, 111

wages: 'gap', 2–3, 21–2; and hours, 176–8, 183–4; and unemployment, 2–3, 13
Warwick Institute for Employment Research, 45–6, 192, 194
welfare, 84–5; *see also* public services
West Midlands Enterprise Board (WMEB), 147–9
work-sharing, 169–98, 200; attitudes to standard work-week, 170–2; benefits of shorter hours, 173–6; determinants of work time, 179–81; early retirement and part-time work, 194–7; economic consequences of reduced hours, 186–9; economists' attitudes, 172–3; employers' attitudes, 182–3; and employment, 189–94; and government role, 185–6; and pay, 176–8, 183–4; reasons for forty-hour week, 176–9

Youth Training Scheme (YTS), 43, 68

LIBRARY OF DAVIDSON COLLEGE

regular loan may be checked out for **two weeks.** Books
Circulation Desk in order to be renewed.